E-Portfolios in Higher Education

Tushar Chaudhuri · Béatrice Cabau
Editors

E-Portfolios in Higher Education

A Multidisciplinary Approach

 Springer

Editors
Tushar Chaudhuri
Hong Kong Baptist University
Kowloon Tong
Hong Kong

Béatrice Cabau
Narbonne
France

ISBN 978-981-10-3802-0   ISBN 978-981-10-3803-7   (eBook)
DOI 10.1007/978-981-10-3803-7

Library of Congress Control Number: 2017930953

Printed on acid-free paper

This Springer imprint is published by Springer Nature
The registered company is Springer Nature Singapore Pte Ltd.
The registered company address is: 152 Beach Road, #21-01/04 Gateway East, Singapore 189721, Singapore

Foreword I

Promoting Diversity Through E-Portfolios

In the second decade of the twenty-first century, we find ourselves in a time of growing diversity in both our urban spaces and our online spaces. Post-Cold War migration and travel, combined with digital mobility, have ushered in an era often described as *superdiverse*. It is an era characterised by a 'diversification of diversity' (Vertovec 2007, p. 1025) stemming from the complex interplay of linguistic, cultural, social, religious, political, economic, educational, gender, sexual and other human variables and affiliations. Preparing students for their future social, working and civic lives in such a diverse and often unpredictable world requires fostering what are sometimes called graduate attributes, or transferrable skills, or twenty-first century skills. These include communication, collaboration, critical thinking, and creativity, coupled with the digital literacies to make effective use of new technologies to support these skills, as well as the linguistic and intercultural abilities to negotiate today's urban and online spaces. In this context, education must make room for students' pre-existing diversities, allowing them to teach and learn from each other, and to play to their strengths even as they address the areas in which they need to develop or improve. In short, we must support our students in undertaking the personalised learning journeys that will best set them up for their future lives.

While many educators recognise the importance of carving out space for their students' diverse learning experiences, a number of questions arise. How can students' scattered learning experiences, taking place both inside and outside the classroom, and across numerous software platforms on multiple digital devices, be captured, collated and evaluated? How can these personal learning experiences be catered for within, or alongside, the standardised learning management systems (LMSs) or virtual learning environments (VLEs) in which educational institutions have invested heavily over the last decade or more? And how can these varied learning experiences be related to the common requirements embedded in courses of study, and the common standards underpinning certifications of achievement?

Portfolios, as collections of artefacts on which learners can reflect, on which they can be assessed, and on which they can base future job applications, are not a new construct. Nor, by the mid-2010s, are *e-portfolios*, the digital versions of portfolios which have also existed for some time. But, in a context of superdiversity, where a premium is placed on the acquisition of twenty-first century skills during personal learning journeys, and where learning can take manifold forms and be demonstrated in manifold ways, e-portfolios are taking on a new salience. This is the right moment to revisit e-portfolios and ask what they might offer higher education; what shapes they might take, both inside and outside the classroom, across different disciplines; and how they might fit in with institutional objectives.

The first part of this book frames the discussion through a conceptual exploration of e-portfolios in higher education. Tushar Chaudhuri outlines the development of a framework which can guide lecturers in the implementation and assessment of e-portfolios across multiple disciplines, neatly summarised in the appendices to the book. Mark Pegrum and Grace Oakley highlight the importance of engaging students, engaging lecturers, and integrating technology to support a successful e-portfolio implementation, while also reflecting on the changes that have occurred in technology and technology users over the last half-decade. Cath Ellis shows how learning analytics, an important development often linked to LMSs, can provide useful individualised feedback for educators and students and, when used in conjunction with e-portfolios, can offer a holistic picture of students' learning and allow them to take greater responsibility for their personal learning journeys.

The second part focuses on e-portfolios employed across a range of disciplines. Chi Shan Chui and Céline Dias indicate the benefits of e-portfolios for students of French and German, showing that language students are able not only to improve their linguistic skills, but to develop twenty-first century skills in areas ranging from digital literacies and intercultural competence through to autonomy and lifelong learning. Turning to the subject of history, Catherine Ladds equally finds support for the idea that students can develop both discipline-specific skills and cross-curricular skills in building e-portfolios. In a chapter about a statistics course, Simon To emphasises the role of e-portfolios in reorienting theoretical subjects towards authentic everyday examples, in helping students to integrate learning experiences, and in promoting sharing and collaboration. Referring to Csikszentmihalyi's work on flow, Warren Linger suggests that employing common, simple tools to underpin e-portfolios makes it easier for educators (and students) to work in a state of flow where they are not distracted by technological issues but can focus on interaction and collaboration around the content and skills being developed. As an ensemble, these papers offer insights into how to address the challenges of effectively implementing e-portfolios, including the need to promote new attitudes to learning and assessment, to ensure students understand the rationale for e-portfolios, and to attend to the technological difficulties that may arise.

Turning to informal, situated, out-of-class learning, Atara Sivan describes the use of reflective, interactive e-portfolios by students acting as 'healthy living ambassadors' in an intergenerational learning community, leading to an enhancement of their twenty-first century skills and digital literacies as well as facilitating their processes of personal self-discovery. Siu Yin Cheung, Heather Kwok and Peggy Choi write about the reflective e-portfolios submitted by sports and recreation students regarding their internship experiences, again emphasising the value of such an exercise in the development of students' twenty-first century skills and digital literacies, and highlighting the use of multimodal e-portfolios to accompany job applications. Béatrice Cabau outlines the use of reflective e-portfolios by students preparing for work in French multinational companies in Hong Kong, emphasising their development of broad twenty-first century skills in tandem with linguistic and intercultural competence, with students being able to gain a greater understanding of themselves as learners while also beginning to develop their professional identities; the next stage of this project will involve orienting the e-portfolios towards employability. Notwithstanding key challenges such as how to scale and manage e-portfolio initiatives, as well as issues of time and technology, the authors of these chapters, like those mentioned earlier, are in no doubt that it is well worth considering implementing e-portfolios more widely than has been the case in the past.

The third and final part presents institutional perspectives on e-portfolios. In their description of a promising pilot project, Eva Wong, Theresa Kwong and Peter Lau insist on the importance of students developing a holistic picture as they build their e-portfolios throughout their study years, integrating both curricular and co-curricular learning into these records of their learning journeys. Likewise, Paula Hodgson emphasises the integrative aspects of e-portfolios used by students as rich showcases of their individual learning journeys across a range of general education courses, where they can build generic twenty-first century skills while also developing personal beliefs and identities. Employing the lens of embedded librarianship, Chris Chan shows how librarians can support an e-portfolio initiative, bringing to bear their information literacy skills—a key component of digital literacies—as well as their technological skills to support students.

As we head towards the end of the second decade of the twenty-first century, it is important to remember that diversity is not a given, but rather is contested terrain. Today, we see many attempts by political, social, religious and military leaders to build barriers to stem human migration, reduce human contact offline and online, and relegate human otherness to the far side of newly constructed, or reconstructed, walls. And at all levels of education, we see attempts to standardise, 'templatise' and circumscribe learning, reducing it to testable, measurable, reportable outcomes linked to the basics of literacy and numeracy. While some standardisation in education is inevitable, and while the basics remain important, this cannot be the whole story of learning in the twenty-first century.

Contemporary digital and especially mobile technologies, coupled with contemporary constructivist, situated pedagogies, can help to support students in undertaking personal learning journeys, engaging with diversity, and representing their emergent understandings in numerous ways. Developing protocols like xAPI will soon make it much easier to track many different kinds of learning and integrate them seamlessly into students' personal learning spaces. The real promise of e-portfolios is perhaps that they constitute a kind of bridge between diversity and standardisation, making room both for diversified learning and standardised evaluations, and for the customisation of learning journeys alongside the multimodal, multifaceted demonstration of core content knowledge and generic twenty-first century skills. As such, they have the potential to play a key, and growing, role in the future of education.

Perth, Australia   Mark Pegrum

Reference

Vertovec, S. (2007). Super-diversity and its implications. *Ethnic and Racial Studies*, *30*(6), 1024–1054.

Foreword II

E-Portfolios and Academic, Structured Communities of Practice: Recommendations for Building Effective Implementation

I am pleased to welcome colleagues to this excellent book about e-portfolios. This collection of chapters is divided into three parts in order to provide educators and researchers with a comprehensive look at e-portfolios in higher education, with a multidisciplinary perspective in classrooms across many disciplines, and with engagement of e-portfolios from an institutional point of view. This book is timely because, internationally, e-portfolios are capturing the attention of educators and researchers in higher education. This book comes at the right moment, providing the research, guidance and resources needed to make e-portfolio applications more productive for both new and experienced instructors and educational developers.

This Foreword offers readers a key recommendation for successful implementation of e-portfolios in courses, curricula and programmes. My recommendation involves the use of academic, structured communities of practice (CoPs) and cites implementation science to confirm why this approach works well. I have confidence in this implementation process due to my 38 years of experience as facilitator and researcher of academic, structured CoPs in higher education. In general, the outcomes of this CoP process have provided colleagues, students and institutions with effective practices and programmes for teaching, learning, research, and organisational development (Cox and Richlin 2004).

My recommendation is that the readers of these chapters employ structured, academic CoPs when implementing the opportunities of e-portfolios described in this book. In the U.S. we call these CoPs by the name of faculty learning communities (FLCs). Membership in FLCs is voluntary, multidisciplinary, of size 8–10 members, and open to those in all disciplines and professions in higher education. FLCs are yearlong and have the goals of building community, developing evidence-based solutions, and disseminating project outcomes, often as the scholarship of teaching and learning (Cox 2004). FLC outcomes include increased student learning in areas high on Bloom's taxonomy and can include design and assessment of new curricula or revised programmes developed by the FLC members or as a group in concert (Beach and Cox 2009). These outcomes have also been confirmed recently at Hong Kong Baptist University (Kwong et al. 2016) and are mentioned here in some of chapters of this book.

For over 38 years in the U.S., topic-based FLCs have engaged hundreds of topics, including e-portfolios. There are two types of FLCs: topic based and cohort based. As an example, a cohort-based FLC could consist of early-career academics. Such an FLC can build institutional capacity by developing leaders and scholars (Cox 2006, 2013). Over the long term, FLCs enable an institution to become a learning organisation (Cox 2001, 2006; Senge 1990).

Implementation science confirms why academics and educational developers are successful in using academic, structured CoPs to implement new, evidenced-based approaches such as e-portfolios. Implementation is the art and science of incorporating innovations, interventions, and evidence-based programmes into typical human service settings to benefit the clients of practitioners. An example is the "bench to bedside" approach in the medical profession. There, evidence-based applications developed by researchers at the bench are to be implemented by doctors (practitioners) for their patients (clients) at the bedside. The purveyor of the implementation is the organisation, staff and process that are engaged by the purveyor to achieve the implementation. In the case of e-portfolios, educational developers attempt to find a purveyor to ensure that their practitioners—instructors, staff, and administrators—implement e-portfolios with fidelity and sustainability for their clients—students, programmes and institutions.

Lacking good information about implementation best practices, policy makers in the U.S. have invested heavily in the science of interventions, not in the science of implementation. The national implementation research network reported that the U.S. federal government invests 99% in intervention research and 1% in implementation of that research, leaving implementation to chance (Fixsen et al. 2005). Purveyor approaches to implementation that have not worked include invitations (Please do X), demands (You must do X), incentives, additional evidence that the evidenced-based programme works, and mass media approaches. What *does* work for successful purveyors is diffusion by people talking to people over time who mentor and show why and how. People follow the lead of others they know and trust (Gawande 2013). This description of what does work describes an academic, structured CoP and an FLC approach. Hong Kong Baptist University used this approach to investigate and implement e-portfolios as well as other innovations (Wong et al. 2016).

The authors of this book have provided research results, resources and guidance with perspectives across higher education, classrooms representing many disciplines, and institutional settings. They have shown that e-portfolios are doable, evidence-based approaches that enhance curricula, organisational development, instructor growth and student learning. The academic, structured CoP model as purveyor is successful here because it employs the effective approaches of implementation: CoP members talk to and mentor each other over time as practitioners, instructors and scholars. They collaborate with their CoP colleagues—members they know and trust—to design, implement, assess and disseminate e-portfolio approaches.

In conclusion, I recommend that readers employ the evidence given in these chapters and use the proven success of the academic, structured CoP model to implement e-portfolios in courses, programmes and institutions.

I extend best wishes for your e-portfolio endeavours.

Milton D. Cox
Miami University
Oxford, USA

References

Beach, A.L., & Cox, M.D. (2009). The impact of faculty learning communities on teaching and learning. *Learning Communities Journal, 1*(1), 7–27.

Cox, M.D. (2001). Faculty learning communities: Change agents for transforming institutions into learning organizations. *To Improve the Academy, 19*, 69–93.

Cox, M.D. (2004). Introduction to faculty learning communities. In M. D. Cox & L. Richlin (Eds.), *Building faculty learning communities* (pp. 5–23). New Directions for Teaching and Learning, No. 97, San Francisco, CA: Jossey-Bass.

Cox, M.D., & Richlin, L. (2004). *Building faculty learning communities.* New Directions for Teaching and Learning, No. 97, San Francisco, CA: Jossey-Bass.

Cox, M.D. (2006). Phases in the development of a change model: Communities of practice as change agents in higher education. In A. Bromage, L. Hunt, & C. B. Tomkinson (Eds.), *The realities of educational change: Interventions to promote learning and teaching in higher education* (pp. 91–100). Oxford, UK: Routledge.

Cox, M.D. (2013). The impact of communities of practice in support of early-career academics. *International Journal for Academic Development, 18*(1), 18–39.

Fixsen, D. L., Naoom, S. F., Blase, K. A., Friedman, R. M., & Wallace, F. (2005). *Implementation research: A synthesis of the literature.* Tampa, FL: University of South Florida, Louis de la Parte Florida Mental Health Institute, National Implementation Research Network (FMHI Publication #231).

Gawande, A. (2013, July 29). Slow ideas: Some innovations spread fast. How do we speed the ones that don't? Annals of Medicine. *The New Yorker, 89*(22), 36–45.

Kwong, T., Cox, M.D., Chong, K., Nie, S., & Wong, E. (2016). Assessing the effect of communities of practice in higher education: The case at Hong Kong Baptist University. *Learning Communities Journal, 8*(2), 171–198.

Senge, P. M. (1990). *The fifth discipline.* New York, NY: Doubleday.

Wong, E., Cox, M.D., Kwong, T., Fung, R., Lau, P., Sivan, A., & Tam, V.C. (2016). Establishing communities of practice to enhance teaching and learning: The case at Hong Kong Baptist University. *Learning Communities Journal, 8*(2), 9–26.

Preface

The subject of this book is the experience of integrating electronic portfolios as assessment tools and as instruments for lifelong learning at the course level. The authors who are both practitioners and researchers in Hong Kong analyse their experience critically and provide empirical data to back up their analysis. The reader will therefore find useful insights into introducing e-portfolios as course work in disciplines such as Mathematics or Business Communications, which are traditionally not considered to be "portfolio-disciplines". At the same time the traditional portfolio disciplines such as Language and Education are also represented and allow a state of the art perspective to the subject. The course level perspective enables the reader to identify challenges faced by instructors and students when implementing e-portfolios in their respective courses but at the same time suggests to them flexible ways of dealing with those challenges.

The second major component of the book from which the interested reader benefits is the introduction to various e-platforms suitable to the hosting of e-portfolios from the point of view of non-IT professionals. Apart from the well-known e-portfolio platforms such as "Mahara" or "My Portfolio" (Blackboard), authors discuss their experiences with Weebly and Google Docs. Thus the book acts as a practical resource for all practitioners who are looking for a non-traditional method of assessment or would like to encourage their learners to engage in self-developmental good practice right at the beginning of or during their educational and formative years. Foremost the book helps teachers who would like to give their students a competitive edge in a world of jobs and careers looking for digitally literate innovators.

But it is not only teachers and practitioners who should be interested in picking up this book. The case studies presented in this book are drawn from a university in Hong Kong. This makes each of these experiences a uniquely Asian one. Therefore each of these case studies also deals with the attitudes towards teaching & learning innovation in the Asian context. In doing so it provides practical insights into teaching and learning in an Asian context. This can translate into useful knowledge for administrators and governance professionals looking for ideas and methods of evaluating the quality of higher education in an Asian context.

Last but not the least the context of this volume is the collective and collaborative work of a community of practice set up to explore the possibilities of implementing e-portfolios in multiple disciplines and come up with a working set of guidelines for all who are interested in the subject of e-portfolios. The volume therefore also addresses administrators and leaders in the academic community who would like to see concrete evidence of the effectiveness of communities of practice within institutions of higher education in Asia.

The editors therefore sincerely believe that the proposed volume will speak to a large target audience drawn from a range of disciplines, roles and geographical contexts within the larger context of higher education in Asia and its relevance to contemporary society.

The book is divided into three parts to better highlight the diverse themes addressed in it. The first part has three chapters which broadly provide the background and the historical development of e-portfolios for assessment purposes. In this part, Chaudhuri provides an overview on research on e-portfolios as assessment tools and asks and answers five essential questions all educators should pose themselves before taking up the e-portfolio challenge; Pegrum and Oakley give an example of how the role and the technology associated with e-portfolios have changed over a five-year period in the education sector, and last but not least Ellis connects up the research on learning analytics with the affordances of e-portfolios thereby putting them right in the centre of outcome-based education and linking the development of e-portfolios to future research in assessment design.

The second part is the core of the book. It includes case studies of implementation of e-portfolios as assessment in academic disciplines at the course level. The case studies included in the former part of this section are drawn from classroom experiences of disciplines such as European Studies (Chui & Dias), History (Ladds), Mathematics (To) and Business Communications (Linger). The chapters in the latter part of this section continue the case studies but look at the out-of-class learning and lifelong learning experiences which can be scaffolded through the e-portfolio implementation. In this part, Sivan analyses qualitative data to reflect on Education students' learning experiences in an intergenerational learning community as reflected in their e-portfolios, Cheung, Kwok and Choi analyse quantitative data from the internship portfolios of Physical Education students and in the final chapter of this section Cabau reflects about her experience in implementing e-portfolios in a final year course in European Studies and the role they can play to ease the transition from university based assessments which students have dealt with and the assessments they have to go through in order to make their mark on the job market.

The third part of the book looks at the university wide efforts of e-portfolio implementation. Wong, Kwok and Lau look at these efforts from an administrator's point of view and pull together other examples of e-portfolio work going on at the university but not highlighted in this volume. They also trace the history and give the rationale of the e-portfolio initiative at the institutional level. This is followed by Hodgson's chapter on how the General Education courses have looked at the potential of e-portfolios for the General Education programme of the university as a whole and how e-portfolios have been used not only to document the students' GE experience but also as a reflection on the transformation potential of the programme itself. In the last chapter in this part, Chan gives an insight into how academic disciplines can collaborate with other teaching and learning units such as the library to give the student a holistic e-portfolio experience which includes essential twenty-first century information literacy skills.

The appendix part of the book is directed squarely at practitioners who are itching to start with their e-portfolio implementation and are looking for a handy step-by-step introduction and or a template on which to build on. Correspondingly this part includes a set of guidelines (Appendix A) to start with student e-portfolios. Appendix B is a rubric which can be extended and or adapted to the needs of the particular practitioner. Finally it includes a short glossary with the terms usually associated with e-portfolios and a short commented list of free platforms which could be used as e-portfolio platforms in case the institution itself has not opted for one.

The book therefore offers a wide range of e-portfolio experiences both in terms of academic disciplines involved and the level of courses (GE vs. final year) and not forgetting the diverse set of voices ranging from researchers and practitioners as well as administrators and teaching and learning officers. But the most important voice in the book is that of the student which features prominently in the chapters of the book and helps to relativize and put into perspective the affordances of e-portfolios in higher education.

We wish all our readers a productive time with this book and extend our heartfelt thanks to all those who have contributed to it.

Hong Kong   Tushar Chaudhuri
October 2016   Béatrice Cabau

Contents

Editors and Contributors

About the Editors

Tushar Chaudhuri is Assistant professor at the European Studies Programme of the Hong Kong Baptist University. He teaches German language and area studies and is interested in looking at contexts and conditions under which technology enhancement in and outside of the classroom is most effective. He holds a Ph.D. in German language pedagogy and a Masters of Arts in German literature.

Béatrice Cabau has been Associate Professor in the Department of Government and International Studies, Hong Kong Baptist University from 1997 until 2016. She has published extensively about language-in-education policy in Sweden. These last years, her research interests were based on her experience as French Stream Coordinator of the European Studies Programme to include pre-departure training for exchange students and the impact of the internationalisation of higher education at the local level in terms of societal ambitions as well as educational perspectives.

Contributors

Christopher Chan is the Head of Information Services at Hong Kong Baptist University Library. He is responsible for overseeing the provision of reference and instruction services, and advises the library's senior leadership team on the future direction of these programmes. His research interests include the assessment of information literacy competencies and the use of social media in academic libraries.

Prof. Siu Yin Cheung is Full Professor of the Department of Physical Education at Hong Kong Baptist University (HKBU). She received her Master's and Doctoral degrees in Physical Education from Springfield College, Massachusetts. USA. Her research areas are sport and exercise psychology, elderly wellness, stress management, motor development and motor learning, as well as physical education.

Peggy H.N. Choi is Lecturer of the Physical Education Department at Hong Kong Baptist University. She is the Director of the HKBU CIE Wellness Promotion Center. Her research has focused on adapted physical activities, sport and recreation for people with special needs, and teaching and learning.

Chi Shan Chui earned her Master's degree in Foreign Language Teaching from the Justus Liebig University in Giessen, Germany. During her studies, she gained practical experience through internships at the adult education centre in Giessen and at Hong Kong Baptist University. She joined the Department of Government and International Studies at the HKBU in 2012 as lecturer and teaches German language courses in the European Studies programme.

Céline Dias holds a degree in Philosophy from La Sorbonne University and a Master degree specialised in Didactics of French as a Foreign Language (FFL) from the University of Rouen.

She joined the European Studies programme (GIS Department) at the Hong Kong Baptist University in 2010 where she is teaching the Bachelor of Social Sciences core French language courses at all levels. Her research interests focus on the influence of new technologies to learning and teaching FFL on learners' intercultural competences.

Cath Ellis is the Associate Dean (Education) in the Faculty of Arts and Social Sciences at the University of New South Wales, in Sydney Australia. Cath has a background in Literature and her current research interests are in the area of higher education, and particularly in learning analytics and academic integrity.

Heather Kwok is Lecturer of the Physical Education Department at Hong Kong Baptist University. She is the Associate Director of the HKBU CIE Wellness Promotion Center. Her research has focused on the biomechanics of Taekwondo, and notational analysis of sports science.

Theresa Kwong, Ph.D. is Assistant Director of the Centre for Holistic Teaching and Learning at Hong Kong Baptist University. Her major responsibilities at the Centre include providing expertise to individuals and departments regarding pedagogical issues, teaching research postgraduate students basic teaching skills and applications of outcome-based approach, taking charge of the evidence collection of student learning and outcomes assessment. Her research interests include faculty professional development, service learning and academic integrity (theresa@hkbu. edu.hk).

Catherine Ladds is Assistant Professor of History at Hong Kong Baptist University, working on the history of colonial communities and China's relationship with the British empire. She has published widely on these themes, including her book, *Empire Careers*, which won the 2013–14 Hong Kong Academy of the Humanities First Book Prize. She is interested in the growth of the digital humanities and in exploring the uses of digital tools in history teaching. She can be contacted at cladds@hkbu.edu.hk.

Peter Lau is Senior Programme Officer of the Centre for Holistic Teaching and Learning, at Hong Kong Baptist University. He is taking charge of various student learning initiatives at the Centre such as arts and cultural education programme, sustainable service learning, creative drama education and graduate attributes ambassador scheme. His research interests include development and assessment of students' generic skills, co-curricular activity outcomes assessment and e-portfolio.

Dr. Grace Oakley is the course coordinator of the Master of Teaching (Primary) at the Faculty of Education, the University of Western Australia. She has been involved in Higher Education for 16 years and is interested in students' use of e-portfolios to reflect on their learning and identify professional learning needs. Grace lectures and conducts research primarily in the areas of literacy, interventions for learning, educational technologies and mobile learning.

Mark Pegrum is Associate Professor in the Faculty of Education at the University of Western Australia, where he specialises in m-learning (mobile learning) and, more broadly, e-learning. His most recent book is Mobile Learning: Languages, Literacies and Cultures (Palgrave Macmillan 2014).

Atara Sivan is Professor and Head of the Department of Education Studies at the Hong Kong Baptist University. Her research includes teaching and learning approaches, adolescents' leisure and education, learning environments and action learning on which she has published extensively. She is the Editor-in-Chief of World Leisure Journal and the recipient of several international awards for her contribution to the field of knowledge and practice.

Simon Kai-Ming To is a Lecturer in the Department of Mathematics of Hong Kong Baptist University (HKBU), with his Ph.D. in Mathematics obtained from the University of Hong Kong in 2011. His teaching focuses on general education in mathematics, and he is particularly interested in the integration of e-learning elements into university courses. He received an honourable mention in the 2014–15 HKBU General Education Teaching Award.

Eva Wong, Ph.D. is the Director of the Centre for Holistic Teaching and Learning at Hong Kong Baptist University. With education and student learning being central to her work, she joined HKBU in February 2010 to take up major responsibilities for the professional development of academic staff, assisting the implementation of the outcome-based approach to teaching and learning and supporting the University's e-learning endeavours, with the main focus on enhancing student learning via a holistic approach.

Part I
E-Portfolios in Higher Education

Chapter 1
(De)Constructing Student E-Portfolios in Five Questions: Experiences from a Community of Practice

Tushar Chaudhuri

Abstract The primary purpose of this lead article in the present volume is to provide the backdrop to the chapters included in the volume and to re-construct the framework, which formed the basis of the work of a Community of Practice (CoP) at the Hong Kong Baptist University (HKBU). The CoP looked into the question of how to develop a model for teachers from different disciplines to introduce e-portfolios as an assessment tool into their courses. It finally came up with a criterion-based model (Appendix A) and a suggestion for an assessment rubric (Appendix B) using an inductive method, where members first designed and implemented e-portfolios for their individual courses and brought back these experiences to the discussion table. The paper will discuss the development of this criterion-based model, which is meant to act as a starting point for practitioners and help them to provide their students with a clear set of outcomes for their respective portfolios. At the same time the criteria laid down in the model and the accompanying assessment rubric provide a scaffolding to the practitioners' existing ideas on the e-portfolios that they would like to have their students create. The criteria are based on a set of key questions that teachers should ask and answer before embarking on the e-portfolio experiment.

Keywords E-portfolios · Assessment · Community of practice · Outcomes-based teaching and learning · Graduate attributes

Using E-Portfolios for Assessment: An Overview

Learning portfolios as an assessment tool is not a new invention by any stretch of imagination. In fact one of the most enduring perspectives on learning portfolios is from the nineties and defines portfolios as "a purposeful collection of student work

T. Chaudhuri (✉)
Hong Kong Baptist University, Kowloon Tong, Hong Kong
e-mail: tusharc@hkbu.edu.hk

© Springer Nature Singapore Pte Ltd. 2017
T. Chaudhuri and B. Cabau (eds.), *E-Portfolios in Higher Education*,
DOI 10.1007/978-981-10-3803-7_1

that exhibits the student's efforts, progress, and achievements in one or more areas. The collection must include student participation in selecting contents, the criteria for selection, the criteria for judging merit, and evidence of student self-reflection" (Paulson et al. 1991: 60). Since then portfolios or their digitized versions, e-portfolios, have been defined as (digitized) collections of artefacts (Lorenzo and Ittelson 2005), repositories of (student) work (Shroff et al. 2013) or even as digital containers capable of storing visual and auditory content (Abrami and Barrett 2005: 1).

The shift, however, from the paper versions to the digitized versions has been evident since the early years of the twenty-first century and have entailed a variety of affordances such as affordability and ubiquity to name just two and is parallel to the shift towards e-learning in general (Light et al. 2012, ix–x). Zubizarreta points out that despite the history of portfolios in certain disciplines, the portfolio approach to gauging student accomplishments and growth in learning—while not entirely new in higher education—has historically received more attention in the K-12 [schools] arena (2009: 4). All authors agree, however, that using portfolios for assessment is gaining momentum in the higher education sector. And this trend is not only restricted to the West but also includes Asian countries such as Singapore, Japan and most importantly for us Hong Kong (Zubizaretta 2009: 4).

The trend of using e-portfolios in higher education institutions in Hong Kong is closely related to the concept of Outcomes-Based Teaching and Learning which has been adopted in Hong Kong since 2010 onwards. This approach is to enable "evaluation and improving quality", (and) "gathering credible evidence for assessing student learning" (University Grants Committee [UGC] 2011).

Since then institutions have worked on their curricula to achieve constructive alignment (Biggs and Tang 2007) between Intended Learning Outcomes, Teaching and Learning Activities and Assessment. Through curriculum planning, the Intended Learning Outcomes of individual courses (CILOS) have been mapped to the matching Programme Intended Learning Outcomes (PILOS), which in turn have been mapped to the Graduate Attributes (GAs) of the institution. The next stage is to ensure that the PILOs and Graduate Attributes are being achieved at an institutional level. This is commonly referred to as outcomes assessment (OA). At the Hong Kong Baptist University, OA has been conceptualised and piloted under the ECI or the Evidence Collection Initiative for outcomes assessment and has 6 testing components distributed over three levels which are by and large quantitative methods using external tests with some elements of course-embedded assessments:

– Course Level: CEA, FRE
– Programme Level: Aggregated CEA, LEI-Programme
– University Level: University Academic Test, LEI-P/Personal and Social Responsibility Inventory

(Hong Kong Baptist University, Centre for Holistic Teaching and Learning Evidence Collection Initiative—Report for AY2012–2013 and Plan for AY2013–2014).

Underlying this concept of OA is the assumption that since constructive alignment clearly defines and assesses outcomes, OA and especially those using course-embedded assessments are a good indicator of student learning (Hernon and Schwartz 2006). It has however been argued that "while the concept of constructive alignment can facilitate instructional planning at the course level to focus on learning outcomes, it may not be able to facilitate the integration of broader sets of outcomes that may be required at institutional or society levels" (Kennedy 2011: 212). For this, an "integrated approach" is proposed in which 'competencies are relational, involve reflective practice and place importance on context' (ibid). Kennedy (ibid: 213) argues that "it follows from such an approach that assessment will be very challenging since its focus will be on the attainment of complex outcomes and the extent to which they have been achieved. Yet this should not be a deterrent from considering such an approach since it can lead to the development of meaningful, relevant and representative outcomes required by institutions and the community". Pelliccione and Dixon (2008: 750) argue further that "quality is a difficult concept to define given the use of a traditional assessment framework and it cannot be simply reduced to a set of easily quantified learning outcomes. Students learn in different ways and assessment which supports learning needs to be flexible and take into account the needs of individuals in order for them to make sense of feedback in the context of their own environment".

The e-portfolio as an assessment tool lends itself very well to this idea of a flexible model of assessment. The outcomes-based approach to teaching, learning and assessment which tertiary institutions in Hong Kong have embraced emphasises learner-centred practices to help achieve higher level outcomes such as evaluation, reflection and inquiry. Student e-portfolios support learners to take an active role in achieving these higher level learning outcomes by giving them ownership of their own learning (Cambridge 2010: 25). In terms of assessment, e-portfolios support criterion-referenced as well as formative assessments. Cambridge (2010: 25) points out that "in giving students a place to reflect on their experiences through the artefacts of those experiences and the ability to creatively express their understanding of who they are and what they have accomplished, e-portfolios take into account the importance of authenticity to deep learning". E-portfolios not only provide students the avenue to demonstrate their accomplishments but also their information communication technologies (ICT) capacities. Their ICT abilities can be illustrated through selected and self-made images, multimedia, blog entries and hyperlinks related to their overall learning experiences. Furthermore, these artefacts should also include student's reflections on their learning and experiences as well as course lecturers, tutors and peers' comments on student's submissions.

E-portfolios are also powerful tools for self-directed evaluation and assessment. For e.g. Johnson et al. (2010: 9) observe that "the development of a portfolio encourages learners to shift from playing a passive role in assessment and evaluation—in which they are pressed to focus on external issues, such as what questions the instructors are going to ask and what they should be studying—to an active role, in which they must engage in more complex thinking and self evaluation in choosing representations of what they learned. This route thus requires students to reflect on and demonstrate their competencies with real world artefacts". Shroff et al. (2013: 144) have summarized the research to find that "the e-portfolio can also be a powerful tool to (1) promote learning (including learning from the process of assembling the portfolio); (2) improve critical thinking and content areas; (3) record accomplishments in an educational context held by the students for their own use; (4) assess long term, ongoing, authentic evaluation, and self-evaluation and self-reflection, and (5) provide evidence of continuous development". In their own research on implementation of e-portfolios for outcome-based assessment Pellicione and Dixon (2008: 759) find that:

> Throughout this research it has become clear that there are several advantages to implementing an ongoing and comprehensive approach to the development of e-portfolios in undergraduate education programs. Not only do they encourage the explicit alignment of organisational generic student outcomes with those of individual programs but it appears that student engagement with this form of selecting, describing, analysing and appraising each chosen artefact empowers students to become the drivers of their own development.

But this is easier said than done. The usual affordances of lifelong learning, personal and professional development, developing reflective practice, etc., associated with e-portfolio integration are valid in the long-term institutional context, but vague in the short term and for the purposes of assessment within a semester or course. This is an issue which affects not only teachers but also students who are required to create an e-portfolio and features prominently in the case study analyses included in this volume. It is a significant factor in accepting or rejecting e-portfolios as a valid teaching and learning exercise, as was shown in the study by Shroff et al. who have described an Attitude Towards Learning (ATL) using E-Portfolios (2013: 143). In fact Ayala (2006: 13) goes as far as claiming that "the ones most hurt by this [e-portfolios as a top-down institutional mandate and without considering the students' needs] would hurt those students the most who created electronic portfolios in response to campus or course requirements established without adequate regard to their effectiveness in higher education". Based on their own empirical research on implementation of e-portfolios in institutions of higher education in Hong Kong, Deneen and Brown (2014: 1) point out that faculties, programmes and universities may depend more on enthusiasm rather than on critical research when it comes to e-portfolio management and adoption.

REFLECT: A Community of Practice on Student E-Portfolios

Enthusiasm did play a big role even at the Hong Kong Baptist University when in May 2014 a Community of Practice (CoP) was set up to exchange ideas on how student e-portfolios could become a tool for assessment and for lifelong learning

公民 Citizenship	Be responsible citizens with an international outlook and a sense of ethics and civility
知識 Knowledge	Have up-to-date, in-depth knowledge of an academic specialty, as well as a broad range of cultural and general knowledge
學習 Learning	Be independent, lifelong learners with an open mind and an inquiring spirit
技能 Skills	Have the necessary information literacy and IT skills, as well as numerical and problem-solving skills, to function effectively in work and everyday life
創意 Creativity	Be able to think critically and creatively
溝通 Communication	Have trilingual and biliterate competence in English and Chinese, and the ability to articulate ideas clearly and coherently
群體 Teamwork	Be ready to serve, lead and work in a team, and to pursue a healthy lifestyle

Fig. 1.1 The HKBU graduate attributes for undergraduate courses

and provide evidence of student achievement of the HKBU Graduate Attributes (Fig. 1.1). The CoP included 12 like-minded colleagues from multiple disciplines and learning centres at the University. They were united by either their experience of working with e-portfolios as assessment tools or their desire to introduce new forms of assessment. The e-portfolios would reflect learning in their respective courses as well as support both formative and summative modes of assessment. (Chaudhuri and Chan 2016: 1).

Although the CoP was set up based on the enthusiasm of colleagues interested in testing e-portfolios in their respective disciplines, its agenda was intended to address some of the issues associated with implementing e-portfolios in university courses as being issues generally associated with integrating technology in higher education. First and foremost the CoP wanted to address the issue that e-portfolios are generally restricted to specific disciplines, where collecting artefacts and reflecting on them to showcase professional and or academic development seems to be an obvious choice. Traditionally some of these disciplines have been Education (pre-service teacher-students), Language (writing courses) and of course Visual Arts. The CoP on the other hand set out to involve colleagues from disciplines where e-portfolios were not the obvious choice for assessment. Disciplines represented in the CoP were History, Mathematics, Business Communication, Physical Education, European Studies and Education Studies, and members included Professors, Assistant and Associate Professors, Lecturers, Learning Officers, Librarians and General Education officers. This eclectic group of members included in the CoP ensured that the discussion on e-portfolios within the campus was multidisciplinary, i.e. additive in nature and was not restricted to certain niche areas. Nor was it a discussion which did not take into account the unique needs of individual academic disciplines. But concentrated on creating a template fit for all which usually brings on the danger that "portfolios are done unto students, rather than being done by them" (Ayala 2006: 13). In other words, the CoP answered the question, why e-portfolios, from a course or discipline perspective rather than from an institutional perspective. It used a more bottom-up approach and contributed to a more democratic model of e-portfolio integration.

Last but not the least, the CoP also paid particular attention to the choice of technology while implementing e-portfolios. Similar to the issue of purpose while introducing e-portfolios, the choice of technology and its implementation plays a major role in students and teachers accepting or rejecting e-portfolios (Shroff et al. 2011). Here also the CoP took an inductive approach to the issue where members were free to choose the technology, which they would use as a platform for their course-level e-portfolios and bring back their and their students' voices to the discussion table of the CoP.

The following sections re-examine the discussion on the above issues within the CoP and the conclusions reached. The sections take the form of questions and answers considered relevant by the CoP on student e-portfolios and which could lead up to an e-portfolio initiative at the course and or programme level at higher education institutions. The chapters in the second section of this volume are not only case studies illustrating the discussion in this chapter but are also carriers of students' and teachers' voices as reflected in their data.

Five Questions for Effective E-Porfolio Practice

Question 1: Why Use E-Portfolios for Your Course?

Any discussion on e-portfolios with a bottom-up approach needs to start with the question of purpose (Barrett 2007). Members of the CoP were asked in one of the very first meetings what to their mind was the primary purpose of introducing e-portfolios to their courses. This is a very different discussion to the one which is found in the literature on the affordances of e-portfolios in general. A good overview of these is provided by Shroff et al. (2013), or a more comprehensive one by Cambridge (2010), and I will not review these here. Individual authors in this volume have referred to the relevant studies in their own fields, which are more useful to the purposes of this volume. The discussion is different because the practitioners were asked to reflect on whether an e-portfolio as a tool (for assessment, reflection, repository or showcase) at all fits the discipline that they were representing. As a previous exercise, the members had already made themselves familiar with the general affordances associated with e-portfolios and were now ready to adapt that discussion to their own practice. In many ways members had to start from scratch as experiences from classical e-portfolio disciplines such as Education or Language could not directly be put to use for disciplines like History or Mathematics. Moreover, they had to consider the value-addition of the e-portfolio exercise both from their own as well as their students' perspectives in order to fulfil the following task:

> Please complete the following statements:
> An e-portfolio would help my students to…
> An e-portfolio (in my course) would help me to…

Task 1: *Identifying Roles for the E-Portfolio*
As expected, courses from diverse disciplines also had diverse expectations of what role an e-portfolio would fulfil in that course, taking into account the existing syllabi, outcomes and assessment schemes in place. These roles ranged from showcasing particular skills such as creativity in a foreign language (Chui and Dias in this volume) to scaffolding a major assessment task such as a term paper by collecting and reflecting on artefacts throughout the semester (To and Ladds in this volume). Courses within disciplines such as Physical Education (Cheung et al. in this volume) or Education (Sivan in this volume) looked at e-portfolios as a reflection and showcase tool for out-of-class learning, whereas in a course on Business Communication it was thought best to integrate the e-portfolio into the day-to-day classroom activities and make it into a sharing platform for collaborative learning (Linger in this volume). On a more macro level, General Education (GE) portfolios were thought to be best open-ended and to serve to showcase the GE experience at HKBU (Hodgson in this volume), whereas final year European Studies students were encouraged to develop a portfolio of skills they thought were most suited to the job market that they were about to enter (Cabau in this volume).

Question 2: Where Should You Start?

Once the role of the e-portfolio at the course level seems to have been defined, a good starting point for the e-portfolio implementation would be to identify specific outcomes for the final product. The CoP being an institutionally funded group with the mandate of identifying the scope of multidisciplinary e-portfolios for the entire institution, it was also essential to find a common denominating factor for all courses of the university and use this as the starting point. A particularly useful set of criteria was found to be the 7 Graduate Attributes (GA) defined by the HKBU.

At first sight these GA are little more than an abstract set of core competencies expected from graduating students representing the university in the job market. Nevertheless core competencies in higher education have been a topic of discussion for quite some time now (Lozano et al. 2012) and are generally read as the antithesis to subject-oriented skill sets; as Gnanam (2000: 148) calls them, they are "subject-neutral" skills. So core competencies are by nature transdisciplinary and speak to a much broader target audience than a particular subject. Yet keeping with the principles of outcomes-based education, these core competencies or in our case the GAs are mapped to each individual course being taught at the university. This fact makes the GA a particularly useful instrument while designing an e-portfolio even at the course level. The CoP sought to capitalise on this fact and the members were asked to identify at least two GAs from the above list, which had been mapped to their individual courses and which they would like to assess based on the e-portfolio they prescribed for their students.

> - Choose a partner from around the room with whom you would like to brainstorm. Try to choose a discipline which is far from your own. The idea is to learn from each other and also to identify common factors of e-portfolios across disciplines.
> - You have a hand-out with the GAs on it. Choose at least two which you think you can use as a starting point for your e-portfolio concept.
> - Ask yourself which course/programme outcome(s) can be mapped to each GA.
> - Explain to your partner(s) why you chose each GA and brainstorm what sort of Artefacts/Student-work you would like to see under this 'Category'.

Task 2: Mapping the GA to the Outcomes of the E-Portfolio
In this particular group of CoP members it was noticed that Knowledge (particularly cultural and general knowledge), Skills (especially information literacy and IT) and Creativity (including critical inquiry) emerged as some of the common GA which members wanted to see reflected through e-portfolios in the courses

irrespective of the discipline. This had something to do both with the understanding of e-portfolios as showcases of student work as well as the difficulty of assessing attributes such as creativity or information literacy through conventional assessment methods. The point to note here is that these attributes were considered important by practitioners of a diverse set of disciplines and found to be relevant to their disciplines.

Question 3: How Is the E-Portfolio Going to Be Structured?

Once the questions have been answered as to what role an e-portfolio should play within the course, its assessment design, and what outcomes the e-portfolio should be assessing, the next logical question to discuss would be the structure and the look and feel of the e-portfolio. The broad question regarding the structure of the portfolio can be further broken down into three main component parts as was evident in the deliberations of the CoP, namely: The nature of the artefacts included in the e-portfolio, the number of such artefacts that should be included so that a clear development of the attribute to be assessed emerges and so that the e-portfolio effectively fulfils its role and last but not the least the question of how the final product is organised and how it should look. An easy answer to these questions is that it depends on the course and its outcomes as well as on the person teaching that course. This is true on the surface. On the other hand, for practitioners just starting out with the idea of e-portfolios it is of vital importance that a set of criteria be provided which act as guidelines for them to develop their own ideas further (see also Pegrum and Oakley in this volume). From the students' perspective it is equally vital that they receive a succinct set of directions to be able to collect, select and present the artefacts to make their e-portfolio most effective for their target audience (Ellis in this volume). The answers presented below therefore do not lay claim to being exhaustive or representative but are the result of the CoP discussions mentioned above and are based on the experiences of 12 different practitioners, the details of which can be found in the chapters of this volume. They contribute to the criterion-based model developed by the CoP and then tested in individual courses.

Question 3a: What Kind of Artefacts Can Be Included?

Broadly e-portfolios would allow for two types of artefacts, namely text-based artefacts, which could include reflective texts, journals, blogs or research logs among others; and multimedia artefacts such as videos, collages, vlogs, etc. The assignments could be course-embedded, i.e. they come from the instructors as part of their teaching or could be specific portfolio assignments.

Systematically one can map these artefacts to specific outcomes of e-portfolios and classify them accordingly. The following table was the result of such a discussion within the CoP, where members were asked to add to the table with more ideas on what kind of artefacts could be linked to the outcomes listed on the left.[1]

Outcome	Examples
Critical inquiry (assignment: small-scale research task)	Journal entries, (video) blogs, bibliographies, evidences of critical use of the Internet
Creativity (assignment: solve a problem)	Case studies, assignments, creating an original piece of work such as a literary text or a multimedia artefact
Citizenship (assignment: discipline-oriented community service)	Multimedia and or reflective essay as evidence of extra-curricular engagement (political/social/creative)
Information literacy	Research log, research assignments, bibliography, use of the Internet

Task 3: Giving Examples for the Nature of Artefacts for the Outcomes
The above table suggests that assignments set within the course are also legitimate artefacts which can be re-used for the purposes of an e-portfolio. Such assignments can be tagged to particular outcomes and pointed out to the students or identified by themselves as artefacts which they can use in their e-portfolios. During the course of the semester a repository is then gradually built up for a particular outcome, out of which the student can select his or her best work. But artefacts can be selected independently of course assignments where the e-portfolio and its contents are an assignment by themselves. These artefacts may showcase independent and autonomous learning (Chui and Dias in this volume) and even encourage the kind of inquiry-based learning which lies at the heart of many of the core competencies set out by higher education institutions for the twenty-first century.

Question 3b: How Many Artefacts Should Be Included?

This is usually the first question asked by students when an e-portfolio is introduced as an assessment component of a course. The question may reflect not so much a desire to know more about the assignment than a nagging concern about workload. And though it is good practice to prescribe a minimum number of artefacts, one needs to constantly keep in mind the feasibility from the student's perspective. On the other hand, it is not realistic to leave it to the student to decide how many

---

[1]On an institutional level such a table could look similar to the table used by the Cleveland State University, where artefacts are mapped to programme standards of the institution.

artefacts he or she would like to include, as only one artefact may not reflect any development of the outcome being assessed over the course of the semester. The CoP experience as reflected in the case studies included in this volume points towards a number ranging from 3 to 5 artefacts in each category of the e-portfolio, depending on the length and time required to acquire each artefact. Finally, it is an individual decision which can be made more democratic by including the students in the decision-making. Asking them to commit to a certain number of artefacts, keeping in mind their individual workloads, fosters the sense of ownership as well as giving the teacher an insight into what the student has actually accomplished given his or her other semester commitments.

Question 3c: How Should the Artefacts Be Organised?

This question has two answers on two different ends of the spectrum of designs available for student e-portfolios. One is that the organisation of the portfolio is best left to the owner of the portfolio, and the other is that a template should be provided to the students where categories to organise the artefacts are pre-determined according to the outcomes that the e-portfolio is intended to assess. The second answer has some obvious advantages. For newcomers, whether students or teachers, it is useful to have a structure or scaffolding on which to build up a portfolio. From the teacher's perspective it helps to keep the outcomes in mind while designing and later assessing the portfolio. It also enables the teacher to present the outcomes better to the students who in turn are better able to understand the expectations of the portfolio. At the very beginners' level where an e-portfolio is being used for the first time, detailed prompts could also be provided in addition to the categories to let the students know what exactly is meant by each category and what types of artefacts are expected from them in a particular category. This kind of scaffolding serves not only to ease the transition into a portfolio-based assessment but also serves as a learning process as to how e-portfolios could look and be organised, a skill that is then transferable to other contexts where an e-portfolio might be used. As the expertise increases and more experience in working with portfolios is gained, such scaffolding can gradually be removed, and the user can eventually decide for himself or herself how he or she would like to organise the portfolio. At this point he or she assumes full ownership of the portfolio.

Generally, the broader the target audience for a portfolio, the less the amount of scaffolding one should use. Whether it is the number of artefacts, their nature or the organization of the end product, less scaffolding is more opportunity for the user to showcase his or her skills and competencies. In the present volume, portfolios showcasing the GE experience in general consciously did not prescribe a template but gave examples of similar portfolios which enabled students to identify the areas they wanted to highlight in their GE portfolios and gave them the space to explore the possibilities (Hodgson in this volume). For purposes of assessments linked to specific competencies which are pre-defined at the institutional or course level, pre-structured portfolios enable a more granular insight into student progress and development, e.g. using student-facing learning analytics (Ellis in this volume).

Question 4: How Should You Assess E-Portfolios?

Assessment of e-portfolios has been discussed in the literature at length (e.g., Bhattacharya and Hartnett 2007; Barrett 2007; Lorenzo and Ittelson 2005a). Through this discussion certain propositions emerge which one must keep in mind while taking up by far the most challenging part of implementing e-portfolios. Barrett (2007) proposes that while assessing e-portfolios one must differentiate between assessment *for* and assessment *of* learning (442). The latter is high-stakes, institutionally prescribed summative assessment, and the former is meant to improve learning and is essentially formative (Barrett 2007: 444). This narrative of the e-portfolio assessment being either summative or formative has become more or less established, leading to the dichotomy of developmental or learning portfolios (Barrett 2007), and showcase or assessment portfolios (Lorenzo and Ittelson 2005a).

On the surface most of the e-portfolios discussed in this volume belong to the latter category of showcase or assessment portfolios as they are prescribed by the institution (even though only at the course level) and are part of the assessment scheme of the particular course and so have to be awarded a grade at the end of the semester. However, it might be wrong to call them positivist as opposed to constructivist (Paulson and Paulson 1994: 8) in a stricter sense, as the process of selecting, organising and presenting the artefacts can still involve a constructivist approach where meaning (of the external GA) could be constructed and students are free to choose or create artefacts that they deem most suited to the GA being assessed in that course. Barrett suggested in 2007 that "in order to approach a balanced solution we must envisage a system that makes it easy for students to maintain their own digital archive of work [...]. Students can then draw from the same collection of evidence as they respond to and create showcase portfolios" (p. 440). This vision is already reality in 2016. The implementation of e-portfolios for pre-service teachers in The Graduate School of Education of the University of Western Australia, which actually prescribes a developmental as well as a showcase e-portfolio, is a shining example (Oakley et al. 2013). E-portfolio management systems such as Mahara and MyPortfolio, which were the two main platforms used for the CoP, enable users to maintain a repository of artefacts which can be drawn upon to create showcase or assessment e-portfolio as the need arises. When these systems are used in conjunction with institutional Learning Management Systems

(LMS) they can also automatically import online assignments into the e-portfolio of the user. Mahara can be plugged into the Moodle LMS and MyPortfolio is built into the Blackboard LMS.

Assessment portfolios are best assessed using a specially constructed rubric fit for the purpose (Bhattacharya and Hartnett 2007). The rubric enables the teacher to assess the portfolio using criteria which have been formulated to describe the skills or outcomes which the e-portfolio is supposed to assess. Sharing the rubric with the students gives them an additional orientation and explains to them what a particular skill or outcome means. In a more democratic process which would make the formative component stronger, one can discuss the skill descriptors of the rubric with the students. The CoP opted to develop a rubric for the core competencies that its members had identified as being relevant to e-portfolios in almost all disciplines. The result was a generic transdisciplinary rubric resulting from a multidisciplinary effort to implement e-portfolios in individual courses (see Appendix B at the end of this volume). The assessment competencies were identified to be Presentation, Reflection, Information Literacy and Critical Thinking. The idea was that teachers would already have the descriptors for the core competencies ready when they embarked upon the e-portfolio experiment and would add to the rubric their discipline's own competencies which the e-portfolio should showcase. They could also remove any of the four core competencies if considered irrelevant.

Question 5: What Electronic Platform Should You Use?

The instinctive web 2.0 answer to this question is "the platform that is easiest to use". Though simplistic this is not an answer that one should just ignore for more sophisticated ones. Using the Technology Acceptance Model (Davis 1989), Shroff et al. have shown empirically that "when students perceive the e-portfolio system as one that is easy to use and nearly free of mental effort, they may have a favourable attitude towards the usefulness of the system" (2011: 610). This is also an important insight which the CoP arrived at after testing four different platforms commonly used as e-portfolio platforms. More importantly, ease of use is a criterion which is relevant to both teachers and students and almost always the first criterion in terms of buy-in and usage for both parties. This is because when it comes to using web 2.0 applications, it is easy to fall into the trap of the digital natives versus digital immigrants divide, which automatically puts teachers on the defensive and assumes magical digital powers in students, though empirical evidence does not support the existence of such a divide. So teachers frequently put in hours of work trying to master the digital platform, often forgetting that students might have to do the same but might not share the same level of motivation especially if the purpose is not yet clear enough.

The CoP tested four different platforms on four different criteria, namely (i) ease of use, (ii) compatibility with the institutional LMS, (iii) fit for purpose (including aesthetics) and (iv) ownership (can the user take the portfolio with him/her?). The first criterion, ease of use, has been discussed above. The question of compatibility with the institutional LMS are important in light of the simple fact that if students and teachers are logged on to the same LMS for their teaching and learning purposes, it might be easier for them to use a built-in e-portfolio system that links to that LMS. Apart from the obvious advantage that no separate log-ins are required, built-in e-portfolio systems also enable students and teachers to seamlessly use their electronically submitted assignments as artefacts for the e-portfolio. Further, as LMS are locked down within the university community, it is an important safeguard for new users against copyright infringement issues, as the teacher can intervene if such infringements are suspected, before the e-portfolio is shared for use outside the course or university domain. Very often LMS-based e-portfolios are the only option which the institution offers, considering costing and logistics involved in hosting and maintaining an entirely different platform exclusively for e-portfolios, especially at the piloting stage as in the case of the HKBU. But such a portfolio platform might not be fit for purpose as it might offer very few tools for organization, presentation or sharing. It might not also be aesthetically pleasing, not offering an adequate number of themes, templates and customization possibilities. Last but not least, it might not enable peer sharing or interaction. On the other hand a simple standard template might be advantageous at the start as it is easy to use and enables both students and teachers to concentrate on the content rather than on the appearance. E-portfolios plugged into the institutional LMS have often an issue with ownership. If an e-portfolio is an instrument of lifelong learning or a showcase for future employers, the students must have complete ownership. However, many institutions do not allow students to take their e-portfolios with them. While some of them allow a certain grace period using an archival system, others might completely block access upon graduation.

It is therefore important to keep in mind how an e-portfolio initiative could be sustained beyond the university experience, and the choice of platforms plays a central role in this issue. The following table[2] gives an overview of the four platforms tested by the CoP, mapped against the four criteria mentioned above. It is interesting to note that it is the commercial websites such as Google sites or Weebly, which offer the most flexibility and features in regard to the CoP criteria. A major weakness however is that commercial platforms, especially Weebly or Wix, which are essentially website builders, do not provide much scope for peer commentary or group sharing in their basic features. Also, not being locked down within a university domain, they expose their owners to the dangers of the open web such as copyright or liability issues, leaving them open to potential lawsuits and other risks (Table 1.1).

---

[2]A similar table but more comprehensive and arranged according to purpose is offered by Barrett (2012).

Table 1.1 Overview of e-portfolio platforms

	Features	Ease of use	Compatibility with LMS	Fitness for purpose and aesthetics	Ownership
MyPortfolio	Part of the Blackboard LMS. Licences required. Cost intensive	✓	✓	X	X
Mahara	Open source. Dedicated entirely to e-portfolios. Compatible with Moodle LMS. Support cost intensive	X	✓	✓	X
Google sites	Free. Not compatible with LMS. No institutional support	✓	X	✓	✓
Weebly	Free. Premium features on payment. Not compatible with LMS. No institutional support	✓	X	✓	✓

Conclusion

Given the amount of literature and good practice examples now available on e-portfolios for student learning, embarking on the e-portfolio experiment can often be a daunting task for individual course leaders or teachers. This is partly because of the very high-level outcomes often associated with e-portfolios, such as lifelong learning or reflective practice. Also, e-portfolios have traditionally been a humanities domain thought to be particularly useful for writing courses and education programmes, or for documenting internship experiences. But as the demand for outcomes-based education and evidence-based assessment grows, especially in the Asia-pacific region, it is essential to explore the affordances of e-portfolios further and to make them more accessible to a wider community of teachers and practitioners as well as students. The community of practice at the HKBU set out to do exactly this, with a multidisciplinary approach as opposed to a transdisciplinary one, so as not to gloss over the details of the e-portfolio implementation process but rather to be able to concentrate on them, in order to reach a maximum number of engaged practitioners.

The CoP experience helped us to break down the implementation process of e-portfolios into its most essential components, which have been discussed in this article. It also gave us an insight into students' perceptions of and teachers' problems with e-portfolios. It brought to light some essential facts which contribute to a low buy-in rate. Like all new teaching and learning initiatives, initiating and sustaining an e-portfolio approach takes up enormous amounts of time both from the teachers' and the students' points of view. Course-embedded e-portfolios cannot therefore be extra-curricular activities but must replace existing and (maybe not so effective) assessment methods such as final exams or term papers, or they might be used to ease the load of such assignments by getting the students to work ahead and prepare to avoid end-of-semester stress. Buy-in can also be ensured by making the e-portfolios legitimate showcases of student learning by giving the students a say in assessing them, both in terms of peer or self-assessment and by giving them an opportunity to negotiate the items of the assessment rubric. A mutually negotiated rubric could serve the dual purposes of giving the users more ownership as well as more orientation. An e-portfolio initiative also cannot be static like most other assessment methods. It must evolve with the needs of the students and the institution. Collecting feedback from students is therefore essential to keep an eye on whether the e-portfolio implementation is indeed working for the students. Last but not least, since e-portfolios are not purely a summative form of assessment but work better when used as a formative tool, it is essential to mentor and scaffold the initial e-portfolios created by students. Regular sharing and submissions throughout the semester go a long way in understanding what direction the e-portfolios are going in before it is too late.

We sincerely hope that the case studies included in this volume will help to allay some initial reservations against e-portfolio practice, and encourage those already thinking about it to take the all-important first step.

Acknowledgements I would like to thank all my CoP members past and present on behalf of whom I am writing this article: Dr. Béatrice Cabau, Ms Céline Dias, Ms Chi-Shan Chui, Ms Chan Wai Yin, Prof. Atara Sivan, Prof. Cheung Siu Yin, Dr. Catherine Ladds, Dr. Simon To, Dr. Lisa Deng, Dr. Warren Linger, Dr. Eva Wong, Mr Chris Chan, Dr. Paula Hodgson and Dr. Ronnie Shroff.

References

Abrami, P. C., & Barrett, H. (2005). Directions for research and development on electronic portfolios. *Canadian Journal of Learning and Technology, 31*(3), 1–15.

Ayala, J. I. (2006). Electronic portfolios for whom? *Educause Quarterly, 29*(1), 12–13.

Barrett, H. C. (2007). Researching electronic portfolios and learner engagement: The reflect initiative. *Journal of Adolescent & Adult Literacy, 50*(6), 436–449. Wiley on behalf of the International Literacy Association Stable. Retrieved from http://www.jstor.org/stable/40015496. Accessed on January 24, 2017.

Barrett, H. (2012). Retrieved from http://www.electronicportfolios.com/eportfolios/tools.html

Bhattacharya, M., & Hartnett, M. (2007). E-portfolio assessment in higher education. In *37th ASEE/IEEE frontiers in education conference*. Milwaukee WI.

Biggs, J., & Tang, C. (2007). *Teaching for quality learning at university*. Berkshire, England: Open University Press.

Cambridge, D. (2010). *Eportfolios for lifelong learning and assessment*. San Francisco: Jossey Bass.

Cleveland State University. Retrieved from http://www.csuohio.edu/cehs/examples-artifacts-for-each-program-standard

Davis, F. D. (1989). Perceived usefulness, perceived ease of use, and user acceptance of information technology. *MIS Quarterly, 13*(3), 319–340.

Deneen, C. C., & Brown, G. T. L. (2014). A critical approach to E-Portfolios in higher education: How research may inform change and adoption. In *40th Annual Conference of International Association for Educational Assessment*. Singapore.

George, L., & Ittelson, J. (2005). An overview of E-Portfolios. In Educause Learning Initiative Paper 1, pp. 1–28.

Gnanam, A. (2000). Core competency and higher education. *SAJHE/SATHO, 14*(2), 147–151.

Hernon, P., & Schwartz, C. (2006). Applying student learning outcomes to an educational programme. In P. Hernon, R. E. Dugan, & C. Schwartz (Eds.), *Revisiting outcomes assessment in higher education* (pp. 181–198). Westport, Conn: Libraries Unlimited.

Johnson, R. S., Mims-Cox, S. J., & Doyle-Nichols, A. (2010). *Developing portfolios in education. A guide to reflection, inquiry and assessment*. Thousand Oaks: Sage.

Kennedy, K. J. (2011). Conceptualising quality improvement in higher education: Policy, theory and practice for outcomes based learning in Hong Kong. *Journal of Higher Education Policy and Management, 33*(3), 205–218.

Lorenzo, G., Ittelson, J., (2005a). Demonstrating and assessing student learning with E-Portfolios. In Educause Learning Initiative Paper 3, pp. 1–19.

Lozano, J. F., Boni, A., Peris, J., Hueso, A. (2012). Competencies in higher education. A critical analysis from the capabilities approach. *Journal of Philosophy of Education, 46*(1), 132–147.

Oakley, G., Pegrum, M., & Johnston, S. (2013). Introducing e-portfolios to pre-service teachers as tools for reflection and growth: Lessons learnt. *Asia-Pacific Journal of Teacher Education*. doi:10.1080/1359866X.2013.854860

Paulson, F. L., & Paulson, P. R. (1994). Assessing portfolios using the constructivist paradigm. Paper presented at the annual meeting of the American Educational Research Association, New Orleans, LA.

Paulson, F. L., Paulson, P. R., & Meyer, C. A. (1991). What makes a portfolio a portfolio? *Educational Leadership, 48*(5), 60–63.

Pelliccione, L., & Dixon, K. (2008). EPortfolios: Beyond assessment to empowerment in the learning landscape. In Hello! Where are you in the landscape of educational technology? In *Proceedings from ascilite Melbourne 2008*.

Shroff, R. H., Deneen, C. C., & Ng, E. M. W. (2011). Analysis of technology acceptance model in examining students' behavioural intention to use an e-portfolio. *Australasian Journal of Educational Technology, 27*(4), 600–618.

Shroff, R. H., Trent, J., & Ng, E. M. W. (2013). Using e-portfolios in a field experience placement: Examining student-teachers' attitudes towards learning in relationship to personal value, control and responsibility. *Australasian Journal of Educational Technology, 29*(2), 143–160.

Tushar, C., & Yin, C. W. (2016). Networked learning communities: A perspective arising from a multidisciplinary community of practice on student eportfolios. *Learning Communities Journal, 8*(2).

University Grants Committee, Hong Kong. (2011). *Annual Report 2010–2011*. Retrieved from http://www.ugc.edu.hk/eng/ugc/publication/report/figure2010/m001.htm. Accessed on September 24, 2016.

University of Waterloo. Retrieved from https://uwaterloo.ca/centre-for-teaching-excellence/teaching-resources/teaching-tips/educational-technologies/all/eportfolios

Zubizarreta, J. (2009). *The learning portfolio: Reflective practice for improving student learning*. San Francisco: Jossey-Bass

Chapter 2
The Changing Landscape of E-Portfolios: Reflections on 5 Years of Implementing E-Portfolios in Pre-Service Teacher Education

Mark Pegrum and Grace Oakley

Abstract E-portfolios are becoming an increasingly common component of higher education programmes, serving as constructivist learning spaces where students can reflect on their learning journeys, as centralised collections of work on which students can be assessed, and as integrated showcases where students can demonstrate their accomplishments to potential employers. At the same time, many working professionals are currently being required or encouraged to build e-portfolios which demonstrate continuing learning for the purposes of maintaining employment, seeking promotion, and applying for new positions. Pre-service teacher education courses are among the higher education programmes where participants are now commonly asked to build e-portfolios which they will be able to continue to expand and develop once they have obtained employment as teachers. This chapter is based on the reflections of two teacher educators in a pre-service teacher education programme in Australia, looking back on the first five years of an e-portfolio initiative, covering the period 2011–2015. They reflect on key lessons learned about engaging students, engaging staff, and integrating technology. They outline changes which have occurred in the e-portfolio space over the past half-decade, due both to the changing nature of technology users and the changing nature of technology itself. It is suggested that e-portfolios may have a role to play in supporting a shift away from today's administratively oriented, pedagogically limited learning management systems (LMSs), and towards personal learning environments (PLEs) where students can engage in more individualised, autonomous learning practices.

Keywords E-portfolios · Pre-service teacher education · Assessment · Reflection · Personal learning environments · Web 2.0 · Multimedia

M. Pegrum (✉) · G. Oakley
The Graduate School of Education,
The University of Western Australia, Perth, Australia
e-mail: mark.pegrum@uwa.edu.au

© Springer Nature Singapore Pte Ltd. 2017
T. Chaudhuri and B. Cabau (eds.), *E-Portfolios in Higher Education*,
DOI 10.1007/978-981-10-3803-7_2

Introduction

With e-portfolios becoming ever more common in higher education as well as in many of the professions into which tertiary students later progress (e.g., Andrews and Cole 2015, on nursing; Winberg and Pallitt 2016, on university teaching), it is timely to reflect on how these have evolved over the past half-decade. E-portfolios are digital collections of artefacts, often assembled to demonstrate competence in a given area or areas. They typically incorporate multimedia resources (Chatham-Carpenter et al. 2009/10; Hallam et al. 2012), allow for flexible organisation and reorganisation (Bartlett 2008; Lin 2008), and facilitate wider networking (ibid.), with considerable scope for supporting reflection on learning (Haverkamp and Vogt 2015; Samaras and Fox 2013; Shroff et al. 2013; Tzeng and Chen 2012).

As such, it has been suggested that e-portfolios may offer a way to balance two competing agendas found within higher education worldwide, namely a completion agenda focused on speed and efficiency, and a quality agenda focused on depth, understanding and complexity:

> thoughtful e-portfolio practice can help build student success (as measured in "hard outcomes" such as retention and graduation) while also advancing reflection, integration, and "deep learning." (Eynon, Gambino & Török, 2014, n.p.)

Building on the notion of deep learning, Haverkamp and Vogt (2015) point out that:

> e-Portfolios provide a constructivist pedagogical approach to learning that allows students to link developed digital content to a framework that illustrates achieved competencies but, more importantly, reflects a contextual understanding of their learning (Ehiyazaryan-White, 2012). This implies a "deep" learning versus a more superficial learning through the integration of new information into prior existing knowledge (Dalal, Hakel, Sliter, & Kirkendall, 2012). (p. 284)

By fostering connections across learning areas and learning experiences, e-portfolios may help students build a more holistic sense of their learning journeys (Martin 2013), while helping higher education institutions to transform themselves into more adaptive organisations which are responsive to today's changing needs (Eynon et al. 2014). Moreover, as will be discussed below, e-portfolios can simultaneously support personalisation of learning and student autonomy, linked to the development of twenty-first century skills. Their implementation is however not unproblematic, and their use may often be fragmented due to a combination of challenges relating to students, staff and technology (Andrews and Cole 2015).

In this chapter, two teacher educators in a pre-service teacher education programme in Australia look back on the first five years of an e-portfolio initiative which commenced in 2011. They reflect on key lessons learned about engaging students, engaging programme staff, and integrating technology into everyday learning practices. They go on to give their perspective on key changes which have occurred in the e-portfolio space over this period, due both to the changing nature of technology users, who are often more comfortable and skilful in the use of technology than they were five years ago, and the changing nature of technology itself, which has become more user-friendly and much more mobile-centric. Finally, it is suggested that e-portfolios, as they have evolved over recent years, may have a role to play in supporting a shift away from today's administratively oriented, pedagogically limited learning management systems (LMSs, also known as virtual learning environments, or VLEs), and towards personal learning environments (PLEs) where students can engage in more individualised, autonomous learning practices.

The Role of E-Portfolios in Pre-Service Teacher Education

In higher education, e-portfolios may serve as constructivist learning spaces where students can reflect on their own learning journeys; as centralised collections of work on which students can be assessed; and as integrated showcases where students can demonstrate their accomplishments to potential employers. At the same time, many working professionals are currently being required or encouraged to build e-portfolios which demonstrate continuing academic and practical learning for the purposes of maintaining employment, seeking promotion, and applying for new positions. Thus, when higher education students are asked to produce e-portfolios, these can serve immediate learning and assessment purposes, a medium-term job-seeking purpose, and the long-term purpose of preparing graduates for an increasingly common professional practice.

Pre-service teacher education programmes are among those where participants are now commonly asked to build e-portfolios (Oakley et al. 2014), which they will be able to continue to expand and develop once they have obtained employment as teachers. Indeed, in the context of teacher education in Australia, there have been recent moves to mandate the use of portfolios (TEMAG 2014). In the programme in question, a Master of Teaching qualification running at an Australian university since 2009, e-portfolios were first introduced in 2011. In the first three semesters of this four-semester programme, the pre-service teachers are invited to work on *developmental e-portfolios,* which are treated much like individualised, student-centred PLEs (Dudeney et al. 2013; Pegrum 2014) where they can assemble multimedia records of their work (including from their teaching practicum placements), reflect on their learning, receive targeted feedback from lecturers and peers, and network both within and beyond their cohort. In the fourth semester, in a unit entitled *Teaching and Learning with ICTs* (Information and Communication Technologies), the pre-service teachers are supported in transforming their developmental e-portfolios into *showcase e-portfolios* where they demonstrate their achievements relative to selected focus areas in the *Australian Professional Standards for Teachers* (AITSL 2014); these e-portfolios are then presented for assessment, and may also be used to accompany job applications in the manner of expanded digital curricula vitae (CVs). The terminological and conceptual division into developmental and showcase stages was instituted to deal with the widely acknowledged tension between e-portfolios' formative/process/constructivist learning aims, and their summative/product/assessment/marketing aims (Farrell and Rushby 2016; Lim and Lee 2014; Trevitt et al. 2014; Yang et al. 2016).

From 2011 to 2014, the e-portfolios were assessed from the perspective of ICTs by the unit lecturer, as well as from a broader employment perspective by a panel composed largely of school principals and deputy principals. By 2015, student numbers had grown too large for it to be feasible to identify enough principals and deputies who could commit the time required to staff the assessment panels, so a more streamlined assessment system was introduced involving only an ICTs-focused assessment by the unit lecturer. However, the pre-service teachers were, and are, encouraged to continue to view their e-portfolios as digital CVs, and anecdotal evidence indicates that many are still using them to support job applications.

Engaging Students

From the very first year, 2011, it was found that in order to engage students in the e-portfolio implementation, it was necessary to provide them with extensive support. First, it became apparent that they were confused about the multiple purposes of the e-portfolios, despite our attempt to introduce more clarity by distinguishing the *developmental* and *showcase* stages, accompanied by an explanation of the intended evolution of the e-portfolios from the former to the latter in a nine-page *E-portfolio Guide*. This corresponds to widespread findings in the literature about confusion over e-portfolios (Chatham-Carpenter et al. 2009/10; Strudler and Wetzel 2011/12). In 2012, this led us to create a flow diagram (see Fig. 1) to be incorporated into the *E-portfolio Guide*. Over the years, the guide grew in size and detail to eventually reach 19 pages in 2015.

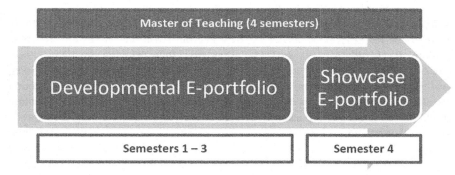

Fig. 1 Flow diagram of e-portfolio evolution over four semesters

Related to this, it has been noted in the research literature that students must perceive the value of e-portfolios for learning and/or career development in order to be motivated to use them (Chen et al. 2012). One of the reasons for the doubling in length of the *E-portfolio Guide* was the gradual expansion of the written rationale for the use of e-portfolios. By 2015, e-portfolios had become more normalised—to borrow a term from Stephen Bax (2011)—for our pre-service teachers, partly because of the embedding of more extensive explanations of their purposes in our programme; partly because of greater staff engagement with the e-portfolios, as detailed below; and partly because of a more widespread familiarity with e-portfolios in educational institutions and in the broader professional teaching community.

Second, our observations echoed findings in the research literature that pre-service teachers may not reflect deeply without adequate learner training (Bartlett 2008; Sung et al. 2009), and that in general guidelines and scaffolding are needed to support students' reflections in e-portfolios (Rafeldt et al. 2014; Yang et al. 2016). More support for pre-service teachers' reflections was provided in a number of ways, including through the use of a structure for reflective thinking based on the work of Bain et al. (2002), introduced both in the *E-portfolio Guide* and in a core first semester unit. Over a number of years, there has been an increasingly strong focus on students using their reflections to link theory with their own practice. This kind of reflecting has many advantages for pre-service teachers: it helps them develop into reflective practitioners who can be more effective teachers (Larrivee 2000; Rodman 2010); it helps them "link academic learning to personal development" (Eynon et al. 2014, n.p., with reference to Rodgers 2002); and it helps them identify their strengths and weaknesses in a way that will stand them in good stead in future job interviews (Andrews and Cole 2015). By the end of the process, while some pre-service teachers still struggle to reach a deeper level of reflection, others' writing clearly shows that they have begun to develop and rehearse a "professional voice" (Rafeldt et al. 2014, n.p.)—partly through peer interactions, as discussed below—which they can take with them into their careers.

Although from the start most pre-service teachers saw the value of reflecting on their learning, some found it tedious (Oakley et al. 2014). It became evident that one issue was the volume of writing and accompanying artefacts needed to demonstrate achievement of the expected graduate level of two to three focus areas for each of the seven professional standards required of Australian teachers. In 2015, we reduced the number of focus areas the pre-service teachers were required to cover. The ensuing drop in quantity correlated with a small but noticeable rise in quality, with an overall improvement in the depth of reflection as pre-service teachers were able to concentrate more closely on their chosen focus areas.

Engaging Staff

In addition to engaging students, it was equally important to engage staff in the e-portfolio implementation. In keeping with broader conversations about the need for educators to see themselves as designers of learning environments and learning experiences for their students (Hockly 2013; Laurillard 2012), one way to view e-portfolio initiatives is as educational design projects (Trevitt et al. 2014; Tur and Marín 2015). This entails a move into more pedagogically creative territory than is typically facilitated in LMSs, as well as a consideration of how best to integrate e-portfolios into programme assessment design (Yang et al. 2016). In the early years, however, we experienced some staff reluctance to get involved, as has been reported in other e-portfolio studies (Andrews and Cole 2015).

At the outset, many staff, much like our students, lacked clarity about the multiple purposes of the e-portfolios. While some made extensive use of them—requiring students to regularly upload work, with a few even providing feedback and conducting assessments within the e-portfolio space—others ignored them almost completely, thus exacerbating the pre-service teachers' confusion about their purposes, relevance and value. This issue was addressed in several ways.

The initial 2011 staff professional development (PD) programme was extended into 2012 in an effort to further upskill those academics who lacked confidence or familiarity with the technology. It was vital, however, for this PD to focus not only on the technology, but on the larger educational value of the e-portfolios, including their link to assessment, in order to ensure the pedagogical 'buy in' of staff (Andrews and Cole 2015). Staff, like students, must see the point of e-portfolios if they are to be motivated to use them (ibid.). Indeed, it has become abundantly clear over the past five years that it is necessary to aim for a point where "learners and teaching staff make the opportunity to acquire an adequately shared understanding of the concept and expectations of an [e] portfolio" (Trevitt et al. 2014, p. 75).

The availability of individualised support for staff, going beyond generic PD, was also important. Some such support was available in 2011–2012 from a dedicated ICTs Pedagogy Officer, a technologically experienced teacher seconded from a local school with funding provided by the Australian Government's *Teaching Teachers for the Future* project (Oakley and Pegrum 2015). After this point, the task of individualised support fell to the *Teaching and Learning with ICTs* lecturer and other programme staff, though in time a dedicated part-time staff member was employed to look after the e-portfolio platform, supporting both students and staff as required. In addition, the growing involvement of programme staff as members of the assessment panels—alongside school principals and deputies —from 2012 to 2014 helped them to perceive the bigger picture of e-portfolio use and to develop a more sophisticated understanding of the then still new *Australian Professional Standards for Teachers,* against which pre-service teachers were asked to reflect. Through this process staff were able to make more explicit connections between their teaching, their students' learning, and assessment.

Integrating Technology

The Changing Nature of Technology Users

In a baseline survey conducted in the first year of implementation, it was observed that although most pre-service teachers were making considerable use of ICTs for social, entertainment and simple information access purposes, very few had ever engaged in more complex activities involving web 2.0 tools (Oakley et al. 2014; cf. Istenic Starcic et al. 2016). This finding dovetails with extensive research that has found little empirical evidence of the existence of a homogenous, digitally accomplished generation of 'digital natives' (Andrews and Cole 2015; Hargittai 2010; Thomas 2011).

Nonetheless, with the spread of mobile smart devices in everyday life, students have generally become more comfortable and more accomplished in their dealings with digital technologies. What is more, during the past five years we have observed the level of peer-to-peer collaboration and support around new technologies growing considerably, and in a very specific way. As pre-service teachers' confidence and abilities increased from cohort to cohort, the reliance on a few expert students, which was noted in the first two cohorts in particular, gradually gave way to a broader sharing between a much larger number of students, all seeking ways to improve the technological aspects of their e-portfolios. In this way, the potential of e-portfolios to support further development of students' technological skills (Lin 2008) has been realised.

Indeed, following on from the *Teaching Teachers for the Future* project (DEEWR, n.d.), and in light of the *Australian Professional Standards for Teachers* and their ICT elaborations (AITSL, n.d.), there is a clear expectation that all Australian teacher educators and teachers, including pre-service teachers, have upgraded or are upgrading their technological knowledge, linking it to their existing or developing content and pedagogical knowledge (Mishra and Koehler 2006). The key aim of the *Teaching and Learning with ICTs* unit, which predated the *Teaching Teachers for the Future* project, has always been to help teachers develop this integrated skillset, but initially there was a strong focus specifically on technology, in large part due to the need to level the playing field for those pre-service teachers who arrived at their fourth semester with an inadequate technological grounding. However, with many now arriving in class with greater technological skills, and most being willing to seek help from peers when necessary, it has become possible over the last two to three years to focus less on technological knowledge per se and more on its integration with content and pedagogical knowledge, which is in line with wider trends in pre-service teacher education (Drummond and Sweeney 2016). This has included promoting pre-service teachers' awareness of the differentiation of technology usage for early childhood, primary and secondary levels, and of their students' typical developmental arcs across these levels.

To the extent that there is still a focus on technology, it involves introducing the pre-service teachers to tools they may not have seen before; showing them examples of how other teachers and students have used them; and encouraging them to explore these, use them with their own students on practicum placements and preserve records of this usage, and employ them to enrich the presentation of their accomplishments in their e-portfolios. The pre-service teachers are thereby encouraged "to explore the use of multimedia to reflect the breadth and depth of learning outcomes" (Haverkamp and Vogt 2015, p. 286, with reference to O'Keeffe and Donnelly 2013). E-portfolios can support the development of multimodal and broader digital literacies as they "encourage[e] deeper learning through the use of multimedia artefacts as richer forms of literacy to express understanding" (Lambert et al. 2007, p. 76, cited in Samaras and Fox 2013, p. 24; cf. Istenic Starčič et al. 2016). A selection of the tools most commonly integrated by recent pre-service teachers into their e-portfolios is listed in Table 1, along with examples of how they have been used.

The Changing Nature of Technology

From 2011 to 2014, each pre-service teacher created his or her e-portfolio on an individual wiki set up by programme staff on the Wikispaces platform, and hosted within a secure, password-protected environment. In line with our observation that five years ago students had limited skills with web 2.0 services, many struggled with uploading material to their wikis, and there was initially little embedding of multimedia artefacts of the kind wikis are designed to support. To our surprise, only a small number of pre-service teachers attended the optional technical workshops offered, though it was noticed that a larger number sought help at the point of need from a few expert peers.

Online peer commentary was restricted in the first year as the pre-service teachers' wikis were private by default and they needed to invite peers to view them, but at their request the wikis were opened up to the whole cohort from 2012; this meant that each individual worked on his or her own wiki, but could view and leave comments on peers' wikis. Due to technical issues the wikis subsequently reverted to invitation-only spaces, but students were repeatedly encouraged to invite peers to view their work, with nearly all opening up their wikis to at least some classmates. While a few students expressed concern over possible plagiarism of their work by others, which aligns with past findings in locations such as Hong Kong and Taiwan (Yang et al. 2016), most preferred a more open structure. Significantly, the process of writing for a wider audience and the ability to access and comment on others' work appear to have led to a deepening of reflections through a process of "reflection in community" (Eynon et al. 2014, n.p.). Furthermore, this has helped foster the kind of networked, web 2.0-supported structure which is becoming common in contemporary e-portfolios (Tur and Marín 2015), where students can interact within their cohorts but also externally with

Table 1 A selection of pre-service teachers' preferred tools for integration into e-portfolios

Purpose of tool	Popular services	Example of usage
Document embedding	• Box (www.box.com) • FlipSnack (www.flipsnack.com) • Scribd (www.scribd.com)	• Embedding lesson plans & essays
Mind mapping	• MindMeister (www.mindmeister.com) • SimpleMind (www.simpleapps.eu)	• Mapping personal learning networks (PLNs)
Image annotation	• ThingLink (www.thinglink.com)	• Annotating photographs of student work
Collage creation	• Cincopa (www.cincopa.com) • PhotoSnack (www.photosnack.com)	• Presenting collages of student work
Slideshow creation	• Prezi (prezi.com)	• Presenting elements of a teaching philosophy
Slideshow embedding	• SlideShare (www.slideshare.net)	• Embedding academic presentations created for other units of study
Animated avatar creation	• Voki (www.voki.com)	• Introducing sections of the e-portfolio
Animated video creation	• PowToon (www.powtoon.com)	• Presenting selections of resources
Video embedding	• YouTube (www.youtube.com)	• Embedding teaching videos
Multimedia poster creation	• Canva (www.canva.com) • Glogster (edu.glogster.com)	• Presenting a self-introduction
Multimedia timeline creation	• Capzles (www.capzles.com) • Timetoast (www.timetoast.com)	• Presenting a study history
Digital storytelling	• Storybird (storybird.com)	• Presenting reflections on teaching

practicum colleagues, mentors, and other educators. In addition, a self-assessment questionnaire, designed to aid the pre-service teachers in maintaining a focus on their e-portfolio contributions, was incorporated into the *E-portfolios Guide* in 2012 and has been used by some to keep their work on track. In brief, the incorporation of elements of both peer and self-assessment can help prepare students (and perhaps pre-service teachers in particular) for future professional practices as well as reducing the pressure on academic staff to provide all the feedback themselves (Trevitt et al. 2014).

In 2011, wikis were seen as state-of-the-art, flexible, generic online spaces which lent themselves to the construction of e-portfolios. By 2014, there were many competitors, including drag-and-drop website building services with clean, contemporary interfaces. Due to an overwhelming number of requests from our increasingly tech-savvy students that year, we decided to offer the pre-service teachers a free choice of platforms from the start of 2015. Around half opted to continue using the Wikispaces e-portfolio spaces provided for them, while the others were willing to risk a lack of technical support in selecting their own services, with the most common choices by far being Weebly (www.weebly.com) and Wix (www.wix.com). The pre-service teachers were generally able to solve their own technical problems, often with the aid of peers, with very few seeking recourse to the lecturer or the part-time support staff member.

Continuing the trend of previous years, the overview of requirements in the *E-portfolio Guide,* echoed in the unit outline, was broadened further, setting general parameters with plenty of illustrative examples, but without closely prescribing the necessary content. In fact, our current approach very much parallels that of Andrews and Cole (2015), who comment:

> When using e-portfolios for assessment purposes, Moores and Parks (2010) advise that assessment guidelines should be transparent but not too prescriptive. There is a fine line between encouraging creativity and innovation, but still providing clarity on structure, size and required elements to include. E-portfolios are consistent with the growth in person-alised and holistic approaches in education (Ellaway and Masters, 2008), and thus assessment guidelines need to be written with this in mind. (p. 571).

In some ways, the pre-service teachers' e-portfolios have come to act as alternative or supplementary spaces to the university's administratively oriented, one-size-fits-all LMS; they are able to function as more "owner-centric" spaces (Shroff et al. 2013, p. 144) aligned with contemporary trends towards the personalisation of learning, and specifically towards PLEs, which can be defined as "appropriate environment[s] centred on the learner, connecting each tool, service, relationship, etc. in the learning process" (Tur and Marín 2015, p. 61, with reference to Adell and Castañeda 2010, & Attwell 2007). Importantly, in these personalised spaces, the pre-service teachers have been able to work semiautonomously to develop the kinds of 'transferable skills' (Simatele 2015), also known as 'generic capabilities' or 'graduate attributes' (Trevitt et al. 2014), which give graduates "enhanced capacity to deal with an unknown and unknowable future" (ibid., p. 70). A related term which has found resonance in recent research is '21st century skills', incorporating for example communication, collabo-ration and critical thinking (Mishra and Kereluik 2011; P21, n.d.) as well as, crucially, creativity (Henriksen et al. 2015; Stansberry et al. 2015). The development of cre-ativity, as often expressed through the innovative use of multimedia web 2.0 tools like those listed in Table 1, certainly goes hand in hand with the freedom and indepen-dence opened up by more personalised learning spaces. In short, the pre-service teachers have been able to fashion their own learning stories, and construct their identities both as students and soon-to-graduate professionals, with the support of their choice of materials presented through their choice of services on their choice of platforms. In 2015, it was found that the best e-portfolios, as assessed by the lecturer at the end of the semester, were roughly evenly distributed across Wikispaces and alternative platforms, and incorporated a wide range of different tools and services, and ways of employing those tools and services.

With the spread of mobile technologies, today's students are not only able to access and work on their e-portfolios using a variety of devices in a variety of locations, but to use those same devices to make multimedia recordings of their learning experiences in their everyday educational and noneducational environments (Pegrum 2014). Such digital recordings can be easily integrated into e-portfolios (Shroff and Linger 2015). Drawing on their practicum placements in school classrooms, our pre-service teachers have been able to create a whole range of artefacts—such as annotated images, audio recordings, and even subtitled videos —to support their reflections on their learning, and demonstrate their growing competence as teachers. At the same time, this has made it all the more pressing a concern to ensure students always consider copyright, as well as confidentiality (Andrews and Cole 2015), with the materials they include.

Future Directions

Much has been written in the last few years about the need for a new generation of LMSs that more closely resemble PLEs. Discussing next generation digital learning environments (NGDLEs), the ELI (2015) suggests that these may take after smartphones where content and functionality can be aggregated in individualised ways for every student and teacher:

> learners and instructors must have the ability to shape and customize their learning environments to support their needs and objectives. By espousing a component-based architecture based on standards and best practices, **the NGDLE encourages exploration of new approaches and the development of new tools.** (n.p; bold in original)

Or, as Ros et al. (2014) write of what they call third-generation LMSs, their features make them:

> user centered and allow building personal learning environments (PLEs) in a simple way. A PLE is as "a set of devices, tools, applications, and physical or virtual spaces associated by learners at a specific time, for a specific purpose, and in a given context" (Gillet, Law & Chatterjee, 2010). In this context, a course is a mash-up of services where students and faculty choose the most appropriate ones for their work. (p. 1252)

Moreover, there would currently seem to be considerable promise for rejuvenating, and even reconceptualising, LMSs thanks to the development of the Experience Application Programming Interface (xAPI, also known as Tin Can API), a still-evolving set of open specifications designed to help track and collate a wide variety of learning experiences within personalised online spaces (Lim 2016). This is an area to watch over coming years.

For now, e-portfolios, as they have evolved over the past half-decade, already foreshadow many of the characteristics imputed to next generation learning environments. If we as educators can give students the autonomy to choose their preferred technological tools, the freedom to express themselves multimodally, the scaffolding they need to author accounts of their own learning journeys, the guidance they require to reflect carefully on those journeys, and the motivation to network with peers and the wider professional community they will enter on graduation, then we have already begun introducing them to some of what the new generation of digital learning environments may offer.

References

AITSL (Australian Institute for Teaching and School Leadership). (2014). *Australian professional standards for teachers*. http://www.aitsl.edu.au/australian-professional-standards-for-teachers/

AITSL. (n.d.) *National professional standards for teachers: ICT elaborations for graduate teacher standards*. http://acce.edu.au/sites/acce.edu.au/files/TTF%20-%20Graduate%20Teacher%20Standards%20-%20ICT%20Elaborations%20-%20201200411.pdf

Andrews, T., & Cole, C. (2015). Two steps forward, one step back: The intricacies of engaging with e-portfolios in nursing undergraduate education. *Nurse Education Today, 35,* 568–572.

Bain, J. D., Ballantyne, R., Mills, C., & Lester, N. C. (2002). *Reflecting on practice: Student teachers' perspectives.* Flaxton, QLD: Post Pressed.

Bartlett, A. (2008). It was hard work, but it was worth it: e-Portfolios in teacher education. In L. Tomei (Ed.), *Online and distance learning: Concepts, methodologies, tools, and applications* (pp. 2049–2060). Hershey, PA: Information Science Reference.

Bax, S. (2011). Normalisation revisited: The effective use of technology in language education. *International Journal of Computer-Assisted Language Learning and Teaching, 1*(2), 1–15.

Chatham-Carpenter, A., Seawel, L., & Raschig, J. (2009/10). Avoiding the pitfalls: Current practices and recommendations for ePortfolios in higher education. *Journal of Educational Technology Systems, 38*(4), 437–456.

Chen, M.-Y., Chang, F. M.-T., Chen, C.-C., Huang, M.-J., & Chen, J.-W. (2012). Why do individuals use e-portfolios? *Educational Technology & Society, 15*(4), 114–125.

DEEWR (Department of Education, Employment and Workplace Relations [Australia]). (n.d.). *Teaching teachers for the future*. http://www.ttf.edu.au/

Drummond, A., & Sweeney, T (2016). Can an objective measure of technological pedagogical content knowledge (TPACK) supplement existing TPACK measures? *British Journal of Educational Technology* [early view].

Dudeney, G., Hockly, N., & Pegrum, M. (2013). *Digital literacies*. Harlow: Pearson.

ELI (EDUCAUSE Learning Initiative). (2015). *7 things you should know about … NGDLE [Next Generation Digital Learning Environments]*. EDUCAUSE. http://net.educause.edu/ir/library/pdf/eli7127.pdf

Eynon, B., Gambino, L.M., & Török, J. (2014). Completion, quality, and change: The difference e-portfolios make. *Peer Review, 16*(1), 8. https://www.aacu.org/publications-research/periodicals/completion-quality-and-change-difference-e-portfolios-make

Farrell, T., & Rushby, N. (2016). Assessment and learning technologies: An overview. *British Journal of Educational Technology, 47*(1), 106–120.

Hallam, G. C., Harper, W., & McAllister, L. (2012). Current ePortfolio practice in Australia. In D. Cambridge (Ed.), *E-portfolios and global diffusion: Solutions for collaborative education* (pp. 129–148). Hershey, PA: Information Science Reference.

Hargittai, E. (2010). Digital na(t)ives? variation in internet skills and uses among members of the "net generation". *Sociological Inquiry, 80*(1), 92–113.

Haverkamp, J. J., & Vogt, M. (2015). Beyond academic evidence: Innovative uses of technology within e-portfolios in a Doctor of Nursing Practice program. *Journal of Professional Nursing, 31*(4), 284–289.

Henriksen, D., Mishra, P., & Mehta, R. (2015). Novel, effective, whole: Toward a NEW framework for evaluations of creative products. *Journal of Technology and Teacher Education, 23*(3), 455–478.

Hockly, N. (2013). Designer learning: The teacher as designer of mobile-based classroom learning experiences. *The International Research Foundation for English Language Education.* http://www.tirfonline.org/english-in-the-workforce/mobile-assisted-language-learning/designer-learning-the-teacher-as-designer-of-mobile-based-classroom-learning-experiences

Istenic Starčič, A., Cotic, M., Solomonides, I., & Volk, M. (2016). Engaging pre-service primary and preprimary school teachers in digital storytelling for the teaching and learning of mathematics. *British Journal of Educational Technology, 47*(1), 29–50.

Larrivee, B. (2000). Transforming teaching practice: Becoming the critically reflective teacher. *Reflective Practice, 1*(3), 293–307.

Laurillard, D. (2012). *Teaching as a design science: Building pedagogical patterns for learning and technology*. New York: Routledge.

Lim, C. P., & Lee, J. C.-K. (2014). Teaching e-portfolios and the development of professional learning communities (PLCs) in higher education institutions. *The Internet and Higher Education, 20*, 57–59.

Lim, K.C. (2016). *Using xAPI and learning analytics in education*. Presented at eLearning Forum Asia, Shanghai, China, June 13–15.

Lin, Q. (2008). Preservice teachers' learning experiences of constructing e-portfolios online. *The Internet and Higher Education, 11*(3–4), 194–200.

Martin, E. (2013). Helping community college students "connect the dots" of their college experience with e-portfolios. *Peer Review, 15*(2). https://www.aacu.org/publications-research/periodicals/helping-community-college-students-connect-dots-their-college

Mishra, P., & Kereluik, K. (2011). *What is 21st century learning? A review and synthesis*. Presented at SITE 2011, Nashville, USA, March 7–11. http://punya.educ.msu.edu/presentations/site2011/SITE_2011_21st_Century.pdf

Mishra, P., & Koehler, M. J. (2006). Technological pedagogical content knowledge: A framework for teacher knowledge. *Teachers College Record, 108*(6), 1017–1054.

Oakley, G., & Pegrum, M. (2015). Engaging in networked learning: Innovating at the intersection of technology and pedagogy. *Education Research and Perspectives, 42*, 397–428. http://www.erpjournal.net/wp-content/uploads/2015/12/1_ERPV42_Oakley_2015_Engaged-in-Networked-Learning.pdf

Oakley, G., Pegrum, M., & Johnston, S. (2014). Introducing e-portfolios to pre-service teachers as tools for reflection and growth: Lessons learnt. *Asia-Pacific Journal of Teacher Education, 42* (1), 36–50.

P 21 (Partnership for 21st Century Skills). (n.d.). *Framework for 21st century learning*. http://www.p21.org/about-us/p21-framework

Pegrum, M. (2014). *Mobile learning: Languages, literacies and cultures*. Basingstoke: Palgrave Macmillan.

Rafeldt, L.A., Bader, H.J., Lesnick Czarzasty, N., Freeman, E., Ouellet, E., & Snayd, J.M. (2014). Reflection builds twenty-first-century professionals. *Peer Review, 16*(1). https://www.aacu.org/peerreview/2014/winter/reflection-builds-twenty-first-century-professionals

Rodman, G. J. (2010). Facilitating the teaching-learning process through the reflective engagement of pre-service teachers. *Australian Journal of Teacher Education, 35*(2), 20–34.

Ros, S., Hernández, R., Caminero, A., Robles, A., Barbero, I., Maciá, A., et al. (2014). On the use of extended TAM to assess students' acceptance and intent to use third-generation learning management systems. *British Journal of Educational Technology, 46*(6), 1250–1271.

Samaras, A. P., & Fox, R. K. (2013). Capturing the process of critical reflective teaching practices through e-portfolios. *Professional Development in Education, 39*(1), 23–41.

Shroff, R., & Linger, W. (2015). Using mobile devices/smartphones to generate creative e-portfolio content. In D. Churchill, T.K.F. Chiu & N.J. Gu (Eds.), *Proceedings of the International Mobile Learning Festival 2015: Mobile Learning, MOOCs and 21st Century Learning*, Hong Kong, SAR China (pp. 229–240), May 22–23, 2015. Hong Kong: IMLF

Shroff, R.H., Trent, J., & Ng, E.M.W. (2013). Using e-portfolios in a field experience placement: Examining student-teachers' attitudes towards learning in relationship to personal value, control and responsibility. *Australasian Journal of Educational Technology, 29*(2), 143–160. http://ajet.org.au/index.php/AJET/article/viewFile/51/48

Simatele, M. (2015). Enhancing the portability of employability skills using e-portfolios. *Journal of Further and Higher Education, 39*(6), 862–874.

Stansberry, S., Thompson, P., & Kymes, A. (2015). Teaching creativity in a Master's level educational technology course. *Journal of Technology and Teacher Education, 23*(3), 433–453.

Strudler, N., & Wetzel, K. (2011/12). Electronic portfolios in teacher education: Forging a middle ground. *Journal of Research on Technology in Education, 44*(2), 161–173.

Sung, Y.-T., Chang, K.-E., Yu, W.-C., & Chang, T.-H. (2009). Supporting teachers' reflection and learning through structured digital teaching portfolios. *Journal of Computer Assisted learning, 25*(4), 375–385.

TEMAG (Teacher Education Ministerial Advisory Group [Australia]). (2014). *Action now: Classroom ready teachers.* Department of Education. https://docs.education.gov.au/system/files/doc/other/action_now_classroom_ready_teachers_print.pdf

Thomas, M. (Ed.). (2011). *Deconstructing digital natives: Young people, technology and the new literacies.* London: Routledge.

Trevitt, C., Macduff, A., & Steed, A. (2014). [E] portfolios for learning and as evidence of achievement: Scoping the academic practice development agenda ahead. *The Internet and Higher Education, 20,* 69–78.

Tur, G., & Marín, V. I. (2015). Exploring student [sic] students' attitudes and beliefs towards e-portfolios and technology in education. *Enseñanza & Teaching, 33*(1), 57–82.

Tzeng, J.-Y., & Chen, S.-H. (2012). College students' intentions to use e-portfolios: From the perspectives of career-commitment status and weblog-publication behaviours. *British Journal of Educational Technology, 43*(1), 163–176.

Winberg, C., & Pallitt, N. (2016). I am trying to practice good teaching: Reconceptualizing e-portfolios for professional development in vocational higher education. *British Journal of Educational Technology, 47*(3), 543–553.

Yang, M., Tai, M., & Lim, C.P. (2016). The role of e-portfolios in supporting productive learning. *British Journal of Educational Technology, 47*(6), 1276–1286.

Chapter 3
The Importance of E-Portfolios for Effective Student-Facing Learning Analytics

Cath Ellis

Abstract The field of Academic Analytics offers considerable potential to Higher Education institutions (HEIs), the academic staff who work for them and, most importantly, the students they teach. This approach to data-led decision-making is starting to have an influence and impact on what is arguably the core business of Higher Education: student learning. As well as being nascent, Learning Analytics is, potentially at least, a very broad area of inquiry and development; the field, necessarily, therefore has significant gaps. It is also just one of a large number of changes and developments that are affecting the way that Higher Education operates. These changes include such things as the introduction of standards-based assessment and outcomes-based education, and the identification and warranting of core competencies and capabilities of university graduates. It is also happening at a time when the affordances of a wide variety of eLearning tools are introducing new possibilities and opportunities to the pedagogy of Higher Education in ways that are demonstrably challenging traditional approaches to teaching and learning, something Sharpe and Oliver famously refer to as the 'trojan mouse' (Sharpe and Oliver In Designing courses for e-learning. Rethinking Pedagogy for a Digital Age, Designing and delivering e-learning, pp. 41–51, 2007, p. 49). This chapter considers the role that one such eLearning tool—the e-portfolio—can play in the implementation of a student-facing Learning Analytics strategy in this ambitious new approach to conceptualising, facilitating, structuring, supporting and assuring student learning achievement.

Keywords Learning Analytics · Assessment Analytics · E-portfolios · Assessment and feedback · Self-regulated learning

C. Ellis (✉)
University of New South Wales, Sydney, Australia
e-mail: cath.ellis@unsw.edu.au

© Springer Nature Singapore Pte Ltd. 2017
T. Chaudhuri and B. Cabau (eds.), *E-Portfolios in Higher Education*,
DOI 10.1007/978-981-10-3803-7_3

Learning Analytics

As I have argued elsewhere, Learning Analytics is a relatively new field of inquiry and its precise meaning is both contested and fluid (Ellis 2013).[1] It is again useful to draw on a definition of Learning Analytics that was offered by the first Learning Analytics and Knowledge (LAK) conference. Its call for papers defines Learning Analytics as:

> the measurement, collection, analysis and reporting of data about learners and their contexts, for purposes of understanding and optimising learning and the environments in which it occurs (LAK n.d.).

Ferguson (2012) nuances this further saying:

> Implicit within this definition are the assumptions that Learning Analytics make use of pre-existing, machine-readable data, and that its techniques can be used to handle large sets of data that would not be practicable to deal with manually (Ferguson 2012 n.p.).

As Ferguson points out, Learning Analytics is synonymous with, incorporates, has grown out of and sits alongside a bewildering array of different terms and analytical approaches.[2] There have been several drivers that have motivated the development of Learning Analytics, including pressure from funding bodies (particularly government agencies but also fee-paying students and their parents) to achieve greater levels of transparency and accountability (Campbell and Oblinger 2007, p. 2). It has also been informed by a wide array of pedagogical and learning theories.[3] At the same time, as Ferguson points out, some of the early work in Learning Analytics was, as she puts it, 'pedagogically neutral' in that it was "not designed to support any specific approach to teaching and learning" (Ferguson 2012, n.p.).

---

[1]See for instance, the 2011 Horizon report. It identifies that Learning Analytics is 'still in its early stages' (Johnson et al. 2011, p. 28). The first conference devoted entirely to Learning Analytics (the Learning Analytics and Knowledge (LAK11) Conference) was held in Banff in the same year (LAK n.d.). As Ferguson points out, however, there is evidence that it has been taking place in some form since the 1970s (Ferguson 2012).

[2]These include (but are not limited to): Educational Data Mining (EDM): "concerned with developing methods for exploring the unique types of data that come from educational settings, and using these methods to better understand students, and the settings which they learn in" (Ferguson 2012); Social Network Analysis (SNA): "explicitly situated within the constructivist paradigm that considers knowledge to be constructed through social negotiation [...SNA allows] detailed investigations of networks made up of 'actors' and the relations between them" (Aviv et al. 2003; De Laat et al. 2006; Ferguson 2012); Content Analytics: "a broad heading for the variety of automated methods that can be used to examine, index and filter online media assets, with the intention of guiding learners through the ocean of potential resources available to them" (Drachsler et al. 2010; Ferguson 2012; Verbert et al. 2011).

[3]For example, SNA draws on the social constructivist pedagogical theories of Dewey and Vygotsky. In contrast, Discourse Analytics draws on, as Ferguson notes, "extensive previous work in such areas as exploratory dialogue, latent semantic analysis and computer-supported argumentation" (Dawson and McWilliam 2008; Ferguson 2012).

Much of the research in the field of Learning Analytics is focussed on questions of improvement in terms of better informed (i.e. data-led) decision-making at the level of the institution (Bach 2010; Campbell and Oblinger 2007; Siemens et al. 2011). As Campbell and Oblinger put it: "In higher education many institutional decisions are too important to be based only on intuition, anecdote, or presumption; critical decisions require facts and the testing of possible solutions" (Campbell and Oblinger, 2007, p. 2). There is, however, increasing emphasis on expanding this data-led decision-making to tutors and students thereby offering a new emphasis on improving student learning.

At this point it is worth dwelling on what student learning actually is. After all, there are a wide variety of answers to the question "what does learning mean?" Theoretically at least, learning and Assessment Analytics is viably applicable to all of them. This chapter, however, works from a constructivist pedagogical perspective, informed by Biggs, that learning and education is "about *conceptual change*, not just the acquisition of information" and that this takes place when "it is clear to students (and teachers) what is 'appropriate', what the objectives are, where all can see where they are supposed to be going, and where these objectives are buried in the assessment tasks" (Biggs 1999, p. 60). In other words, this chapter works from the principle of constructive alignment whereby constructivism is, from a teaching perspective, "used as a framework to guide decision-making at all stages in instructional design: in deriving curriculum objectives in terms of performances that represent a suitably high cognitive level, in deciding teaching/learning activities judged to elicit those performances, and to assess and summatively report student performance" (Biggs 1996, p. 347). This chapter proposes that to be most effective, and to align with the growing emphasis on and enthusiasm for self-regulated and self-directed learning, Learning Analytics needs to attend to and place emphasis on the role that student-facing information might play in a constructivist educational paradigm.

Whether it is institution-, student- or tutor-facing, a significant proportion of Learning Analytics is preoccupied with predictive strategies based on identified patterns of behaviour and activity that indicate a higher likelihood of certain outcomes. As Ferguson points out, in its early incarnations, the impetus for a lot of the work in Learning Analytics came from a desire to improve student retention rates and as such, the dominant outcome upon which a great deal of this work has been and remains focussed is a reduction in student attrition through withdrawal or failure. For instance, the opening statement of Campbell and Oblinger's report makes the assertion that student success is "commonly measured as degree completion" (Campbell and Oblinger 2007, abstract). This chapter proposes that student success should be understood as something more than this: as students having been inspired, challenged and stretched such that they emerge from the educational experience with skills, abilities and knowledge that they did not have prior to enrolment but also with a strong sense of self-awareness, alongside drive and commitment. Further, I contend that success should mean that they are also able to communicate this learning attainment to others in a way that is both compelling and supported with evidence. While some would argue that this evidence of learning attainment is implicit within a completed degree, I argue that being able to reflect on their learning achievement, synthesise it from atomised courses into a whole degree of achievement and to compose the specificity and distinctiveness of their achievement into a compelling and well-evidenced story is becoming increasingly important to university graduates in a highly competitive employment and post-graduate study market. It is here that the role of e-portfolios is becoming so crucial. Before I go on to consider the specific affordances of e-portfolio tools and the pedagogy that these tools make available to teachers and students, it is important to consider the limits of Learning Analytics and the challenges that it presents.

The Limits of Learning Analytics

Getting Learning Analytics established as 'business as usual' at scale has proven challenging. The reasons for this are widespread but one of the key issues is to do with the availability of data. On the one hand, a significant barrier to achieving successful operationalisation is the huge and growing volume of data that is potentially available for analysis. The 2011 *Horizon Report*, for instance, refers to "an explosion of data" (Johnson et al. 2011, p. 29) in the Higher Education sector, something Ferguson argues is an example of 'big data' (Ferguson 2012, n.p.; Maryika et al. n.d.). Ferguson asks the important question: "*How can we extract value from these big sets of learning-related data?*" (Ferguson 2012, n.p.). On the other hand, and completely counter-intuitively, another challenge and limitation of Learning Analytics is a *paucity* of data. As I have argued elsewhere, there are specific and significant gaps in the available data sets in the area of assessment and feedback (Ellis 2013). I have considered several reasons for this 'gap' in the available data, but I suggest that the most likely reason is

> That the more finely granular level of data (such as student achievement against assessment criteria) has been, up to now, too difficult to collect and collate. This is a direct product of the continuing prevalence and persistence of paper-based marking systems that [...] are difficult if not impossible to use for the purposes of Learning Analytics. [...U]ntil relatively recently, the possibility of collecting and collating assessment data at a level of granularity that is meaningful and useful has simply been unthinkable. With the advent of useable, affordable and reliable electronic marking tools and the upsurge in interest across the sector to move towards Electronic Assessment Management, this is, arguably, about to change (Ellis 2013, p. 663).

As I will go on to discuss below, Assessment Analytics, as a subset of Learning Analytics, is an as yet untapped but potentially hugely significant area of future development, particularly as a way of developing student-facing analytics strategies.

The next issue that arises is what to do with the information, or data. Ferguson points out that while most online learning tools provide data on student behaviour, activity and interaction, what they offer to teachers or learners is often difficult to interpret and also difficult to put to use in a way that can have a beneficial impact on student learning (Ferguson 2012, n.p.). This returns us to the issues she identifies as 'pedagogic neutrality'. While it is difficult to understand precisely what 'neutrality' might mean in this context, or whether pedagogical neutrality is even possible, the point Ferguson is making here is, perhaps, better understood as having limited or ill-defined usefulness. At least part of the problem relates to the tendency of Learning Analytics to measure things that teachers and students may not identify as being centrally significant to learning, such as interaction in online social learning networks.

The over-abundance of data in some areas alongside the paucity of it in others, accompanied by uncertain or unclear uses to which this data might be meaningfully put, offers an important reminder of some of the risks we face as we embark upon Learning Analytics strategies. One of the potential pitfalls of Learning Analytics is that it can be driven by the wrong motivating factors. Key amongst these is the risk of measuring the wrong things, measuring things that are not meaningful, measuring things simply because they are measurable and/or not measuring the right things. Arguably, when it comes to Assessment Analytics, it is most appropriate to work from first principles and for those principles to be pedagogical rather than statistical. As we approach the design of Learning Analytics strategies, it is worthwhile heeding George Siemens's call to take "a holistic view of L[earning] A[nalytics] that includes […] practical issues, but also aspects related to the data, such as openness, accessibility, and ethics, as well as the particular pedagogical goals and usage context of the L[earning] A[nalytics] tools (e.g., detecting at-risk students, supporting self-awareness, or enhancing instructor awareness)" (Siemens cited in Martinez-Maldonaldo et al. 2015, p. 10). As Campbell and Oblinger point out, knowing why you are doing analytics is an important starting point (Campbell and Oblinger 2007). Martinez-Maldonado et al. have identified "the need for new design methodologies for L[earning] A[nalytics] tools, providing a pedagogical underpinning and considering the different actors (e.g., instructors and students), the dimensions of usability in learning contexts […] (individuals, groups of students, and the classroom), the learning goals, data sources, and the tasks to be accomplished" (Dillenbourg cited in Martinez-Maldonado et al. 2015, p. 11). Their LATUX workflow offers a useful set of questions to guide the early design process including the particularly pertinent "what are the (unexplored) possibilities?" (Martinez-Maldonaldo et al. 2015, p. 17). This question is an important reminder of the fact that Learning Analytics has the potential to allow us to know things and therefore do things that have previously been impossible or unthinkable. This growing body of work on the methodological aspects of Learning Analytics implores us to consider the factors that motivate what is measured, how it is measured, what patterns are identified, how it is acted upon, who acts upon it and when. Most importantly, it reminds us of the importance of ensuring that these considerations should be derived from pedagogy rather than simply by what data is available or obtainable.

It is also important to consider some reasons as to why Learning Analytics might not be undertaken in order to consider how best to mitigate against potentially negative or 'backwash' effects. While it is outside the scope of this chapter to consider these possible objections in detail, it is worth identifying them at this point. Prime amongst these is the issue of ethics for both students and tutors. The concern that some may have at being 'surveilled' through an analytics strategy may raise concerns about privacy and academic freedom and may raise the spectre of a 'big brother' institution. Mitigating these concerns with clear lines of consent and strategic purposes (to improve student learning rather than to 'police' poor teaching) will be important. Another concern may be that the aggregation of information for students is an instance of infantilising or 'spoon feeding' them. Ensuring that analytics automate, make easier, more convenient or more obvious things that they are offered anyway and, as Campbell and Oblinger argue, are designed to "steer students toward self-sufficiency" are important (Campbell and Oblinger 2007, p. 10). Finally, concerns that a Learning Analytics strategy might have a 'flattening' effect by leading the pedagogy (rather than responding to or supporting it) are significant. Amongst these concerns, in the area of Assessment Analytics we can usefully include concerns focused on grade integrity and the use of assessment criteria and rubrics to evaluate student work (Sadler 2007, 2009a, b, 2010b). It is also important to consider concerns about the potential impact this might have on knowledge acquisition and accumulation (Avis 2000; Clegg 2011; Maton 2009).[4] Arguably it is only worth pursuing a Learning Analytics strategy if, and only if, we can mitigate against these concerns.

Finally, it is important to remember that for any analytics strategy to be useful, and therefore effective, it is ultimately not the data in and of itself that matters. That is because just providing data and an analysis of it does not, ultimately, accomplish anything. It is the set of actions that happen because of, informed by and based on the analysis that has the impact. This brings to mind the work of David Boud who has argued for the importance of closing the feedback loop in assessment. He suggests that what we tend to think of as feedback on assessment only becomes feedback when a student acts upon it. He and Elizabeth Molloy draw on Sadler's pithy observation that without that subsequent action, feedback is only 'dangling data' (Sadler quoted in Boud and Molloy 2013 loc 434). While I will return to this later, the same is true of student-facing Learning Analytics. Ultimately, analytics without interventions or actions is a fundamentally pointless activity. So, for Assessment Analytics to be effective, students need the guidance, support and motivation to engage with, interpret and act on what it is telling them. It is here that we can begin to see the important role that e-portfolios can play in a Learning Analytics strategy because in order to deal with the information that has been made available to them, students need a space in which to do that.

---

[4]It is worth noting that, within Maton's research into cumulative knowledge, Assessment Analytics are used as part of the analytical methodology in the form of the 'analyses of students' work products' (Maton 2009, p. 43).

E-Portfolios

Like Learning Analytics, the term 'e-portfolio' is contested and it is not easy to get a good, stable working definition of what it means. As Hughes suggests, the discussion about e-portfolios has often been dominated by the "tools used rather than the transformations in learning and teaching that such a domain and conceptual shift might support" (Hughes 2008, p. 437). The definition Hughes prefers comes from the Centre for Recording Achievement and proposes that an e-portfolio is, or might be: "a repository, a means of presenting oneself and ones skills, qualities and achievements, a guidance tool, a means of sharing and collaborating and a means of encouraging a sense of personal identity" (CRA quoted in Hughes 2008). Another, pithier, definition that she points us towards, which I commend for both its efficacy and efficiency, is taken from La Guardia Community College who identify their e-portfolio as a place to "collect, select, reflect and connect" (Hughes 2008, p. 439). It is around these four key purposes of the e-portfolio that I will later turn to further explore how Learning Analytics and e-portfolios can, and arguably, should connect and work together to bring about important transformations in student learning and our educational model as a whole.

Assessment Analytics within a Learning Analytics Strategy

In terms of developing student-facing Learning Analytics strategies, assessment seems an obvious place to start. As I have argued elsewhere, the key value in including assessment data in a Learning Analytics strategy is because, as far as students are concerned, assessment is very meaningful. That is largely because it provides students with tangible evidence of their learning attainment and progress. For students, assessment results are the return on their investment of both time and money (see Taras 2001). As the SOLAR concept paper puts it: Learning Analytics can "contribute to learner motivation by providing detailed information about her performance" (Siemens et al. 2011, p. 6). Finding ways to get more value out of students' investment is well worth pursuing.

What form the actual data takes and the way that it is generated and later harvested or mined for the purposes of analytics is wide and varied. As outlined above, it is really only with the advent of eMarking and Electronic Assessment Management (EAM) tools, such as Grademark available within the Turnitin tool developed by iParadigms, that it has become feasible to collect these data sets. Of course, e-portfolio tools themselves now incorporate assessment tools, such as the Gateways available within PebblePad. It is fair to say, however, that the assessment tools within e-portfolios are fairly unsophisticated in comparison to specialist EAM tools. Most e-portfolio tools also integrate with Learning Management Systems (LMS), such as Blackboard and Moodle, which have well established EAM tools such as rubrics and grade management functions. The data sets for assessment analytics can therefore be generated inside, outside and through e-portfolio tools. Whether they are generated inside or outside of e-portfolios, these data could usefully include the frequency of common comments that are made by tutors on student work as part of the marking and feedback process. These comments often relate to common errors or areas of weakness, or they relate to areas of improvement and strength. When appended to student work as annotations, these comments can serve the dual purpose of providing useful information to students on the strengths and weaknesses of that piece of work, while also laying down a data trail that can be available for later analysis. Within Grademark, the comments, which are known as Quickmarks, can be customised to suit a particular assessment task, a specific set of learning outcomes, or even to suit the aims of an individual teacher or a group of teachers.[5] It is therefore possible to create a set of Quickmarks that cover a range of achievement levels or scenarios (e.g. a set that identifies if work is not meeting, approaching, meeting or exceeding a particular competency) that tutors can use to evaluate particular characteristics of students' work. If these are used systematically it is possible to gather a rich picture of such things as the competencies students are struggling with the most. In a similar way, the selection of 'cells' in a marking rubric, such as that available within Grademark and also with other tools such as ReView and most LMSs, provide ways to record and gather this information at the same time as communicating it to students. Many of these tools also allow for the collection of peer and self-evaluation data that can be compared to each other and to tutor evaluation decisions. Even apparently incidental information, such as the date and time of assessment submission, could be incorporated into an Assessment Analytics strategy.

There is a wide variety of different ways that assessment data can be useful as part of such a strategy. It can be aggregated and then 'cut' in many different ways so that it looks across a cohort as well as between them, while also being able to focus into the level of an individual student within and across courses and levels, as well as across time. At the individual level, this can include such things as providing students with information about where their result places them in the cohort (in terms of final results, achievement against specified learning outcomes and even in the frequency of common problems). This may have the potential to motivate students to improve and aspire to higher levels of achievement. Evidence of common errors and cohort-wide weaknesses may also turn students' attention to areas they have previously neglected or considered to be unimportant or insignificant. By comparing self- and peer-evaluation data to tutor evaluations, it is possible to identify the development of self-evaluation skills as well how well assessment criteria are understood by individual students and by the cohort as a whole. Pre-submission feedback that is informed by evidence from the strengths and weaknesses of previous student cohorts in response to a specific assessment task, can guide students when they approach that same assessment task (see Boud and

---

[5]For more information on building customised Quickmarks and Quickmark sets within Grademark, see the user guide available on the iParadigms website ("Home - Guides.turnitin.com," n.d.).

Molloy 2013, loc 500). Post-submission feedback may be effective in motivating students to engage with their feedback, take steps to understand it and to act upon it. These data sets can become artefacts in themselves that can be imported into e-portfolio tools. In the near future we will almost certainly see dashboard tools being built that aggregate these data sets into user interfaces (e.g. that are student and tutor facing) that could be incorporated within e-portfolio tools.

While the principles of assessment feedback are to give students an indication of their learning achievement at a particular point in time, this information is almost always provided in isolation. One of the key benefits of providing students with Assessment Analytics data as part of a larger Learning Analytics strategy is that it might help both students and teachers join these isolated pieces of information together to see a bigger picture. This bigger picture has the potential to help students and teachers appraise student performance across all their assessment tasks in all of their courses, and even across degrees if they are undertaking a dual degree program, and then locate this performance against a set of standards, learning outcomes and assessment criteria. But it also allows students to locate their current performance against their previous performance—their former self—and against concurrent performance in different contexts—their other selves. It could also allow students and teachers to get a sense of students' performance relative to their peers and also to track and trace their performance against their own self-evaluation and their personal goals—their future self. These kinds of comparisons are, for the most part, unexplored in the way that Higher Education courses and assessment are currently designed, delivered and administered. This approach is aimed at providing a more holistic view of student performance and attainment.

By providing this more holistic 'bigger picture' view, Assessment Analytics coupled with an e-portfolio have the potential to mitigate one of the biggest challenges that we currently face across the Higher Education sector. This challenge comes from the fact that our undergraduate degrees tend to be structured in ways that are deeply and perhaps dangerously atomised. By this I mean that while a student, as Geoff Scott puts it, comes to university to study a particular degree with a particular name and a particular purpose (Scott 2015, pers. comm.), we have a tendency to break these degrees up into smaller 'chunks.' These 'chunks' can be 'streams' (such as specialisations or majors and minors that are common in American and Australian degrees) and/or levels (such as the foundation, intermediate and honours years that typify British undergraduate degrees). In almost all university degrees, these are further broken down into individual subjects, courses or modules. Within these subjects learning is further 'chunked' into topics, which often coincide with weekly timetabled class sessions and/or assessment tasks. Piecing all of these 'chunks' back together to make the whole can be challenging for both academic staff and students. As the principles of constructive alignment and curriculum coherence are encouraging more HEIs to introduce well aligned, outcomes-based education, more degrees are being 'mapped' such that both students and their teachers can get a clear sense of how all of these atomised 'chunks' fit together to constitute the whole. Where sets of program or degree learning outcomes and statements of graduate attributes or capabilities have often been constructed as aspirational or desirable, increasingly institutions are not only out-lining what they intend their graduates in and across their degrees to achieve, but they are also setting out to assure stakeholders (students, their parents and the graduate employment market) that graduates have indeed achieved them. Such assurance-of-learning requirements are now quite standard in accredited degrees (such as qualifications in medicine). It is no coincidence that it is these discipline areas that lead the way in the use of portfolios, and latterly e-portfolios, for students as a means of managing, tracking and providing evidence of their learning achievement (see Van Tartwijk and Driessen 2009).

This more holistic approach that Learning Analytics can make available to students and their teachers aligns usefully with what Sadler argues we should be aspiring to in our approach to assessment and feedback; he refers to it as a "full-bodied concept of quality" (Sadler 2010a, 548). Providing students with support and guidance at this holistic, full-bodied level, in a joined-up way, is arguably becoming something an increasing proportion of students expect, if not feel entitled to, as part of their higher education experience. After all, they are becoming very accustomed to this kind of holistic view of their lives and behaviour, supported by data analysis, in many other aspects of their lives; this is most obvious in their experiences of social media, but it is also becoming a common place in other areas such as shopping, finance, and exercise and fitness. The fact that their higher education providers are not able to provide them with this bigger picture of their own behaviour is almost certainly making what we do seem increasingly out dated and unsatisfactory.

Many institutions are now turning to use Assessment Analytics as a way of making their assurance-of-learning strategies both more efficient and reliable. For the time being at least, the dominant means by which students demonstrate their learning attainment in a way that can then provide assurance that learning outcomes have been met, is through their performance in assessment tasks. Using EAM to record the professional judgements of academic staff regarding student performance in assessment tasks against standards-based assessment criteria makes the har-vesting of that data, even across large, team-taught and/or geographically dispersed student cohorts, relatively quick, cheap and easy. Again, it is possible to 'cut' the data in different ways to not just ascertain which individuals have met, not met or even only partly met specific learning outcomes. It is also possible to ascertain which learning outcomes have been most (or least) frequently met across the cohort. This means that proactive steps can be taken by teachers to provide targeted (be-spoke) educative just-in-time interventions at both the individual and cohort level to address areas of weakness at the point of need.

The Role of E-Portfolios in a Learning Analytics Strategy

While this ability to assure learning achievement is useful from an institutional point of view, particularly when needing to report to professional, statutory and regulatory bodies for accreditation purposes, it stands to reason that pairing student-facing Assessment Analytics data (in the form of a report or even a dashboard) with an e-portfolio makes it possible for students to begin to take responsibility for assuring their own learning. I would go as far as to say that in order to provide this holistic, 'bigger picture', it is *essential* that Assessment Analytics be coupled with an e-portfolio. It is here that I return to the La Guardia definition of the key affordance of the e-portfolio in teaching and learning: collect, select, reflect and connect. First is the role of the e-portfolio as a place for students to collect evidence of their learning achievement. Providing students with a curriculum map, which can be used to measure their progress through a program of study by measuring their learning attainment against a set of learning outcomes, moves Learning Analytics into the realm of self-regulated learning. This approach helps students and teachers move beyond what Sadler refers to as the *"one-way telling"* that characterises so much of what is understood as 'feedback' (Sadler 2015, p. 16). It also sets students "on the path to more informed self-monitoring and [...] connoisseurship' (Sadler 2015, p. 18). It also resonates once again with Boud's important and influential work on assessment and feedback where he advocates for "closing the feedback loop" and to seek "evidence of effects" with "both teachers and students seeing the outcome of feedback on improved performance in subsequent tasks" (Boud and Molloy 2013, loc 154).

It is at this point that the usefulness of the 'reflect' and 'select' elements of e-portfolios becomes apparent. In the first instance, as suggested earlier, a fundamental truth of any analytics strategy is that data in itself is useless unless a set of actions happen as a result of and based on it. In other words, for analytics to be effective, the data needs to have somewhere to go and to be dealt with further. Prompting and rewarding students for reflecting on what their data are showing them is the first step. As Van Tartwijk and Driessen put it: "a portfolio can [...] stimulate reflection, because collecting and selecting work samples, evaluations and other types of materials that are illustrative of the work done, compels learners to look back on what they have done and analyse what they have and have not yet accomplished" (Van Tartwijk and Driessen 2009, p. 791). A Learning Analytics strategy that aggregates data from a large number of diverse assessment activities into an e-portfolio gives students a space in which to consider their performance and improvement across both tasks and time. This allows them to measure their own competence development and, more importantly, to set detailed and realistic goals towards which they can work in the future. It is important to consider, however, that while e-portfolios can provide students with a space in which to develop their reflective skills, and particularly their reflective writing skills, e-portfolios in and of themselves cannot teach students these skills. Offering students dedicated and targeted guidance and support on the development of their reflective capacities is an important component of any reflective learning strategy (see Buckley et al. 2009; Moon 2007).

Second, another way that students can use e-portfolios to take responsibility for assuring their own learning achievement is to use them to select which pieces of work best demonstrate their achievements. This role of e-portfolios sets up an inevitable tension between their purpose for reflection, on the one hand, and assessment on the other. As Van Tartwijk and Driessen put it, "an argument against this dual function is that […] Learners may be reluctant to expose their less successful efforts at specific tasks and to reflect on strategies for addressing weaknesses if they believe they are at risk of having 'failures' turned against them in an assessment situation. Portfolios that are not assessed, on the other hand, do not 'reward' learners for the time and energy they invest in them" (Van Tartwijk and Driessen 2009, p. 793). This is an important reminder to find ways to structure e-portfolios and their use such that they can achieve these multiple functions and purposes. The idea of students self-selecting work that they feel best demonstrates their achievement of learning outcomes and competencies is, as Hughes argues, one of the ways that e-portfolios are playing such an important role in the destabilising of traditional notions of teaching and learning (Hughes 2008). This movement from tutor-assured to student-assured learning is part of an important sector-wide shift towards a more participatory and collaborative pedagogical approach.

The final component that makes e-portfolios so useful and valuable is their ability to help students 'connect'. These connections can be established both during a student's program of study but also, importantly, beyond graduation as they enter the world of work. Integrating e-portfolios into a social learning context could allow students to develop and harness folksonomies whereby such things as the attitudes and behaviours of high-achieving students are visible to and shared with everyone, thus guiding and motivating their behaviour. Gamification (whereby students are 'rewarded' for achieving against markers which are known to be attendant to student success such as making regular use of the library) may also have some use. In these contexts, Learning Analytics could operate as a kind of nudge analytics: by making plain which pathways, behaviours and strategies are most likely to result in success. Using the affordances of e-portfolios to facilitate students making and maintaining connections might be useful in facilitating these interactions.

Beyond graduation, by making possible the collection and selection of a series of artefacts, combined with a space in which to undertake effective reflection on how these artefacts constitute evidence of learning achievement, e-portfolios enable and empower students to first curate evidence of their successful learning journey and then to compose distinctive and compelling stories of themselves that they can tell to the graduate employment market. At this point it is useful to clarify what I mean by the term 'graduate employment market' because, of course, an increasing pro-portion of graduates from HEIs will never be, or even aspire to be, employees. So, when I speak of the graduate employment market, I take this to mean all aspects of entrepreneurship including venture capital, seed funding, crowd sourcing and partnership so on. It also acknowledges that some students pursue higher education qualifications for the reward of learning alone and have no attendant career aspi-rations. Their requirements for composing a 'story' of their learning journey and achievement is just as important and legitimate. One of the affordances of e-portfolios that makes them so compelling and ultimately so valuable to higher education is their persistence and their availability and accessibility. In terms of persistence, e-portfolios as a means of showcasing student work and achievement, remain available to students even after graduation. Because they are online, they are widely shareable, being available and accessible to anyone, anytime, anywhere. As such, they can provide a flexible and attractive 'shop window' through which graduates can display the 'wares' of their learning achievement, alongside their distinctive qualities and capabilities.

Conclusion

It is clear that Academic and Learning Analytics offer an exciting and powerful new strategic direction in Higher Education. It is vital, however, that Learning Analytics embrace student- and tutor-facing strategies. In order to do this, it stands to reason that data from assessment and feedback—Assessment Analytics—is central. It is important that the design principles for an Assessment Analytics strategy should be informed by the pedagogical theory of assessment and feedback. This should concentrate on retaining the fundamental principles of assessment but also, and perhaps more importantly, should encourage a move away from guess work, anecdote and speculation towards providing *informed* answers to questions relating to student attainment and achievement. It should also deliberately work towards outcomes like students' self-regulated learning and students assuring their own learning in order to facilitate the development of collaborative and participatory pedagogies that are so important to the future relevance and therefore value of higher education. As a tool to help students collect, select, reflect and connect, e-portfolios play a vital role in supporting and facilitating these endeavours. What remains, now, is to begin the practical work of piloting and evaluating these strategies to establish which are both practicable *and* effective in achieving the outcomes envisaged here. This is an exciting area for future research and development.

References

Avis, J. (2000). Policing the subject: Learning outcomes, managerialism and research in PCET. *British Journal of Educational Studies, 48*(1), 38–57. doi:10.1111/1467-8527.00132

Aviv, R., Erlich, Z., Ravid, G., & Geva, A. (2003). Network analysis of knowledge construction in asynchronous learning networks. *Journal of Asynchronous Learning Networks, 7*(3), 1–23.

Bach, C. (2010). *Learning analytics: Targeting instruction, curricula and student support*. Office of the Provost: Drexel University.

Biggs, J. (1996). Enhancing teaching through constructive alignment. *Higher Education, 32*(3), 347–364.

Biggs, J. (1999). What the student does: Teaching for enhanced learning. *Higher Education Research & Development, 18*(1), 57–75.

Boud, D., & Molloy, E. (2013). *Feedback in higher and professional education: understanding it and doing it well*. London and New York: Routledge.

Buckley, S., Coleman, J., Davison, I., Khan, K. S., Zamora, J., Malick, S., ... & Sayers, J. (2009). The educational effects of portfolios on undergraduate student learning: A Best Evidence

Medical Education (BEME) systematic review. BEME guide no. 11. *Medical teacher, 31*(4), 282–298. http://doi.org/10.1080/01421590902889897

Campbell, J., & Oblinger, D. (2007). Academic analytics. EDUCAUSE Centre for Applied Research. Retrieved from http://connect.educause.edu/library/abstract/AcademicAnalytics/45275

Clegg, S. (2011). Cultural capital and agency: Connecting critique and curriculum in higher education. *British Journal of Sociology of Education, 32*(1), 93–108. doi:10.1080/01425692.2011.527723

Dawson, S., & McWilliam, E. (2008). Investigating the application of IT generated data as an indicator of learning and teaching performance. Australian Learning and Teaching Council. Retrieved from http://olt.ubc.ca/learning_tools/research_1/research/

De Laat, M., Lally, V., Lipponen, L., & Simons, R. J. (2006). Analysing student engagement with learning and tutoring activities in networked learning communities: A multi-method approach. *International Journal of Web Based Communities, 2*(4), 394–412.

Drachsler, H., Bogers, T., Vuorikari, R., Verbert, K., Duval, E., Manouselis, N., … others. (2010). Issues and considerations regarding sharable data sets for recommender systems in technology enhanced learning. *Procedia Computer Science, 1*(2), 2849–2858.

Ellis, C. (2013). Broadening the scope and increasing the usefulness of learning analytics: The case for assessment analytics. *British Journal of Educational Technology, 44*(4), 662–664. doi:10.1111/bjet.12028

Ferguson, R. (2012). *The state of learning analytics in 2012: A review and future challenges (technical report)*. UK: Knowledge Media Institute, The Open University.

Home—Guides.turnitin.com. (n.d.). Retrieved April 22, 2016, from https://guides.turnitin.com/

Hughes, J. (2008). Letting in the Trojan mouse: Using an e-portfolio system to re-think pedagogy. Retrieved from https://wlv.openrepository.com/wlv/handle/2436/47434

Johnson, L., Smith, R., Willis, H., Levine, A., & Haywood, K. (2011). *The 2011 Horizon report*. Austin, Texas: The New Media Consortium.

LAK. (n.d.). First international conference on learning analytics and knowledge 2011 (conference). Retrieved from https://tekri.athabascau.ca/analytics/call-papers

Martinez-Maldonado, R., Pardo, A., Mirriahi, N., Yacef, K., Kay, J., & Clayphan, A. (2015). The LATUX workflow: Designing and deploying awareness tools in technology-enabled learning settings. In *Proceedings of the Fifth International Conference on Learning Analytics and Knowledge* (pp. 1–10). ACM. Retrieved from http://dl.acm.org/citation.cfm?id=2723583

Martinez-Maldonado, R., Pardo, A., Mirriahi, N., Yacef, K., Kay, J., & Clayphan, A. (2016). Latux: An iterative workflow for designing, validating and deploying learning analytics visualisations. *Journal of Learning Analytics, 2*(3), 9–39. doi:10.18608/jla.2015.23.3

Maryika, J., Chui, M., Brown, B., Bughin, J., Dobbs, R., Roxburgh, C., & Byers, A. H. (n.d.). Big data: The next frontier for innovation, competition, and productivity| McKinsey Global Institute| Technology & Innovation| McKinsey & Company. Retrieved April 22, 2012, from http://www.mckinsey.com/Insights/MGI/Research/Technology_and_Innovation/Big_data_The_next_frontier_for_innovation

Maton, K. (2009). Cumulative and segmented learning: Exploring the role of curriculum structures in knowledge-building. *British Journal of Sociology of Education, 30*(1), 43–57. doi:10.1080/01425690802514342

Moon, J. A. (2007). *Learning journals* (2nd ed.). Taylor & Francis.

Sadler, D. R. (2007). Perils in the meticulous specification of goals and assessment criteria. *Assessment in Education, 14*(3), 387–392. doi:10.1080/09695940701592097

Sadler, D. R. (2009a). Grade integrity and the representation of academic achievement. *Studies in Higher Education, 34*(7), 807–826. doi:10.1080/03075070802706553

Sadler, D. R. (2009b). Indeterminacy in the use of preset criteria for assessment and grading. *Assessment & Evaluation in Higher Education, 34*(2), 159–179. doi:10.1080/02602930801956059

Sadler, D. R. (2010a). Beyond feedback: Developing student capability in complex appraisal. *Assessment & Evaluation in Higher Education, 35*(5), 535–550. doi:10.1080/02602930903541015

Sadler, D. R. (2010b). Fidelity as a precondition for integrity in grading academic achievement. *Assessment & Evaluation in Higher Education, 35*(6), 727–743. doi:10.1080/026029309029 77756.

Sadler, D. R. (2015). Backwards assessment explanations: Implications for teaching and assessment practice. Springer International Publishing. Retrieved from http://link.springer.com/chapter/10.1007/978-3-319-10274-0_2

Sharpe, R., & Oliver, M. (2007). *Designing courses for e-learning* (pp. 41–51). Rethinking Pedagogy for a Digital Age: Designing and delivering e-learning.

Siemens, G., Gasevic, D., Haythornthwaite, C., Dawson, S., Buckingham Shum, S., Ferguson, R., … Baker, R. S. J. d. (2011). Open learning analytics: An integrated and modularized platform. Society for learning analytics research. Retrieved from http://solaresearch.org/OpenLearning Analytics.pdf

Taras, M. (2001). The use of tutor feedback and student self-assessment in summative assessment tasks: Towards transparency for students and for tutors. *Assessment & Evaluation in Higher Education, 26*(6), 605–614.

Van Tartwijk, J., & Driessen, E. W. (2009). Portfolios for assessment and learning: AMEE guide no. 45. *Medical Teacher, 31*(9), 790–801. doi:10.1080/01421590903139201

Verbert, K., Drachsler, H., Manouselis, N., Wolpers, M., Vuorikari, R., & Duval, E. (2011). Dataset-driven research for improving recommender systems for learning. In (LAK 2011). Retrieved from http://dl.acm.org/ft_gateway.cfm?id=2090122&type=pdf

Part II
E-Portfolios in the Classroom and Beyond: The Multidisciplinary Perspective

Chapter 4
The Integration of E-Portfolios in the Foreign Language Classroom: Towards Intercultural and Reflective Competences

Chi Shan Chui and Céline Dias

Abstract This article examines the implementation of e-portfolio (ePF) as an innovative and alternative form of assessment in the French and German language courses of the European Studies undergraduate programme at HKBU. It focuses on the potentials of ePF in achieving Course Intended Learning Outcomes (CILO): how it helps students improve their language skills and, at a broader level, how it helps students develop their intercultural and reflexive competence in handling an increasingly diverse variety of situations in our increasingly globalized world. To begin with, we believe in the necessity to implement innovative teaching to foster our graduates' capacity for lifelong learning through ePF. A qualitative and quantitative research was then conducted to analyse samples of our students' reflexive and critical essays in their ePFs, along with questionnaires distributed to study their views towards portfolio keeping. The results obtained are in favour of the implementation of ePF in foreign language classes although they also reveal the issue that students could be disorientated in using ePF, which initially requires attention.

Keywords E-portfolio · Foreign language teaching & learning · Intercultural competences · Reflection · Alternative assessment · Students' perception

Introduction

Portfolios (PF), which gained prominence in higher education in the 90s (Lorenzo and Ittelson 2005: 3) and their modern versions, E-portfolios (ePF), which are electronic versions of physical PF that contain digital objects instead of physical

C.S. Chui (✉) · C. Dias
European Studies Programme, GIS, Hong Kong Baptist University,
Kowloon Tong, Hong Kong
e-mail: cs_chui@hkbu.edu.hk

C. Dias
e-mail: cdias@hkbu.edu.hk

© Springer Nature Singapore Pte Ltd. 2017
T. Chaudhuri and B. Cabau (eds.), *E-Portfolios in Higher Education*,
DOI 10.1007/978-981-10-3803-7_4

objects, have become a mainstream activity in education. They "address many issues such as lifelong and personalized learning, flexible and student-centered pedagogies" (Stefani et al. 2007: 7) which are much needed to adapt to new academic, professional, cultural environments. Compiling ePF, which can be defined as "digitized collections of student work and reflections" (Stefani et al. 2007: 17), is "learner-centered (…) and involves higher-order cognition" (Lee 1997: 358). In producing ePF, learners need to "collect, sort, select, describe, analyze and evaluate" multiple concrete artefacts to "demonstrate their skills and knowledge (…) and they must engage in a reflection on these evidences" (Cummins and Davesne 2009: 849). This active process of reflection "enhances learning" (Cambridge et al. 2005: 17), as it can help "turn information into knowledge (…) in moving beyond surface learning to deep learning" (ibid: 3). Hence, it can "cause new types of thinking (…) and expression" (Gibson 2006: 144).

Specifically, ePF play an important role in Foreign Language (FL) teaching & learning, as portfolios can be used to assess both language and culture learning (Allen 2004: 233; Lee 1997: 232). This is with this objective in mind that an ePF pilot project has been implemented since 2013 with the students of both French and German streams of the European Studies Programme of Hong Kong Baptist University, followed by the creation, in May 2014, of the Community of Practice (CoP) on Student E-Portfolios—*REFLECT*—which was established to enable academics from various disciplines to share their experiences on ePF and learn from each other to improve this teaching & learning activity. This article will showcase the intended learning outcomes of this new e-learning activity in our language courses (German and French) and the challenges of its implementation seen through our learners' comments.

Context

Globalization increases the necessity for higher education institutions to form well-rounded citizens. HKBU's mission & vision—the Whole Person Education (WPE)[1]—is to provide students with a liberal and holistic education.[2] That is why a drastic change has been operated in the nature of the curriculum and in the teaching and learning activities (TLA) since 2008 in order to acquire the 7 Graduate Attributes promoted by the University (citizenships, knowledge, learning, skills, creativity, communication, teamwork).[3] These "softer skills" (Stefani et al. 2007: 27), which could be defined in terms of knowing how to do and how to be, are essential in a world constantly changing, to adapt not only in the workplaces of tomorrow but also in all kinds of life situations. In the language classes of the

---

[1]http://chtl.hkbu.edu.hk/main/wpe/.

[2]http://vision2020.hkbu.edu.hk/.

[3]http://chtl.hkbu.edu.hk/main/hkbu-ga/.

European Studies programme which is "multilingual and multidisciplinary" (Hess 2012: 38) as it combines two major axes: social sciences and intensive language learning, either French or German, the approach is a constructivist one: it implies a high level of learner autonomy and initiative through active learning, critical thinking, problem-solving, reflective practices, etc. Each learner is seen as a "social agent", "i.e. a member of a society who has tasks (not exclusively language-related) to accomplish in a given set of circumstances, in a specific environment and within a particular field of action" (Council of Europe 2001, cited in Cabau 2015: 167). That is why "all language courses (...) have been re-titled "Language in Context" to illustrate that language learning is multi-purposed and context-oriented" (Cabau 2015: 173). French and German teaching & learning puts emphasis not only on the language itself but also on historical, political and social aspects of the French- and German-speaking societies of Europe. That also explains why the teaching & learning method in our courses is based largely on the Content & Language Integrated Learning (CLIL) approach (Hess 2012: 52) since it offers many advantages such as

> building intercultural knowledge and understanding, (...) opportunities to study content through different perspectives, possibility of having more contact with the target language, [increasing] learners' motivation and confidence in both the language and the subject being taught (...) (Cabau 2015: 168).

We can see that TLA such as "spoon-feeding" learning and assessment-oriented teaching are undoubtedly not adequate anymore to acquire these "resilient skills". That is why ePF have been introduced in our French and German language courses, in order to go beyond "passive learning, knowledge transmission, regurgitation of course content" (Stefani et al. 2007: 20). It is an innovative tool with multiple assets not only for language learning but also to acquire these intercultural competences and reflective skills mentioned above.

Intended Learning Outcomes for E-Portfolios in Language Teaching & Learning

In implementing ePF in French and German language courses as an alternative and authentic assessment, three objectives were targeted in line with the CILO, PILO and GAs: improving language, intercultural and reflective skills.

Language Learning

The benefits of ePF in language learning are well evidenced in the literature. Aydin (2010: 195) presents different studies that all pinpoint the contributions of PF/ePF in terms of language-related skills. According to his own findings:

PF keeping in EFL writing contributes considerably to vocabulary and grammar knowledge, reading, research and writing skills. In other words, it can be stated that PF keeping benefits EFL students' language skills and knowledge, and is useful in developing their rhetorical skills (ibid: 198).

Obviously, while creating their ePF, students will have to investigate and select various resources (e.g. reading materials or videos) for their collection. Then, they will be assigned a written reflection on these artefacts which includes description, analysis, evaluation, etc. In doing so, we can see that students are much more in contact with the target language, and in a much more integrated way than in doing any other kind of "traditional" French or German exercise which mobilizes only one competence at a time, such as in writing assessment tests for example.

Intercultural Competences

Since "learning about FL cultures is becoming an important objective in FL curricula" (Su 2011: 230), teaching and learning a foreign language goes beyond the acquisition of grammatical rules, vocabulary, etc. But neither is teaching culture distributing a list of facts to be memorized (list of people's traditions, customs, beliefs, behaviours or art, civilization, history, art of a nation, etc.) (Lee 1997: 356). That would lead to simplistic cultural explanations (Dervin and Hahl 2014: 3). Hence, as Abrams et al. underline, teaching culture is challenging as culture is elusive, it is not a solid entity (2006: 80), due to the fact "that language is embedded in a myriad of sub-cultural/social contexts, extremely diverse, depending actually on individual's affective and attitudinal orientation and interpersonal skills" (Little and Simpson 2003: 4). That is why, although teaching cultural knowledge to some extent is relevant, what should really be done in language classes is to provide an intercultural education understood as a "protéophilic" model (Dervin 2010) which could help appreciate the variety, the diversity of the culture understood as a perpetual social construction. Accordingly, intercultural education should not be understood as a culturalist approach but rather should make understand that "the individual is no longer the product of his culture, he is instead the actor of his culture, he elaborates it, and he builds it, with diversified strategies, according to the needs and circumstances" (Abdallah-Pretceille 1999: 55).[4] In this sense, ePF projects are "seen as effective tools for integrating these situations of construction, identification and uncertainty" (Dervin & Hahl 2014: 7). In fact, several practitioners who conducted cultural PF projects in Spanish, French, German, Korean or English language classes (Lee 1997; Allen 2004; Abrams et al. 2006; Byon 2007; Su 2011, respectively) pinpointed numerous benefits of PF keeping in terms of

---

[4] « L'individu n'est plus le produit de sa culture, il en est au contraire l'acteur, il l'élabore, la construit en fonction de stratégies diversifiées, selon les besoins et les circonstances » (Abdallah-Pretceille 1999: 55).

intercultural awareness. Su summarizes them well: ePF helps gain insight on a specific aspect of the culture; modify one's stereotypical impressions; develop open attitudes towards the target culture; recognize the impact of one's perspectives on understanding another culture; and demonstrate an understanding of target culture from emic perspectives (2011: 233). Indeed, collecting and evaluating multiple sources over time will not only improve language skills as we have seen above. In the same way, the FL learner, facing and confronting all these various information about diverse aspects of the foreign culture, will be more sensible to the fact "that culture is not static and may vary according to the forces at play in the society" (2011: 232). Furthermore, particular attention must be paid to the fact that the reflection of the students is "the fruit of their own explorations, based on both the target culture as well as their own culture" (Allen 2004: 232). In doing so, they engage themselves in "a process of discovery, social construction and meaning negotiation" (Su 2011: 231) in which they can appreciate the complexity not only of the foreign culture but also of their own culture.

Reflection

Students are individuals with their own personalities, habits and beliefs, which influence their way of learning enormously. Therefore, it is hardly possible to design lessons and tasks in which every student can profit best. In other words, teachers have to make students aware of "how they understand their roles as learners, how they work and how they might improve their learning skills" (Kohonen 2000: 4). According to Zubizarreta, "reflective thinking and judgment are effective stimuli to deep, lasting learning" (2009: 10). However, it is important to answer the following questions: what does reflective thinking mean and how does it work?

Reflection can be summarized as follows:

> *Reflection is one way to bridge the divide between thought and action - an opportunity for students to describe their internal processes, evaluate their challenges, and recognize their triumphs in ways that would otherwise remain unarticulated.* (Allan and Driscoll 2014: 37).

Figure 1 describes Schön's understanding of a human process in action. To carry out an action, one reverts to prior knowledge but reality shows that changes are made due to reactions or other circumstances. Therefore, a person reflects (un-) consciously on the executing action while this is still in process, which is labelled as "reflection-in-action" by Schön. Following the completed action, a reflection on the whole action takes place that can be done by analyzing and interpreting it, which then leads to a revised "knowing-in-action" step to be applied for a similar situation happening. Figure 1 emphasizes the perpetual process of lifelong learning through experience.

According to Zubizarreta (2009: 24), a learning portfolio "consists of a written narrative section in which the student reflects critically about essential questions of

Fig. 1 Adapted from Schön
(1987)

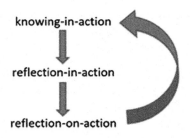

what, when, how, and why learning has occurred". Doig et al. (2006: 164) describe the advantage of "using an ePF as the basis for reflection [as it] provides a structured opportunity to take stock of personal development, accounted for and justified by reference to evidence". Furthermore, since the contents of the ePF are generated by the students themselves, it offers them the opportunity to become actively involved in the learning process, which encourages students' self-evaluation and reflection (Su 2011).

To summarize, our French and German ePF is seen as an alternative and authentic assessment which emphasizes the process of learning. ePFs have a lot of similarities with cultural PFs as described by Lee (1997), Allen (2004), Abrams et al. (2006), Byon (2007) or Su (2011) and contributes to a more effective and comprehensible *reflection-on-action*. Indeed, Stefani et al. (2007) and Farr (1991) point correctly to the fact that by selecting pertinent contents from multiple resources, students will gain an understanding of the ideas and then construct their own responses, conceptualizations and solutions to problems and therefore support their understanding of their role as learners. We will now give a detailed presentation of both ePFs' structures, followed by concrete examples of ePFs implemented in language courses (French and German) to illustrate students' achievements.

Case Study 1: French Stream E-Portfolio

Structure

In the French stream, the ePF is divided in three categories.

The first category—*Learning Experiences outside the classroom*—in which students are asked to reflect on something they have seen, read, heard in the target language is directly inspired from the European PF (Little and Simpson 2003) which describes the benefits of such an activity:

> In his ePF, the owner [of the PF] will categorize various sources (painting, music, movie, mass-media...) which contributed to his knowledge of the studied society and culture. In doing so, the learner will articulate his impressions, his observations and experiences whose some of which may be fleeting (for example when watching a film). (...) That will

gradually develop his IC awareness by capturing experiences over time. (…) He will
realize also the variety and frequency of such IC opportunities and that will draw his
attention to the different ways in which [he/she] comes into contact with the other culture
(ibid: 8, 10, 16).

The second category which is called "*Journal*" is used to deepen a topic seen in class. The idea in this category is to restructure and refine the knowledge transmitted in class by collecting and evaluating new data from multiple sources that will provide students with a deeper understanding of the subject. The students conduct an exploration through various media on a specific theme discussed in class. In doing so, they find out—by themselves—new information on a specific topic. In addition, they will make their own perception of the "Other" "instead of relying on outsider's perception" (Abrams 2002: 149). Indeed, as Stefani et al. (2007: 61) point out, students will relate it to what they already knew, to their own experiences in their reflective essay. In trying to understand by observing, describing, questioning new material they encounter, they will create links to new ideas and, consequently, they will have an overview of the subject much wider and complex than what was presented by the teacher. We think that it will encourage them to be more open to the diversity and to understand "the dynamic nature of the culture" (Byon 2007: 2).

Last but not least, the third category—*Creativity*—is presented in these terms: "anything that you [the student] have created individually or with someone in French; a song, a poem, a video, a comic, an animation, an original translation etc." To use the words of Duffy et al. (1999: 34), what is at stake in this category is truly "to celebrate the individuality" of learners in giving them a total liberty of expressivity in the target language/culture. It helps them build a personal relationship with foreign language/culture and create meaning of external facts, information (Fig. 2).

Fig. 2 Screenshot from a student's ePF

Example 1: Learning Experiences Outside the Classroom

To illustrate the first category, we can take as an example, the ePF of a student who presented three experiences with the target culture: a movie, a graphic novel and a sculpture exhibition. Each artefact related to a specific and different aspect of the French society: the movie was about homosexuality, the graphic novel about police repression and the exhibition was about women's rights. We can say that without the ePF, our student would probably have watched, read, seen this movie, book, exhibition, all presenting a particular angle of France, but she would not have taken the time to pause and reflect on these different facets of society. Although the level of reflection differs from one artefact to another, sometimes failing to go beyond the level of description (we will see later the difficulty of achieving reflexive skills), she can gradually sense the diversity of the target culture she is studying. Thus, the ePF plays its role in increasing cross-cultural awareness through a process of distanciation (Holliday et al. 2004) which consists in describing and questioning different cultural facts. This interrogative approach on the other culture which often leads to take into consideration one's own culture, allows students' interpretations to evolve and to move away from culturalist constructions that essentialize and solidify the other. This is particularly remarkable in the reflection of our student on the graphic novel about a true event which happened in Paris in the 1960s related to police repression. She starts saying that *she wants to talk* about this tragic event because she *found it very surprising*. Then she describes with more details what happened to conclude her first paragraph by saying *she knows now more and better* about this. Nevertheless, she adds that *she was very surprised that such thing could happen* in France and that this story *recalls her* something similar which took place in her own country. This leads her to say that *she would never have thought* that France could do such similar thing because *she always thought that* France was different from her country. We can see through her discourse (highlighted in *italic*), how the ideas she had about France are set in motion and evolve from an image of France rooted in common symbols (*Liberté, Egalité, Fraternité*) to a reconstructed image which is not as fixed and stable as it was (Fig. 3).

Example 2: Journal

Let us take here, as an example for the second category, the ePF of a student who decided to reflect upon a topic discussed in class about suburbs in France. This decision is motivated by the fact that *the student is surprised* that such a problem exists in France. Therefore, *she would like to know more* to try to get a clearer picture of this aspect of the society. Particularly, she would like to know more about what solutions have been put into place, how the young generation lives, etc. Without an ePF, most likely the student would not have undertaken such a research unless asked to do so for a formative assessment in a term paper or an essay. Here,

Les Banlieues

Dans la classe,   on a étudié le sujet des **banlieues**. J'étais un peu surprise que un problème social comme ça existe en France, un pays développé et riche. Je suis très ignorante des affaires arrivent là, les journals hongkongais n'en rapportent pas beaucoup. Même si je n'aime pas faire les devoirs, c'est une bonne chance pour moi de savoir mieux la france en écrivant ce journal. J'aimerai apprendre plus sur les banlieues, comme le premier pied que je marche vers une image claire de la société française.

Je sais que les banlieues sont originairement construites pour la classe moyenne qui travaillent à Paris, mais comme la condition de vivre n'est pas bien, ils y quittent. Après, les benlieues devient un ensemble de logement sociaux avec beaucoup d'immigres. Mais la région a nombreux de problèmes, notamment *l'isolement de la societé, la violence, le chômage* etc, et les banlieues sont maintenant un problème social en France.

Je voudrais savoir plus comme ce que le gouvernement fait pour résoudre les problèmes, comment les jeunes vivent aux benlieues etc.

Je vais *regarder les videos* de ce sujet sur YouTube et je vais *lire les journals concernés*. J'espère que dans l'article prochain je sera plus au courant des banlieues.

Fig. 3 Screenshot from a student's ePF

ePF allows the students to conduct research based on their own interests and questions. That seems to us a positive starting point. Then our student talks about a video she found on YouTube *where she learns more* on how people live in Paris suburbs. In her discourse in this second entry, she says *that this is absolutely what she wanted to know* but she adds immediately after that, *still, she doesn't understand why* nothing has been done to improve the situation. She continues saying that after watching this documentary, *she doesn't feel well*. This aspect of the society does not leave her satisfied. That brings her to *compare* this situation in France to HK and *she notices similar issues that reinforce her discomfort*: how two well-developed countries can leave wide parts of society abandoned? Finally, our student pursues her research citing a French newspaper article highlighting another point of view that puts forward the role that civil society can play in this issue, *an aspect she had never taken into consideration before.* We can see in this ePF, the work (highlighted in *italic*) of a dynamic, critical thinking student that goes beyond the description of a simple cultural fact. The reflection presents the impact that the different perspectives of this fact have on the person, on her knowledge and on her own experience.

The reflective writing allowed by the ePF shows that the way of seeing things has been destabilized. According to us, this is a first step towards acquisition of intercultural competences in the sense of ePF is a means to help us take a non-rigid look at the otherness.

Fig. 4 Screenshot from a student's ePF

Example 3: Creativity

The students, after a class dedicated to French art history, learnt about the scandal of the famous painting of Edouard Manet created in 1862, *Le Déjeuner sur l'herbe* (*The Luncheon on the Grass*). The photo below, taken by a group of students to be included in the third category of their ePF, is a perfect example of the learner autonomy and initiative (Stefani et al. 2007: 11) implied in ePF. Students reclaimed, remixed the painter's codes to reinterpret them, to integrate their own subjectivity. This means that, the history, the different elements which compose this masterpiece are not only known by the students but also reused by them in a new product retitled here *Réviser sur l'herbe (Revise on the Grass)*. Pegrum talks about "appropriation": "in becoming creative actors rather than passive consumer" (2011: 13), they develop a way of learning where the knowledge is no more external, but on the contrary, becomes a knowledge whose they take ownership, that belong to them (Fig. 4).

Case Study 2: German Stream E-Portfolio

Structure

In the German language classes, the tasks are divided into two main parts for each semester. In semester one, students are supposed to watch a movie that dealt with German Reunification and then decide to concentrate their work on a specific topic taken out of the movie, e.g. the cultural differences between West and East Germany. During this activity, they are expected to write a descriptive text, which was a summary of a movie. This is followed by a brief reflection on why they had chosen the topic and to describe their prior knowledge about it. The core of the second part is research on the topic. A template of an ePF was created as a tool support to help students grasp what the design could look like and to guide them. The documentation of their research task and the reflection on the challenges they faced are also parts of the first semester (cf. Appendix).

As for the second semester, students now being more familiar with reflective skills, have to document their learning process on their "German identity": every student is given a year of birth and a German town name, the remaining personal information in provided categories like education, family background, profession and hobbies are completely up to themselves. During class, they had time to present their "lives" and on their ePF, the assignment is to describe their new character in general and concentrate on three categories they did research on. Then, a reflection on what they found out and their process in doing research has to be documented. Concluding the students' first year of creating an electronic portfolio, they had to comment on what they think was positive and negative (e.g. the tasks themselves, their own learning habits and time management skills) with suggestions how the whole project could be improved or changed. To sum up this class' first attempt to work with an ePF, the tasks are created in order to support their research skills and especially to stimulate reflective thinking. The task design is to encourage students to work effectively and autonomously in specific. As an in-class stimulus, students are provided with explicit questions on a template they could use as a guideline (cf. Appendix). Therefore, the provided scaffold was a helping hand throughout their first year with an ePF.

Example 1

Let us take a German stream student's product as an example for the first semester's task. The student chose the topic "freedom of travel" as his focus of research after watching the movie "Go Trabi Go" which is about an East German family travelling to Italy for the first time after the reunification of Germany. Figure 5 shows the screenshot of a newspaper and video source he used to explore more about the topic.

After he did some research on this topic, the student compares the situation with his own life, as he comes from mainland China and is now enjoying the freedom to travel to Hong Kong. This is not what his mother experienced when she came to visit in 2003. At that time, she was not allowed to travel on her own but rather was obliged to join a group of other tourists. This task allows the student to recognize the similar situation between Germany and his home country. Therefore, he concludes that the regulations for travel are part of the history and that this sort of freedom he did not use to have allows him now to make new experiences. By

Quelle 6: Reportage in den Zeitungen (*Süddeutsche* und *Die Welt*)

Auch heutezutage sind die Reisegewohnheiten von Ost- und Westdeutschen und die Unterschiede Dazwischen häufig zu besprechen. Alle dies können nicht von dem Thema Reisefreiheit getrennt werden. In großen Zeitungen wie *Süddeutsche* und *die Welt* kann man Reportage darüber finden, dadrin stehen auch viele Ergebnisse der wissenschaftlichen Studien, die man gut gebrauchen kann.

  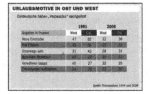

Quelle 7: Videomaterial
Animation ist eine besondere Art von Film, die schweres Thema immer gut erklären kann. Dieser kurze Film über die Flucht der DDR-Bürger finde ich Interessant.
Link: http://www.zeitklicks.de/ddr/zeitklicks/schau-mal/video/der-duft-des-westens/

"Visafrei nach Hahwai(Hahwaii)". Die fehlende Reisefreiheit war eine sehr wichtiger Grund für den Zusammenbruch der DDR. Lassen wir uns von dem damals Parteileiter Günter Schabowski erzählen.

Fig. 5 Screenshot from a student's ePF

realizing this, he describes how he appreciates this privilege and nothing should be taken for granted. Besides this topic-related research, this student explains that this task helps him to improve his language proficiency especially in learning a regional dialect since the main characters in the movie are inhabitants of the federal state Saxony. During his research, he could enhance his knowledge in the usage of synonyms and colloquial language. The whole ePF simplifies the process of returning to one's written texts and realize the progress students made when rereading the artefacts. Due to the online access of his ePF, students can easily return to the first task to reflect on the artefacts which make the student in this example discover his linguistic mistakes. Still, in his opinion he made progress since there are less grammar mistakes by the end of the first semester. In addition to that, how to summarize information is a skill that he could practice with Weebly. It was necessary to do so in order not to forget important aspects while reading a long text. Using an ePF helps the student to realize his own weakness: he now understands how important it is to pay attention to design and layout because he is aware of the fact that someone will be looking at his product. He adds it would be a pity if the content is good but no one wants to read it because of its bad design. So, he suggests adding pictures in order to visualize the content. In his concluding statement, he describes his ePF as a present he made himself and he is happy when realizing his own development in a year. To be more precise, regarding the development, he states that this does not only include positive advancements but also problems he had encountered through the whole activity. Creating an ePF helps him to perform better in the foreign language (practice of written articulation), to develop research skills (selection of resources), to work autonomously and most importantly how to reflect critically on his own actions. In his opinion, the ePF's value is beneficial for the learning process of both the language and the life style because the webpage allows him to reread it whenever and wherever he wants to recap on his thoughts in the past. A comparison between the past and the present makes changes visible. According to his point of view, the implementation of an ePF in the FLC is not a waste of time at all.

Example 2

In the following, we will take a look at another student's ePF. An excerpt of a student in Fig. 6 shows two of the resources he makes use of, namely a survey and a newspaper article. With this information, he could form an idea on how both parts of Germany see the other side after the reunification. With his documentation, he does not only present the source but also summarizes and draws a conclusion from the content.

Before the research, he would not have thought and expected that the situation between both parts of Germany would be that complicated. He assumed that every inhabitant would have welcomed the reunification. So, he was surprised there are still many people who have a negative opinion about East Germans although this event took place 25 years ago. This fact leads him to become curious about the prejudices within Germany for which he tries to find reasons. In his opinion, prejudices cannot exist on their own: "I think that the media is responsible for the current situation, because people accept these statements if they are confronted with propaganda every day. A lie becomes truth when it has been told 100 times". Furthermore, he compares the reunification with Hong Kong's handover to China in 1997. The relationship between Hong Kongers and the Chinese is not harmonious and both are struggling with prejudices from the other side. A similar atmosphere can be found in Germany between the Eastern and Western part of the country as well. This research task helped him to obtain information about Germany's culture, history and social situation. He has learned that both life and history have an important impact on a society. Nevertheless, the biggest finding was that the feeling of a unity in Germany is not as strong as he had imagined before. When summing up his learning achievements, he mentions that he is really proud to be able to find and handle many resources in a foreign language. Linguistically, the ePF helps him —according to his own perception—to construct long and complex sentences, which he would never have been practised in classroom. Although he thinks that the whole project lasted too long and was too intensive, he noted that he would still continue using this platform for similar tasks in the future.

Through these different examples, we have seen that ePFs offer an interesting and effective interface to let emerge linguistic, intercultural and reflective skills.

Quelle C Umfrage

Top 10 der gesamtdeutschen Vorurteile zu
Ossis und Wessis (aus Sicht aller Befragten):

1. Ossis heißen häufig Mandy, Cindy, Sandy,
Enrico,
Maik etc. 48%
2. Wessis sind Besserverdiener: 46%
3. Ossis können kein Hochdeutsch: 36%
4. Ossis sind sparsamer als die Westdeutschen:
35%
5. Ossis haben alle schon mal Urlaub an der
Ostsee
gemacht. 35%
6. Wessis würden am liebsten die Mauer wieder
hochziehen. 30%
7. Wessis sind arrogant: 28%
8. Ossis sprechen schlechtes Englisch: 27%
9. Ossis meckern viel: 27%
10. Wessis denken nur ans Geld: 25%

Tag der Deutschen Einheit: Top 10 Ossi- und Wessi-Klischees
Presseportal.de   24.09.2013

Die Daten zeigt das Top 10 der gesamtdeutschen Vorurteile zu
Ossis und Wessis. Die Umfrage wurde im Jahr 2013 durch
Deal.com gemacht. Die Anzahl hindeutet, dass die Deutsche
heute noch viele Vorurteile haben, weil fest die Hälfte der
beklagten Personen denken, die Wessis verdienen mehr Geld.
Es meint, dass die Gesellschaft eine Existenz der Prosperität
zwischen die Westdeutsche und die Ostdeutsche glaubt,
obwohl die Wiedereinigung schon passiert ist. Außerdem denkt
jeder dritte Deutsche, dass die Ossis kein Hochdeutsch
sprechen können. Es reflktiert die alte Meinung an der
Gesellschaft, weil sie scheinen, in der Vergangenheit zu leben,
aber der Staat ist jetzt in einer Einheit.

Quelle D Zeitungsartikel

Bilanz zur Wiedervereinigung: Ostdeutsche
Wirtschaft hinkt dem Westen hinterher

**Fast 25 Jahre nach der Wiedervereinigung zeigt ein
Bericht der Bundesregierung den Nachholbedarf in
den neuen Ländern auf. Laut "Bild"-Zeitung liegt die
Wirtschaftskraft dort noch immer 30 Prozent unter
dem Niveau im Westen.**

Bilanz zur Wiedervereinigung: Ostdeutsche Wirtschaft hinkt
dem Westen hinterher
Spiegel Online   24.09.2014

Dieser Artikel zeigt die Unterschiede in dem wirtschaftlichen
Aspekt zwischen die Westdeutsche und die Ostdeutsche nach
der Wiedereinigung. Eigentlich ist das Gehalt von Wessis
doppelt die Ossis, deswegen sind die Vorurteile manchmal
richtig. Außerdem gibt der Artikel an, dass es viele Leute gibt,
die dem Mauer erhalten wollen, denn jeder vierte sieht den
Mauerfall wie einen Nachteil. Es meint, dass nicht alle
Menschen die Wiedervereinigung haben möchten.

Fig. 6 Screenshot from a student's ePF

Views of Our Students on This New TLA

At the end of the semester, we have conducted a survey that was provided by the Centre of Holistic Teaching and Learning (CHTL) to examine students' feedback about the ePF's implementation. In Figs. 7 and 8, graphs present the distribution of the classes' reply of 15 and 18 students in French and German, respectively.

Q 1 *Overall, I found constructing the e-Portfolio valuable to this course.*
Q 2 *I acquired useful skills in creating my e-Portfolio.*
Q 3 *The e-Portfolio helped me improve my writing, reading and listening skills.*
Q 4 *The use of the e-Portfolio as part of the course helped me learn French in a meaningful way.*
Q 5 *The process of developing my e-Portfolio increased my awareness of aspects of French/European culture.*
Q 6 *The process of developing my e-Portfolio increased my awareness of my own culture.*
Q 7 *I was able to engage with e-portfolio interface in a worthwhile manner.*
Q 8 *The process of creating my e-Portfolio helped me to take responsibility for my own learning.*

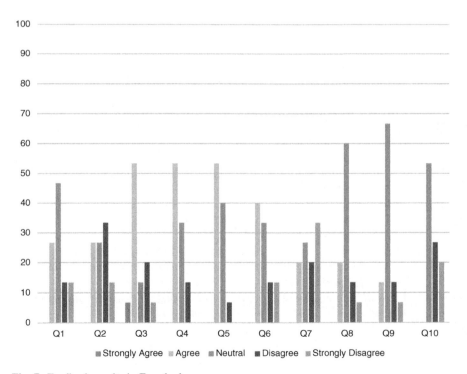

Fig. 7 Feedback results in French class

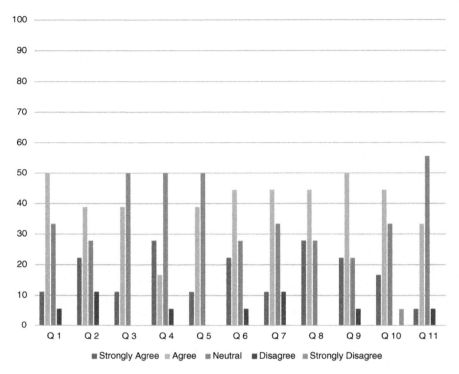

■ Strongly Agree   ■ Agree   ■ Neutral   ■ Disagree   ■ Strongly Disagree

Fig. 8 Feedback results in German class

Q 9   *I became more aware of my learning process.*
Q 10 *I have a generally favourable attitude toward using the e-Portfolio.*
Q 1   *Overall, I found constructing the e-Portfolio valuable to this course.*
Q 2   *I acquired useful skills in creating my e-Portfolio.*
Q 3   *The process of creating my e-Portfolio helped me to take responsibility for my own learning.*
Q 4   *Showcasing electronic media (i.e. text-based, graphic or multi-media elements) in my e-Portfolio allowed me to demonstrate a more meaningful understanding of my course.*
Q 5   *Overall, I valued the integration of the e-Portfolio into this course.*
Q 6   *Overall, I am satisfied with the way my learning is assessed using the e-Portfolio in this course.*
Q 7   *I was able to engage with e-portfolio interface in a worthwhile manner.*
Q 8   *I could exercise choice in how I customized my e-Portfolio entries.*
Q 9   *Constructing the e-Portfolio helped me to reflect upon my achievement.*
Q 10 *I have a generally favourable attitude toward using the e-Portfolio.*
Q 11 *Using the e-Portfolio enhanced my effectiveness in learning.*

According to our students' views and feedback comments, we can recognize the potential of an ePF although it includes challenges as well. Some of the negative comments were about the "user-friendliness" of the platforms and that the implementation of such an ePF only means "extra work" and is "really time-consuming".

Platforms

At first, the French and German streams worked with the platform Mahara. However, after one year, taking into account various technical difficulties reflected in students' feedbacks (e.g. "(…) the interface could be more direct, simplified and user-friendly"), both streams decided to explore different tools to integrate students' reflection. The French stream decided to opt for an ePF platform integrated in the Learning Management System (LMS) of the university—Blackboard (Bb)—which was put in service in 2014. This decision echoed the view of Stefani et al. on the ePF part in students' task:

> the most important way to make the ePF an integral part of a learner's daily routine is to ensure that the software is integrated into the tasks students regularly perform for their courses in their electronic learning environments (2007: 59).

Indeed, instead of multiplying the interfaces (Bb for their courses and Mahara for their ePF), we thought that students would find it a lot easier and more stimulating to compile an ePF in an environment they are used to work with. But still, complaints increased with the Bb platform as students mentioned that the ePF interface was not convenient, too slow to use, not intuitive enough to upload documents or too complicate to share them with their instructors and peers. If we refer to question 7, related to the interface of the French students' feedback (cf. Fig. 7), one can see that almost half of the students were unsatisfied with the Bb platform and this although one session at least was spent at the beginning of the semester to go through the different technological aspects of this software. Students and instructors got support from the ITO and the CHTL officers who came to our class to show in detail how to log in, how to insert documents, how to share them, etc.

Stefani et al. (2007) discussed these disadvantages. Regarding the use of technologies, for example, the researchers pointed out the importance of interfaces for ePF: they need to be usable, accessible, and to inspire confidence if we want ePF projects to be successful. Unfamiliar and unfriendly technology will discourage the use of ePF and may act as a brake on ePF implementation (ibid: 33). That is why the German stream, observing that "the reflective components of ePF have great similarities with blogging (…) and that a personal webpage carries many of the presentational functions of ePF" (ibid: 16), opted for Weebly. The assumption here was that students were much more familiar with a "blog type" platform which allows much more space for freedom and creativity. Other reasons for choosing Weebly were the easy access (log in with a Facebook or Google+ account), the possibility of possessing the product after graduation, the intuitive usage and the attractive interface with its large variety of designs. If we refer now to question 7, related to the interface of the German students' feedback (cf. Fig. 8), one can see that more than half of the students were here satisfied with the Weebly interface. We are inclined to think, from these results (Q. 7 and 8 in Figs. 7 and 8 respectively), that technology played a significant role in the implementation and in the success of maintaining our students' ePF: if we refer to Q 10—*I have a generally favourable attitude towards using the e-Portfolio*—(cf. Figs. 7 and 8), we can see that, in the French stream, not a single student out of 15 agreed on this, whereas, on the contrary, 60% of the German class that used Weebly as their ePF platform were of the mind that they have a favourable attitude towards using this tool. Taking this vast contradiction into account, we believe that an unsatisfactory technology, like Blackboard in our case study, might have had a great impact on students' perception and their exposure to ePF.

Meaningful Assessment

Practitioners also pinpoint another important issue to be addressed to achieve the full potential of ePF: the necessity to promote ePF to the learner as a purposeful activity, "not something bolted on to their studies as an added extra" (Stefani et al. 2007: 34). Students need to be made aware of the benefits of ePF production for them (Lee 1997: 34) if they want to think that it is worth to spend time on it and to motivate them (Cummins and Davesne 2009: 858). Hung (2006: 7) also gives an example of an unsuccessful tentative of ePF which was due to unclear explanation of the purposes, criteria and outcomes. That is why, in both streams, instructors spend a great deal of time at the beginning of the semester to introduce this new e-learning project. We insist on the specificity of this assessment because, as Stefani et al. remind us, we "need to be careful that students don't see the PF as just another chore with no real value for them" (2007: 21). Despite this, we can find some particularly critical remarks from students that do not find any interest in completing their ePF: "E-Portfolio is really useless and a waste of time. I don't understand the meaning of doing this". Or "E-portfolio used in this course is useless, waste of time and adding unnecessary workloads to the students, we found that the e-portfolio has nearly no effect in improving our language level".

This difficulty could come actually from "students' unfamiliarity with PF assessment", as underlined by Hung (2006: 7). Certainly, reflective thinking is not easy and it can be quite challenging and painful (Zubizarreta 2009: 10) because it goes beyond collecting and simply presenting representative samples of experiences. Students may lack the skills of reflection (Moon 2006). This is particularly well shown in the surveys conducted with our students of both streams: we can see that for the questions related to reflective thinking [Q 3, 4, 5 & 11 for German stream (cf. Fig. 8) and Q 8 & 9 for French stream (cf. Fig. 7)], more than half of the students have a neutral opinion regarding this issue. The ePF is not seen for them as a specific tool to improve one's reflective skills. Thus, becoming an autonomous learner who takes initiatives does not happen by itself. Students need guidance not only for the tasks to be accomplished but also for the understanding of reflection in an academic context (Stefani et al. 2007). Zubizarreta (2009: 10) points to the importance of prompts and rubrics in the teacher's guidance task: "To guide students toward the metacognitive work necessary for strong critical thinking skills, one's need directed questions for reflection". Prompts and rubrics play a crucial role to orient students in an activity they are not familiar with and to raise cross-cultural awareness. Yet, the provision of particularly detailed guidelines (cf. Appendix) is not sufficient for some students, as exemplified in the following comment: "Maybe we can spend more time (…) working on our (…) e-portfolio together [students and instructors] so that we have more instructions, which can also reduce our stress".

Nonetheless, a large majority of students see the benefits of an ePF as part of their learning. In the German stream for example, over 60% of the students declare to be favourable toward the ePF, a TLA that they find valuable (Q 1 & 10) (cf. Fig. 8). In the French stream, a large majority appreciates the ePF as a TLA helping them to learn the target language in a meaningful way (Q 3, 4 & 5) (cf. Fig. 7). In this sense, despite important issues that need to be addressed, it seems to us that "ePF can act as a vehicle for meaningful formative assessment" (Stefani et al. 2007: 21). This is also the feeling expressed in some students' feedbacks. One wrote for example that "writing/constructing his ePF allowed him to showcase his skills better than in class or assignments as it is a bigger project in which he spent more time on it". Another described an ePF as "a good medium as it is environmental friendly and students can review their works easily after". At the end, the satisfaction, when they look at their products after two semesters, seems to overcome their frustration. Once they realize what they are actually able to master in a foreign language, they portray their work for their ePF as a "proud moment".

Outlook

Although we were facing many challenges, we observed the success students achieved by the end of their work. So if teachers decide to implement ePF, they need to be aware of the fact that it may frustrate students at some point, but all in all the benefits will predominate.

Surely, ePFs have several advantages. One is definitely the online access which makes the students able to show how much they can master multimedia and digital literacies which are key components nowadays. Furthermore, the ePF is also a strong potential support tool for the acquisition of intercultural skills which are essential in an increasingly multicultural world. And finally, to have a product that documents students' learning process and progress makes it worth through the enhancement of lifelong learning skills. This trend is corroborated by a research done by Chaudhuri in 2014 in our programme. In his article, in which he analysed the distribution of 14 German language students' responses using the same template as our CHTL survey, he observed a predominant agreement concerning students regarding the work with ePFs as useful in the sense of encouraging their autonomy and self-directed learning (Chaudhuri 2015: 113). For us, it is the biggest asset of this TLA in line with the GAs of our university mentioned at the beginning: enabling students to stand on their own and show their creativity and versatility.

Appendix: Prompts

French	German
What to write in learning experiences?	Part 1: About the movie
In this category, you are required to reflect about an experience you had in the target language (movie, documentary, article, blog, Facebook post, book, radio program etc.). You are required to write at least two entries	There are three movies on the list that deal with "reunification". Choose one of them • Go Trabi Go • Good Bye, Lenin! • Sonnenallee
• What did you see/read? • Names: director, author, actors, main characters, year of publication/production • Write a short summary • Why did you choose this film? Why did you read it? • What is the main theme of the film/book? • Your comments: this is your reflection. (ca. 150 Words), e.g.: – What surprised you? – What did you not understand well? Why? – What do you think about the topic, the characters? Is it the same/different in your country? – Did you read more about this topic? – How much of the language did you understand? Did you use the subtitles? – Was there a dialog/a sentence or a word that you would like to use in your everyday life?	1. Write a summary after you have watched the movie (200–250 words) 2. Describe and explain the topic of the movie 3. Answer the following questions: • Did you like the movie? What exactly did you like? What did you not like? • How difficult was it to understand the movie? • Why did you choose this movie? • Have you encountered anything about the movie or the topic itself before watching? • How difficult was it to recognize the topic of the movie? • What do you already know about this topic? • Which information do you want to explore?
What to write in the journal?	Part 2: Research
In the journal you are required to reflect in depth about a topic seen in class. You are required to write at least three journal entries • Tell us what topic you chose and why? • Tell us what you know about this topic and what you would like to know further. What resources are you going to use to learn more?	You are expected to do a research on your chosen topic and establish a contemporary connection. Use as many resources as possible (literature from the library, literature from the internet, audio files, videos, contemporary witness reports, interviews with German-speaking students, …) Document and reflect this activity: • What have you done at the beginning to get more information? • Which resources helped you the most to get information the easiest? • How did you select the information?

(continued)

French	German
• Tell us what more you have now learnt about this topic. What resources have you used till now? • Tell us what more you have now learnt about this topic. What is the difference in your knowledge now than it was in your first entry? • Tell us how you feel about this topic now? Was it an important topic? Did you find enough resources to learn more? Do you want to know more still? Or is this enough? <u>What to write in creativity?</u> You need to produce an artefact that show you're using creatively the target language/culture and you need to reflect on your 'creation' in a short text (±200 words): why did you choose to do this, what did you learn doing so about the language, the culture, how was the process of the creation	• Which challenges did you encounter? • Did you expect these challenges? • How could you cope with them? <u>Part 3: Learning process</u> • Could you benefit from your prior knowledge? • What did you learn about the topic with the research? • To what extent is this topic of current interest? Describe this in detail. • Did you learn anything about the German language? • Do you think, you could enhance your intercultural competence? If so, how? If not, why not? • What did you learn that you definitely want to keep for your next research task and which aspects need to be changed, improved or neglected?

References

Abdallah-Pretceille, M. (1999). L'Education interculturelle, Paris, PUF, coll. « Que Sais-je? » , n° 3487, 4ème éd., 2013.

Abrams, Z. I. (2002). Surfing to cross-cultural awareness: Using internet-mediated projects to explore cultural stereotypes. *Foreign Language Annals, 35*(2), 141–160.

Abrams, Z. I., Byrd, D. R., Boovy, B., & Morhing, A. (2006). Culture portfolio revisited: Feedback from students and instructors. *Die Unterrichtspraxis/Teaching German, 39*(1/2), 80–90.

Allan, E. G., & Driscoll, D. L. (2014). The three-fold benefit of reflective writing: Improving program assessment, student learning, and faculty professional development. *Assessing Writing, 21,* 37–55.

Allen, L. Q. (2004). Implementing a cultural portfolio project within a constructivist paradigm. *Foreign Language Annual, 37*(2), 232–239.

Aydin, S. (2010). EFL writers' perceptions of portfolio keeping. *Assessing Writing, 15,* 194–203.

Byon, A. S. (2007). The use of cultural portfolio project in Korean classroom: Evaluating stereotypes and enhancing cross-cultural awareness. *Language, Culture, and Curriculum, 20,* 1–19.

Cabau, B. (2015). The intercultural approach in Hong Kong academic setting. *The Language Learning Journal, 43*(2), 165–179.

Cambridge, B.L; Kahn, S., Tompkins, D.P. and Yancey, K. B. (Eds.), (2005). Electronic portfolios: emerging practices in student, faculty, and institutional learning. Sterling, VA: Stylus Publishing.

Chaudhuri, T. (2015). Mehr Autonomie wagen. Elektronische Portfolios im DaF-Unterricht. In: C. Merkelbach (Ed.), *Mehr Sprache(n) lernen—mehr Sprache(n) lehren* (pp 97–116). Aachen: Shaker Verlag GmbH.

Cummins, P. W., & Davesne, C. (2009). Using electronic portfolios for second language assessment. *The Modern Language Journal, 93,* 848–867.

Dervin, F. (2010). « Pistes pour renouveler l'interculturel en éducation », in Recherches en éducation, ALAOUI D. (coord.), Education et formations interculturelles: regards critiques, No. 9.

Dervin, F. & Hahl, K. (2014). Developing a portfolio of intercultural competences in teacher education: The case of a finnish international programme. *Scandinavian Journal of Educational Research, 59*(1), pp 95–109.

Doig, B., Illsley, B., Mcluckie, J., Parsons, R. (2006). Using e-portfolios to enhance reflective learning and development. In A. Jafari & C. Kaufman (Eds.), *Handbook of research on e-portfolios* (pp 158–167). Hershey, PA: Idea Group.

Duffy, M. L., Jones, J., & Thomas, S. W. (1999). Using portfolios to foster independent thinking. *Intervention in School and Clinic, 35*(1), 34–37.

Farr, R. (1991). Portfolios: Assessment in language arts. Eric Digest: 3.

Gibson, D. (2006). E-portfolios decisions and dilemmas. In A. Jafari & C. Kaufman (Eds.), *Handbook of research on E-portfolios* (pp 135–145). Hershey, PA: Idea Group.

Hess, H. W. (2012). Understanding Europe—understanding yourself: European studies in Hong Kong. In Josê E. Borao Mateo Vassilis Vagios (Ed.), *Interfaces: EU studies and European languages programs in East Asia,* Taipei: NTU Press, pp 33–62.

HKBU websites: CoP: http://chtl.hkbu.edu.hk/main/cop-eportfolio/ Vision 2020: http://vision2020.hkbu.edu.hk/ WPE & GAs: http://chtl.hkbu.edu.hk/main/hkbu-ga/

Holliday, A., Hyde, M., & Kullman, J. (2004). *Intercultural communication: An advanced resource book.* London: Routledge.

Hung, S. (2006). *Alternative EFL assessment: Integrating electronic portfolios into the classroom.* (Doctoral Dissertation). Indiana University, Bloomington.

Kohonen, V. (2000). Student reflection in portfolio assessment: Making language learning more visible Babylonia. *The Journal of Language Teaching and Learning.* N1. Available online at: http://www.cndp.fr/crdp-dijon/IMG/pdf_3-_Portfolio_Assessment_V_Kohonen.pdf

Lee, L. (1997). Using portfolios to develop L2 cultural knowledge and awareness of students in Intermediate Spanish. *Hispania, 80*(2), 355–367.

Little, D. & Simpson, B. (2003). European language portfolio: The intercultural component and learning how to learn. Council of Europe (DG IV/EDU/LANG/4).

Lorenzo, G. & Ittelson, J. (2005). An overview of institutional e-portfolios. In D. Oblinger (Ed.), *Educause learning initiative.* Available online at: https://net.educause.edu/ir/library/pdf/ELI3001.pdf

Moon, J. A. (2006). *Learning journals: A handbook for reflective practice and professional development.* Florence, KY, USA: Routledge.

Pegrum, M. (2011). Modified, multiplied, and (Re-)mixed: social media and digital literacies. In M. Thomas (Ed.), Digital education: Opportunities for social collaboration (pp. 9–35). Basingstoke: Palgrave Macmillan.

Quality Assurance Concil. (2009). http://www.ugc.edu.hk/eng/qac/publication/report/hkbu200909e.pdf

Schön, D. A. (1987). *Educating the reflective practitioner.* San Francisco, CA: Jossey-Bass.

Stefani, L., Mason, R., & Pegler, C. (2007). *Educational potential of e-portfolios: Supporting personal development and reflective learning.* Abingdon, UK, New York: Routledge.

Su, Y. (2011). The effects of the cultural portfolio project on cultural and EFL learning in Taiwan's EFL college classes. *Language Teaching Research, 15* (2), 230–252. Available online at: http://dx.doi.org/10.1177/1362168810388721

Zubizarreta, J. (2009). *The learning portfolio: Reflective practice for improving student learning. The Jossey-Bass higher and adult education series* (2d ed.). San Francisco, CA: Jossey-Bass.

Chapter 5
E-Portfolios and History Teaching: Supporting the Development of Information Literacy and Research Skills

Catherine Ladds

Abstract This chapter explores the utility and limitations of student academic e-portfolios in learning and assessment in the humanities. Whereas a substantial literature exists on the benefits of e-portfolios in education, language learning, and writing courses, the potential usefulness of e-portfolios in humanities education is lightly trodden ground. Using two case studies of the implementation of student academic e-portfolios in Hong Kong-based university history courses, this chapter considers how the e-portfolio format can support the development of both discipline-specific research ability and cross-curricular skills, such as information literacy. Furthermore, because of their online nature, e-portfolio assignments are well positioned to exploit recent developments in the digital humanities. Nevertheless, student feedback on the experience of creating an e-portfolio suggests that, while non-history major students were receptive to the low stakes and graduated nature of the assignment, a significant shift in disciplinary cultures of learning and assessment is required in order to implement e-portfolios successfully in advanced-level history courses.

Keywords Humanities education · Research portfolio · Information literacy

Introduction

Over the past ten years, e-portfolios have gained increasing acceptance as a means of showcasing learning in vocational subjects and traditional portfolio fields such as the creative arts. E-portfolio platforms enable the user to demonstrate the achievement of specific competencies by both uploading evidence in the form of 'artefacts' and reflecting upon their learning, thereby making it a useful tool for

C. Ladds (✉)
Department of History, Hong Kong Baptist University,
Hong Kong, Hong Kong
e-mail: cladds@hkbu.edu.hk

© Springer Nature Singapore Pte Ltd. 2017   75
T. Chaudhuri and B. Cabau (eds.), *E-Portfolios in Higher Education*,
DOI 10.1007/978-981-10-3803-7_5

assessing competencies in teacher and healthcare education (Boulton 2014; Peacock et al. 2012; Zinger and Sinclair 2014). Beyond vocational subjects, language and writing portfolio assignments can showcase increasing proficiency over time, while also presenting learners with an opportunity to reflect upon this journey (Desmet et al. 2008; Acker and Hasalek 2008). Furthermore, the combination of concrete evidence of achievement and reflection in e-portfolios make them beneficial to graduate jobseekers (Moretti and Giovannini 2011), meaning that constructing an e-portfolio that integrates evidence and experiences from across the entire period of degree study is now a graduation requirement at certain universities. Yet, the potential applications of student e-portfolios in humanities classes have so far been neglected, perhaps because of the perceived gulf between the training of IT specialists and scholars in the arts and humanities (Bartscherer and Coover 2011). Furthermore, the traditional focus on long research papers as the primary method of assessment of student learning in humanities teaching cultivates a perception that portfolio-based assessment is incompatible with the aims and methods of humanistic inquiry. However, the structure of e-portfolios, which enable the user to compile source materials, ideas, and commentary gradually over time, makes them an appropriate platform for conducting and demonstrating in-depth preparatory work for research projects (Källkvist et al. 2009; McGuinness and Brien 2006). Similarly, the reflective component of the e-portfolio compels users to consider the merits and demerits of different learning approaches, thus potentially leading them in creative research directions.

Beyond augmenting conventional history papers, e-portfolio users are poised to take advantage of the learning opportunities proffered by recent developments in the digital humanities, a subfield which marries humanistic inquiry with computing methods. In the discipline of history, digital humanities projects have created vast digital repositories of textual, visual, and audio primary sources, including more than 50 collections published by Adam Matthew Digital, while also pioneering new methods of historical analysis. For example, text mining tools use algorithms to extract data, such as language patterns, from historical sources. These text mining techniques can be combined with GIS mapping to create spatial histories (Schwartz 2015). Visualizing past environments using computational techniques, such as the 3D scanning of historical artefacts, can aid museum conservation and enable a more precise analysis of material cultures (Warwick et al. 2012). As an online platform equipped with tools to create hypermedia, e-portfolios encourage and enable learners to engage with digital humanities projects and incorporate these initiatives into their own work. Furthermore, e-portfolios provide learners with an opportunity to develop their own digital humanities projects by incorporating a range of simple digital tools into the portfolio in order to, for example, record oral histories or analyze visual maps of the content of historical documents. As Lauren (2011, 38) observes, although the digital humanities are usually associated with large-scale projects such as the Google Ngram Viewer, 'the ideas and methods associated with digital humanities research can now be implemented by sole practitioners, and in individual classrooms, by utilizing an array of off-the-shelf tools' in a way that can 'reintegrate ways of teaching and knowing in the digital age.'

Using two case studies of the implementation of e-portfolio-based assessment in university history classes, this chapter demonstrates how student e-portfolios can both enhance the development of conventional research papers in advanced courses and provide a low-stakes method of assessing the attainment of basic historical skills in learners who have little-to-no background in the discipline. In both cases it emerged that e-portfolio assignments support the acquisition of both cross-curricular skills, such as information literacy, and discipline-specific methodologies. Furthermore, the online nature of e-portfolio platforms means that they are well situated to take advantage of the explosion of digital humanities resources, which can be easily incorporated into the portfolio content. Nevertheless, student feedback on the experience of creating an e-portfolio suggests that, while non-history major students were receptive to the low stakes and graduated nature of the assignment, a significant departmental—or even disciplinary—shift in cultures of learning and assessment is required in order to implement e-portfolios successfully in advanced-level history courses.

Fostering Information Literacy and Learner Autonomy Through E-Portfolios

Above and beyond their potential use as a tool for assessing student understanding of course content, e-portfolios are most useful as a means of fostering non-discipline-specific skills and learning habits. Besides demonstrating the attainment of learning objectives, most e-portfolios have a reflective component, which usually entails reflection upon the examples of work showcased in the portfolio ('artefacts') or deliberation on the learning process. The value of reflective journals in promoting deep thinking about the learning process is well documented (McGuinness and Brien 2006). As Moon (1999) summarizes, reflective journal-writing requires higher level engagement with the material rather than the simple restatement of fact, leads students to a greater understanding the advantages and disadvantages of their individual learning approaches, and enables students to explore and form new ideas through the process of informal writing. In an e-portfolio, which is usually designed as an ongoing project constructed over a period of time ranging from several weeks to several years, the author's reflections should ideally form a narrative identifying changes, continuities, and setbacks in learning over time. As Abrami and Barrett (2005) have observed, ongoing reflection in portfolios enables students to 'evaluate their own growth over time as well as discover any gaps in their development.' This process of reflection and self-monitoring prompts learners to take responsibility for her or his own learning, (Kennedy et al. 2011) thereby fostering the autonomous learning strategies that are essential to practicing the discipline of history, the cornerstone of which is the writing of independent research papers.

E-portfolios can be a powerful tool for developing and showcasing digital literacies, particularly information literacy, the significance of which has increased in the face of the information overload that has accompanied the digital age. In the discipline of history, the conventional practice of which involves collecting, analyzing, and synthesizing large amounts of textual material, information literacy is especially important. When used as a method of formative assessment over a period of time, e-portfolios encourage learners to explore multiple methods of searching for information, evaluate these methods, reflect on the credibility and biases of different materials, and discuss appropriate usage of different types of source materials (Fourie and Niekerk 1999). By emphasizing the *process* of developing a research project in addition to the final product, e-portfolios can introduce discipline-specific methods of academic research in a structured way, thereby preparing learners for higher level work.

Designing E-Portfolio Assignments for History Learners

E-portfolios can be used for both formative and summative assessment, although, as Abrami and Barrett (2005) suggest, using them for high-stakes assessment is problematic. The author designed two e-portfolio assignments for two different undergraduate history classes at Hong Kong Baptist University, the first being an advanced-level course called International Relations since 1945 and the second a general education class called Modern China and World History. Rather than seeing an opposition between the reflective and assessment components of an e-portfolio (Kennedy 2011), the assignments emphasized both the process of creating the portfolio (formative assessment) and the end product (summative assessment). Each portfolio was designed to support the acquisition or enhancement of historical research skills through a process of analysis and reflection while also developing students' information literacy. Blackboard's My Portfolios was selected as the platform because of its technical simplicity and its integration into a Learning Management System that was already familiar to students at HKBU. In order to provide formative feedback, the instructor commented on each e-portfolio halfway through the semester and conducted a final assessment at the end of the semester.

Using E-Portfolios to Support a History Research Project

'International Relations Since 1945,' introduces students to recent historical events and contemporary political theories pertaining to the conduct of international politics. Twelve students completed the class, comprising eight history majors ranging from their second to fourth years of study and four non-history majors, majoring, respectively, in creative writing, government and international studies, sociology, and business studies. Nine students were pursuing degrees at Hong Kong Baptist

University, while three were overseas exchange students hailing from the Netherlands, Sweden, and the United States. Each student designed and completed a research project, consisting of an e-portfolio, presentation, and paper, which analyzed the historical roots of a contemporary international issue of his or her choosing. Each project required the synthesis of secondary historical accounts, primary sources, and international relations theory.

The aims of the e-portfolio component, which accounted for fifteen percent of the final course grade, were to support the research project by providing a repository for source materials and reflection. In particular, the assignment was designed to:

a. enhance information literacy skills by locating relevant source materials and critically evaluating their arguments and biases. Learners were also asked to reflect upon the differences between academic, mass media, textual, visual and discipline-specific materials and their appropriate uses. Periodic reflection upon the process of conducting research, such as the difficulties encountered and potential solutions to these difficulties, was also encouraged.
b. encourage a departure from the institutional and departmental culture of summative, semester-end assessment by introducing students to a graduated, reflective method of conducting a research project that mirrors the practice of professional historians and can thereby prepare learners for higher level history work.

The assignment was loosely structured, requiring each student to include some critical evaluation of both mass media and scholarly sources related to their research topic and reflection upon at least two academic 'artefacts', including a bibliography of sources and a video recording of his or her presentation. Students were also strongly encouraged to engage in general reflection on the research and writing process.

Using E-Portfolios to Support General Education History Learning

General education students without a background in history required a more structured e-portfolio assignment, which would build confidence through a series of low-stakes segments. Modern China and World History introduces students to a multifaceted history of China's interactions with the wider world in the modern period. In order to emphasize the diversity of these interactions, students were required to construct an e-portfolio consisting of six of more segments, each of which analyzed a different category of primary source: a photograph, a historical simulation game, a secondary narrative, an oral history, a cartoon, and an artwork or decorative object. 38 mainly first-year students, none of whom were history majors and all of whom were enrolled in full-length degree programs at Hong Kong Baptist

University, completed the e-portfolio. The major learning objectives of the assignment were to:

a. foster information literacy and autonomous learning in first year students by requiring them to locate, analyze and cite historical sources. A library workshop run by another member of the community of practice lent practical support to this objective.
b. engage with recent digital humanities initiatives by incorporating these materials into the e-portfolio. By creating a multimedia portfolio, students would also become digital humanities practitioners.
c. develop core skills of historical analysis by asking students to use appropriate methodologies in discussing each source and to evaluate the uses, limitations, and misuses of different types of sources.

The e-portfolio built upon a series of in-class activities, each of which was directly linked to a specific portfolio segment, which introduced different categories of sources and the skills needed to analyze them. Periodic instructor feedback during the semester enabled students to revise previous work and incorporate advice into future posts.

Instructor Evaluation of Student E-Portfolios

In terms of student achievement as evaluated by the instructor, the general education class e-portfolio was considerably more effective than the assignment designed for the advanced-level class, exhibiting both a higher degree of student success in achieving the learning objectives and a greater degree of enthusiasm for the project. Enhancing information literacy was an objective of both assignments. In International Relations Since 1945, the majority of students engaged in only cursory discussion of their sources, often describing rather than evaluating the materials. Similarly, while all students posted some form of reflection on the learning process, only a few engaged in deep reflection, which can be explained by history students' lack of experience at reflective writing coupled with a perceived lack of academic value in reflection within the discipline. Nonetheless, the assignment did prompt students to collect and engage with a range of sources, thereby confirming Snavely and Wright's (2003, 301) point that one of the most important results of using a portfolio to support a research project is 'the structure which it provides for students in developing a template for the present and future information gathering aspects of their research.' In the general education class, most students' information literacy skills improved markedly over the course of the project, partly because as first year students they began the project from a lower baseline of ability than the advanced-level class. For instance, while most students defaulted to using online search tools such as Google at the beginning of the semester, by the end of the project more than 50% had utilized the digital databases introduced in the library workshop. The rigidly scaffolded nature of the assignment, which required students to locate specific categories of sources, combined with the opportunity to act upon mid-semester instructor feedback also accounts for this improvement.

In order to successfully implement e-portfolio assignments, especially in fields where assessment is usually paper-based, instructors and students alike must be convinced of the value added by the electronic nature of the portfolio. In the advanced-level class, the main advantages were that:

a. the online platform formed a digital repository of research materials that could be updated from any location and easily shared with the instructor.
b. the electronic format enabled the showcasing of mass media sources, such as video documentaries, radio broadcasts and photojournalism, in order to help students analyze the contemporary aspect of their research topics.

However, only around 60% of students utilized the multimedia capabilities of the e-portfolio, suggesting that more instructor support is needed to highlight the ways in which different types of media can enhance conventional text-based history writing. Perhaps because of their multidisciplinary backgrounds in largely non-text-based fields, students in the general education class were more receptive to the 'e' dimension of the portfolio. Despite experiencing an array of technical glitches, almost all students incorporated multimedia into their assignment, thereby successfully creating their own digital humanities projects.

Learner Responses to E-Portfolios

During the final week of the course, the instructor distributed a student feedback questionnaire designed by the community of practice in order to gauge student responses to using the e-portfolio. Students were asked to indicate whether they agreed or disagreed with ten statements about the appropriateness of e-portfolios as an assessment tool, the skills acquired by constructing an e-portfolio, its effectiveness at enhancing learning, and the overall value that it added to the course. Respondents selected one of five options on a sliding scale from 'strongly agree' to 'strongly disagree.' The seven statements deemed to correlate most closely with the objectives of the e-portfolio assignments have been selected for discussion here (see Tables 5.1 and 5.2). Additionally, students were given an opportunity to provide qualitative comments and were requested to furnish details of their previous experience of using e-portfolios, the frequency of their engagement with the portfolio during the course, and a self-assessment of their technological skills.

A striking disparity between the questionnaire results for the two courses is immediately apparent. While students in Modern China in World History reported a largely positive experience of creating an e-portfolio (with statement 1 about the overall value of constructing an e-portfolio receiving an average score of 4.2 out of 5),

Table 5.1 Student responses to the e-portfolio assignment in 'International Relations Since 1945'

Statement	Strongly agree (%)	Agree (%)	Neutral (%)	Disagree (%)	Strongly disagree (%)
1. Overall, I found constructing the e-Portolio valuable to this course	11.1	22.2	22.2	44.4	0
2. Overall, I am satisfied with the way my learning is assessed using the e-portfolio in this course	11.1	22.2	33.3	22.2	11.1
3. I acquired useful skills in creating my e-portfolio	0	22.2	44.4	33.3	0
4. The process of creating my e-portfolio helped me to take responsibility for my own learning	33.3	33.3	22.2	11.1	0
5. Showcasing electronic media in my e-portfolio allowed me to demonstrate a more meaningful understanding of my course	11.1	11.1	44.4	33.3	0
6. Constructing the e-portfolio helped me to reflect upon my achievement	11.1	11.1	44.4	11.1	22.2
7. Using the e-portfolio enhanced my learning	22.2	22.2	0	33.3	22.2

Table 5.2 Student responses to the e-portfolio assignment in 'Modern China and World History'

Statement	Strongly agree (%)	Agree (%)	Neutral (%)	Disagree (%)	Strongly disagree (%)
1. Overall, I found constructing the e-Portolio valuable to this course	34.3	54.3	8.6	2.8	0
2. Overall, I am satisfied with the way my learning is assessed using the e-portfolio in this course	25.7	60.1	11.4	2.8	0
3. I acquired useful skills in creating my e-portfolio	22.9	54.3	20	2.8	0
4. The process of creating my e-portfolio helped me to take responsibility for my own learning	34.3	48.6	14.3	2.8	0
5. Showcasing electronic media in my e-portfolio allowed me to demonstrate a more meaningful understanding of my course	20	68.6	11.4	0	0
6. Constructing the e-portfolio helped me to reflect upon my achievement	40.1	45.7	11.4	2.8	0
7. Using the e-portfolio enhanced my learning	31.4	51.4	14.4	2.8	0

the responses of students enrolled in International Relations Since 1945 were variegated, but overall skewed towards the negative (an average score of 3.0 in response to the same statement). One explanation for this divergence is the differences in the assignment structures and objectives, suggesting that students creating an e-portfolio for the first time are more receptive to highly structured assignments with narrow parameters clearly defined by the instructor. Furthermore, the demographics of each group possibly influenced the responses, with the advanced-level class of mostly history majors proving less receptive to the assignment than mainly first-year, non-history major students in Modern China in World History.

International Relations Since 1945

The responses of the nine students who completed the questionnaire were variegated, mirroring the instructor's assessment of student achievement of the assignment's learning outcomes. As indicated in Table 5.1, only one third of students agreed or strongly agreed that constructing the e-portfolio was both valuable to the course as a whole and was a satisfactory way of assessing learning. One student elaborated on this negative response:

> Frankly speaking, I think the use of e-Portfolio is a good way if no research paper is added on it. This is because the addition of e-portfolio is a distraction for me to focus on research paper. The use of e-portfolio might be good if it used as the only major way to count my grade.

From the perspective of this respondent, rather than enhancing the development of the research paper by encouraging early reflection on source materials, the e-portfolio created an onerous burden of additional work.

When asked about their learning experiences, a majority of respondents (seven out of nine) indicated that the electronic aspects of the portfolio (for example, the ability to integrate multimedia elements) did not enhance student ability to demonstrate understanding, thus raising doubts about the value of the 'e' in e-portfolios for this type of assignment. Despite the fact that only two respondents had used an e-portfolio previously, most students indicated that they did not acquire useful skills by completing the assignment, a negative response that in part stemmed from technical frustrations with the Blackboard My Portfolios platform. As another student commented, 'it is too difficult for the beginners and I find that I use too much time for settling technical problems.'

Nonetheless, while most students disagreed that the assignment enhanced overall effectiveness in learning, two-thirds conceded that it helped them to take responsibility for their own learning, thus demonstrating the attainment of the assignment's objective of encouraging independent learning. The three international exchange students in the class demonstrated significantly more favorable attitudes toward the assignment than those enrolled in three- and four-year degree programs at Hong Kong Baptist University, expressing appreciation for the gradual approach to completing the research paper and the reflection the e-portfolio encouraged. One student observed that:

> I especially liked working with an e-portfolio because it more or less forced me to work on the research project throughout the semester, instead of leaving it to the last weeks/days. It is useful because it made me reflect and analyse sources in an early stage of the project which now gives me confidence in actually writing the paper.

Similarly, another respondent commented that the assignment 'forced me to reflect upon the various sources,' while also appreciating the process of constructing the portfolio: 'you get a feeling of creating something!' The divergent responses of these two demographic groups suggest that the reception of Hong Kong-based students to the e-portfolio is filtered through deeply rooted conventions in assessing the learning of history majors in Hong Kong. As David Carless has demonstrated, the dual-pronged heritage of exam-oriented British colonial educational traditions and the Chinese civil service examinations have fostered an entrenched suspicion of formative learning and assessment in the Hong Kong higher education context (Carless 2011).

Modern China and World History

The relative enthusiasm of students in this course toward the e-portfolio assignment was paralleled by the high number of written comments in response to the feedback questionnaire: 17 out of 35 respondents provided qualitative comments. As indicated in Table 5.2, the vast majority of students expressed a favorable attitude toward both the e-portfolio's value to his or her own learning and to the course overall, with over 83% of respondents agreeing or strongly agreeing with all statements except number three. Several students commented positively on the close integration of the e-portfolio assignment with in-class content, observing that the multi-pronged assignment helped learners to view historical events 'in wider perspective' and to 'understand history from different angles.' A recurring comment was that the assignment reinforced other teaching and learning activities by requiring students to put into practice and 'review the knowledge and concepts' learned in class. In contrast to the lukewarm response of the advanced-level history class to the e-portfolio, students with little-to-no background in history appreciated how the portfolio structure enabled them to test out new discipline-specific skills learned in class and to construct a multifaceted analysis of a historical topic in a way that a research paper with a singular focus might not. Furthermore, a few comments noted the cross-curricular skills developed during the project, particularly the technical skills needed to use the e-portfolio platform and the ability to locate sources and reference them accurately. Although the vast majority of respondents in both classes perceived themselves as intermediate users of technology in general, the mainly first year students in the general education class appreciated the opportunity to develop unfamiliar digital literacies and technical skills specific to the higher education environment, such as the ability to negotiate library search engines and troubleshoot online learning management systems.

In a general education class consisting of students from various disciplinary backgrounds, multiple respondents appreciated the segmented structure of the e-portfolio and the formative nature of the assessment, which enabled less confident learners to hone their skills over time in response to instructor feedback. 'It is a gradual assessment and we can learn from our mistakes,' summarized one student. Learners who lacked a prior disciplinary knowledge appreciated the opportunity to 'test' their newly acquired skills through several low-stakes components instead of one high-stakes research paper.

While several students expressed similar technical frustrations with the My Portfolios platform as those noted by respondents in the advanced-level class, overall they exhibited a more positive attitude toward the 'e' aspects of the e-portfolio. 88.6% of those surveyed agreed or strongly agreed that showcasing electronic media allowed them to demonstrate a more meaningful understanding of the course, compared with only 22.2% of respondents in International Relations Since 1945. The library workshop, which introduced students to digital resources that could be incorporated into the portfolio, partly explains this positive perspective. Furthermore, we can speculate that students who are not acculturated into the text-focused conventions of the discipline are more ready to accept the use of digital media.

Conclusions and Future Directions

Contrary to received wisdom, which assumes that creative and relatively unstructured e-portfolio assignments are most effective at promoting learning, this case study found that a highly structured e-portfolio that was closely integrated with in-class activities was most successful in supporting history learners at Hong Kong Baptist University. A combination of regional, institutional, and entrenched disciplinary cultures can explain the resistance of advanced-level history majors to the e-portfolio. Many third year and fourth year history students are acculturated into the conventions of high-stakes, summative assessment common to university history teaching in Hong Kong, and therefore view the e-portfolio as a distracting sideshow from the main event of the semester-end research paper. By contrast, general education history learners, who were not acculturated into these disciplinary norms, valued the way in which the e-portfolio provided a highly structured, low stakes means of developing discipline-specific and cross-curricular skills. The segmented, reflective, and revisable nature of e-portfolio assignments builds confidence as well as competencies in novice learners.

In order to foster greater acceptance of the e-portfolio's uses in supporting research papers, a dramatic cultural shift, brought about through the department-instructor-library-institution nexus, is needed. Promoting the benefits of the digital format of the e-portfolio, such as the ability to compile and reflect upon source material and integrate digital humanities initiatives into history work, is one potential path. Indeed, requiring students to create an online portfolio incorporating digital historical materials could foster a greater understanding of how technologies are transforming scholarly enquiry in the humanities (Bartscherer and Coover 2011). Integrating the e-portfolio into existing research projects which emphasize process as much as the final product, such as the final-year honors project, would legitimize this new form of assessment through departmental and institutional endorsement. Because the discipline of history is by its very definition focused on past events that are supposedly far removed from present-day experiences, personal reflection is not usually valued. However, an emphasis on the *process* of developing a project, as encouraged by e-portfolios, could lead practitioners to a clearer view of problems, solutions, and strategies in history research.

References

Abrami, P., & Barrett, H. (2005). Directions for research and development on electronic portfolios. *Canadian Journal of Learning and Technology, 31*(3), 001.

Acker, S. R., & Halasek, K. (2008). Preparing high-school students for college-level writing: Using E-portfolio to support a successful transition. *JGE: The Journal of General Education, 57*(1), 1–14.

Bartscherer, T., & Coover, R. (2011). *Switching Codes: Thinking through digital technology in the humanities and the arts.* Chicago: University of Chicago Press.

Boulton, H. (2014). E-portfolios beyond pre-service teach education: A new dawn? *European Journal of Teacher Education, 37*(3), 374–389.

Carless, D. (2011). *From testing to productive student learning: Implementing formative assessment in Confucian-heritage settings.* New York: Routledge.

Desmet, C., Miller, D. C., Griffin, J., Balthazor, R., & Cummings, R. E. (2008). Reflection, revision, and assessment in first-year composition E-portfolios. *JGE. The Journal of General Education, 57*(1), 15–30.

Fourie, I., & van Niekerk, D. (1999). Using portfolio assessment in a module in research information skills. *Education for Information, 17,* 333–352.

Källkvist, M., Gomez, S., Andersson, H., & Lush, D. (2009). Personalised virtual learning spaces to support undergraduate students in producing research reports: Two case studies. *Internet and Higher Education, 12,* 35–44.

Kennedy, F., Bruen, J., & Péchenart, J. (2011). Using an e-portfolio to facilitate the self-assessment of both language and intercultural learning in higher education: A case-study approach. *CercleS, 1*(1), 229–247.

Klein, L. (2011). Hacking the field: Teaching digital humanities with off-the-shelf tools. *Transformations: The Journal of Inclusive Scholarship and Pedagogy, 22*(1), 37-52.

McGuinness, C., & Brien, M. (2006). Using reflective journals to assess the research process. *Reference Services Review, 35*(1), 21–40.

Moon, J. (1999). *Learning journals: A handbook for academics, students and professional development.* London: RoutledgeFalmer.

Moretti, M., & Giovannini, M. (2011). E-portfolios as a jobseeking tool for universities. *Journal for Perspectives of Economic, Political and Social Integration, 17*(1–2), 87–104.

Peacock, S., Scott, A., Murray, S., & Morss, L. (2012). Using feedback and E-portfolios to support professional competence in healthcare learners. *Research in Higher Education Journal, 16,* 1–23.

Schwartz, R. M. (2015). Digital partnership: Combining text mining and GIS in a spatial history of sea fishing in the United Kingdom, 1860 to 1900. *International Journal of Humanities and Arts Computing, 9*(1), 36–56.

Snavely, L. L., & Wright, C. A. (2003). Research portfolio use in undergraduate honors education: Assessment tool and model for future work. *The Journal of Academic Librarianship, 29*(5), 298–303.

Warwick, C., Terras, M., & Nyhan, J. (Eds.). (2012). *Digital humanities in practice*. London: Facet Publishing.

Zinger, L., & Sinclair, A. (2014). Starting an E-portfolio: A multi-disciplinary approach. *Contemporary Issues in Education Research, 7*(4), 249–252.

Chapter 6
Integrating Student E-Portfolio into a Statistics Course: A Case Study

Simon Kai-Ming To

Abstract The element of e-Portfolio was integrated into a general education (GE) course in elementary statistics consisting of mainly first year undergraduate students from different disciplines. While building an appropriate statistical sense in daily life scenarios was a key learning outcome, there was a need for a platform for constant reflections throughout the course. Introduced as a continuous assessment component leading to the end-of-semester group presentation, the student e-Portfolio provided not only such a platform, but also a foundation for further interactions among students. Moreover, the e-Portfolio played a major role in linking up other existing components of the course, while feedback suggested that such integration was generally valued by the students and the overall effectiveness in learning was enhanced. However, students also demonstrated mixed attitudes toward using e-Portfolios, with technical difficulties possibly a major obstacle. Both benefits and drawbacks of the implementation of the e-Portfolio are discussed and directions for possible improvements and further investigation are also explored.

Keywords E-portfolios · Mathematics education · Peer learning

Introduction

As a part of the major reform of the secondary and postsecondary educational systems of Hong Kong (the 3 + 3 + 4 reform), the undergraduate programs in Hong Kong switched from 3-year to 4-year curricula in 2012. Among many changes that came along with the overhaul of the academic structure, HKBU introduced the General Education (GE) Program to enhance Whole Person Education (WPE). Particularly, one important Program Intended Learning Outcome

S.K.-M. To (✉)
Department of Mathematics, Hong Kong Baptist University,
Kowloon Tong, Hong Kong
e-mail: simonkmto@hkbu.edu.hk

© Springer Nature Singapore Pte Ltd. 2017   89
T. Chaudhuri and B. Cabau (eds.), *E-Portfolios in Higher Education*,
DOI 10.1007/978-981-10-3803-7_6

(PILO) of the GE Program focuses on the application of appropriate mathematical reasoning to address everyday life problems.

The role of context in the teaching and learning of mathematics has been studied by many mathematics educators (see Boaler 1993 for example). Different social or cultural contexts significantly affect the understanding of mathematical concepts (see Oughton 2013 and Bishop 1988 for discussions on social and cultural contexts respectively), while very often a clear linkage to the real world provokes mathematical thinking (see Gibney 2014 for example). Thus the GE courses in numeracy were designed to offer students insights and raise students' awareness in the use of quantitative methods and data in addressing different practical issues. Such courses cover aspects of numeracy including but not limited to probability, statistics, and information technology numeracy, highlighting their applications in daily life.

After the first semester of the new curriculum, four GE courses in numeracy were selected to assess the impact on students in terms of the achievement of the aforementioned PILO. Results showed that while students performed well in most elements of quantitative reasoning, the aspect of communication, which is defined as "expressing quantitative evidence in support of the argument or purpose of the work" in the AACU rubric used in the assessment, seemed to be a relative weakness (To 2013).

Communication, in a broader sense, is not only seen in mathematics education as a demonstration of the level of proficiency but also an integral part of the process of achieving deep understanding (Stahl 2009). Through studying young children learning mathematics, Sfard argued that mathematical cognition does not only come from an individual rationalist process but also from a discursive social one (Sfard 2008). She suggested that mathematical objects such as formulas are products of discursive constructions constantly adding to the objects' complexity, and deconstructions of such collective processes would be beneficial to the understanding of the objects themselves (Sfard 2008). Other studies also support that collective effort has a major impact in the process of establishing mathematical sense and acquiring mathematical problem solving skills (Martin et al. 2006; Powell 2006).

As a means of communication of knowledge and reflective comments among students and teachers, e-Portfolio has been used in many different disciplines (see Fitch et al. 2008 and Lorenzo and Ittleson 2005 for example). While the use of e-Portfolios as an assessment is still a relatively less common practice in the field of mathematics education, it is not entirely new to the discipline and has shown potential. Bairral and dos Santos used e-Portfolio to extend the scope of mathematical learning to cover not just skill-based aspects but also communication in the context of training for preservice mathematics teachers (Bairral and dos Santos 2012). In a more recent large-scale implementation of the e-Portfolio assessment of the college-wide learning outcome of quantitative literacy at Salt Lake Community College, Hubert and Lewis concluded that e-Portfolios lead to an assessment that is supported by authentic evidence (Hubert and Lewis 2014).

Implementation

Overall Structure

We integrated the use of student e-Portfolios into the GE course "Speaking of Statistics" in the first semester (September to December) of 2014–15 (pilot implementation) and in 2015–16 (second implementation). The course has four Course Intended Learning Outcomes (CILOs), while three of them are directly related to the daily life or daily situations:

1. Explain basic statistical terms and concepts behind valid statistical arguments
2. Interpret quantitative data in daily life from the appropriate statistical point of views
3. Identify and demonstrate statistical methods used in daily life examples
4. Evaluate statistical claims in commercial advertisements or daily situations for their truthfulness.

E-Portfolio element was incorporated into the course as a new teaching and learning activity to mainly address CILO3 and CILO4. Prior to the incorporation, activities such as written classwork and assignments were together addressing almost all CILOs without a very clear continual focal point, at times making reflection more challenging. With e-Portfolios introduced alongside the existing written assignments, it was hoped the e-Portfolios could help students keep track on the buildup of their statistical sense in daily life, while other written assignments could address on other important aspects such as computations, basic statistical terms and concepts, giving a clearer structure to the organization of the teaching and learning activities.

Before the introduction of e-Portfolio, detailed instructions for the group presentation component were usually given to the students in the last month or so of the semester, while some students tended to put in significant effort only days before their scheduled date of presentation. It was also observed that the group presentation component itself was considered by some students as more of an isolated component of the course that demands attention and effort only in the last part of the semester. The selection of presentation materials was therefore sometimes done without thorough discussion and consideration among group members as it was not uncommon for students to settle with the first feasible choice they came across, especially with a relatively tight schedule. On the other hand, the level of contribution of different members of the group in such selection process could also vary greatly. It was possible that some students, intentionally or not, did not actually contribute any alternative choices of materials for presentation. Such uneven contributions among different group members might also be seen in the subsequent preparation of the presentation in some cases. As a common group dynamics problem encountered in many occasions involving group work, freeriding, which is an extreme form of uneven contributions within a group with potential hindrances to team performance and learning process, has been studied extensively in the literature, not only in the field of education but also in other disciplines such as business (see Albanese and Van Fleet 1985 and Joyce 1999 for example). The freeriding phenomenon could be explained economically (Albanese and Van Fleet 1985). Practical solutions have been suggested, with the level of delegation of power to students being one of the key choices to make for teachers (see Joyce 1999 for example) (Fig. 6.1).

In light of the above observations, e-Portfolio was introduced to the course as an extension of the end-of-semester group presentation. It took the form of an individual online journal with four blog entries. Each of the first three entries had a theme and consisted of tasks that the students had to complete according to some guiding instructions. After finishing the first three entries, students formed groups of two to five, and each group prepared a 10-min presentation on selected materials from members' individual e-Portfolios. Such an arrangement was meant to promote the exchange of ideas via e-Portfolios among different students, and to ensure baseline contribution of group members in the preparation process, partially addressing the freeriding problem. Such exchange of ideas was expected to be facilitated by the accessibility of the online nature of the e-Portfolio.

In the final entry of the individual e-Portfolio, students were asked to reflect on aspects such as challenges met in the preparation process, their own performances and possible improvements. This entry served as a guided overall reflection on both the group presentation and the course as a whole. It was designed to extend the learning process beyond the end of the group presentation. Figure 6.2 shows the structure of the implementation.

A pilot implementation was completed in the first semester of 2014–15. Students' feedback was collected before the end of the teaching weeks. Table 6.1 shows the distribution of the results (questionnaire adopted from Shroff et al. 2013).

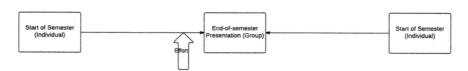

Fig. 6.1 Before implementation: last-minute effort (To 2015)

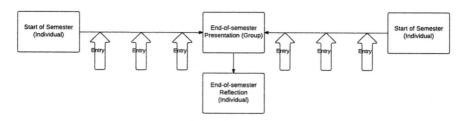

Fig. 6.2 Implementation: constant effort and reflection (To 2015)

Table 6.1 Students' feedback on pilot implementation

#	Question	Strongly agree (%)	Agree (%)	Neither agree nor disagree (%)	Disagree (%)	Strongly disagree (%)	Mean
2	I acquired useful skills in creating my e-Portfolio	23.53	55.88	14.71	2.94	2.94	2.06
3	The process of creating my e-Portfolio helped me to take responsibility for my own learning	32.35	41.18	17.65	2.94	2.94	2.00
5	Overall, I valued the integration of the e-Portfolio into this course	17.65	50.00	29.41	0.00	2.94	2.21
6	Overall, I am satisfied with the way my learning is assessed using the e-Portfolio in this course	20.59	44.12	20.59	8.82	5.88	2.35
10	I have a generally favorable attitude toward using the e-Portfolio	11.76	52.94	20.59	14.71	0.00	2.38
11	Using the e-Portfolio enhanced my effectiveness in learning	17.65	50.00	23.53	5.88	2.94	2.26

The structure of the second implementation in 2015–16 was very similar to that of the pilot implementation of the e-Portfolio component in 2014–15, with minor adjustments made based on feedback obtained in the pilot run:

- Entry 1 (Early October): The first entry of the e-Portfolio in the pilot implementation focused on misleading statistical presentations. Each student was asked to identify two items (images or videos) with some misleading statistical elements. The students described the items and commented on the abuse or misuse of statistics therein. During the pilot implementation, students occasionally reported confusion regarding the instructions given due to the lack of restrictions on the nature of the multimedia to be used for the task. In response to that, in the second implementation, this entry's focus was then further restricted to the use of numbers/statistics in commercials. Instead of any multimedia example, each student was asked to find two examples of a print advertisement in which numbers/statistics were used. Moreover, students were also given more guiding questions, as they were prompted to describe the roles of such

Tutorial School - Geography Tutor

When and where did I see it?
This picture was taken by me on the bus in Sham Shui Po on 27 Sept 2015

How were numbers/Statistics used in this commercial?
The statistics were used to show how popular the tutor is by stating he has the largest number of students and students who getting 5**/5*/5.

On a 1/2/3/4/5 scale (5 being most convincing), how convincing do you find this commercial? Why?
3. Firstly, there are three sentences with a relatively small font size of words showing the evidence which supports its claim of statistics. Besides, while i believe that both two claims are true, it does not mean that the tutor has the highest percentage of having 5**/5*/5 students. This is because he

Fig. 6.3 Student's work: entry 1

numbers/statistics in the advertisements, as well as to explicitly rate their level of convincingness in a 5-point scale (Fig. 6.3).

- Entry 2 (Late October): The theme of the entry for the second implementation, which consisted of two tasks, was the use of averages in news. In the first task, students were given two articles related to the two different concepts of poverty lines, namely the absolute poverty line set by the World Bank and the relative poverty line, which is defined to be half of the median of the household income by the Hong Kong Government. They then answered simple questions related to the articles and commented on the suitability of the two poverty lines for the Hong Kong society. In the second task, each student was asked to identify another news article involving the use of averages from a local news agency, and to rate both the importance and the suitability of such use of averages in the article. This entry in the second implementation was different from the one in the pilot run, which simply required each student to find and comment on two local news articles, one involving the use of mean and one involving the use of median, without much limitations on the nature of the news. The amendments made to the entry were due to the observation that students tended to feel more on a familiar ground with more concrete guidelines on the choice of materials, taking into account that the task involved choosing from a relatively much wider range of materials compared with Entry 1. The poverty-lines-related articles provided in the first task offered students insights and a concrete example for their search of their own materials for the second task.

- Entry 3 (Mid November): The third entry focused on questionnaire design. In the pilot implementation, each student was asked to identify a news article reporting on a questionnaire survey done by a local organization. The student then had to find the actual questionnaire and identify two mistakes in its design. In the revised version of the entry, an extra part, with a news article and a questionnaire provided as a starting point, was introduced. This extra part of the revised entry involved a given questionnaire designed by the Hong Kong Public Opinion Poll for a survey chartered by a local political party and a related news article. Students answered simple questions related to the survey which high-lighted some standard sampling procedures and standard survey practices such as random selections of interviewees within selected households. The second part of the entry required more active input from students. To make instructions more specific than the ones in the pilot implementation, each student was asked to identify one questionnaire designed by a local political party, instead of any survey agencies, with at least one element of improper design. The student then commented on one such problematic aspect of the questionnaire and rated the overall quality of the questionnaire design in a 5-point scale.

- Group Presentation (Late November): Each group consisted of two to five students and was required to do a 10-min presentation with optional Q&A. In the pilot run, each group could either choose a questionnaire collected for Entry 3 among all its members or look for another questionnaire for the presentation, in which they had to provide a thorough critical analysis on the questionnaire design. However, with the option of using materials not from the e-Portfolios, there was less incentive for students to share and read each other's work, potentially undermining the benefit of peer learning. In the second implementation, such an option was no longer available, and each group had to choose a questionnaire collected for Entry 3 to carry out a thorough critical analysis. While Entry 3 only required indication of one problematic aspect of the questionnaire, some collective inputs were expected for completion of this part. Unlike in the pilot run, the presentation in the second implementation had an extra part, in which the groups were required to choose, from all advertisements collected for Entry 1 by the members, two commercials to present. While each group could base the presentation on the contributors' e-Portfolio entries, input from all members, instead of mere repetitions of the content of the contributors' e-Portfolios, was expected.

- Entry 4 (Early December): The fourth and final entry for the pilot run was a reflection on the group presentation, while the revised version included also a reflection on the course as a whole. Individually each student reflected on the problems the group encountered during the preparation process. Students were

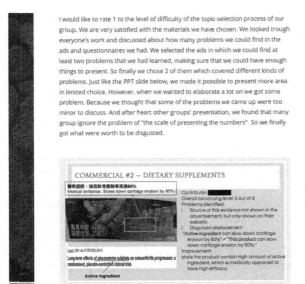

I would like to rate 1 to the level of difficulty of the topic-selection process of our group. We are very satisfied with the materials we have chosen. We looked trough everyone's work and discussed about how many problems we could find in the ads and questionnaires we had. We selected the ads in which we could find at least two problems that we had learned, making sure that we could have enough things to present. So finally we chose 2 of them which covered different kinds of problems. Just like the PPT slide below, we made it possible to present more area in limited choice. However, when we wanted to elaborate a lot on we got some problem. Because we thought that some of the problems we came up were too minor to discuss. And after heart other groups' presentation, we found that many group ignore the problem of "the scale of presenting the numbers" So we finally got what were worth to be disgusted.

Fig. 6.4 Student's work: entry 4

asked to state if they had considered any alternative choices, and elaborated on the rationale behind the final decision and whether or not they were satisfied with the choice. They were also guided to reflect on the impact, if any, of reading the e-Portfolios of other group members. Strengths and weaknesses of the group's performance in the presentation were also discussed. For the reflections on the course itself, students stated things they learned from the course and what they thought would be interesting to investigate more (Fig. 6.4).

Assessment

Assessment for the pilot run was on an entry-by-entry basis, using a slightly different rubric for different entries and with each entry assessed separately after its deadline. However, such a practice seemed to work against the continual nature of the e-Portfolio as an organic and coherent collection of artifacts and reflections. Completed entries tended to be static after the assessments, and the e-Portfolios generally looked more disjointed, potentially with entries scattered across different pages in a less organized manner. To address such problems, the assessment of the e-Portfolios in the second implementation came in two parts. Throughout the semester, comments were given by the instructor using the blog's online commenting function. Students were free to make changes, taking into account of the instructor's and other students' feedback, before the end of the semester and the deadline of the final entry of the entire e-Portfolio. The complete e-Portfolio was then formally assessed according to the rubric consisting of four main categories:

- Information: accuracy and clear indication of sources
- Subject knowledge: proper statistical view point
- Organization: clarity, coherence and logic of presentation
- Language and communication: effective delivery of ideas and use of multimedia.

Choice of Platform and Technical Support

Weebly, with its relatively intuitive drag-and-drop interface, was selected as the platform for the implementations. A briefing session of 30 min to 1 h on the use of the site-building tool was given to the student. The session was conducted in a standard lecture room setting without desktop computers provided. Students mainly used their own electronic devices with access to the internet for hands-on tasks during the briefing session, in which accounts were set up and web addresses were collected on the spot.

Results and Discussions

Students' Perception and Self-assessment

A questionnaire survey (adopted from Shroff et al. 2013) for the second implementation was conducted near the end of the first semester. The questionnaire consists of two parts, with the first part focusing on students' feedback on various aspects of the implementation and the second part on the general background of students, including their level of expertise related to the use of e-Portfolio. Table 6.2 shows the result of Part I.

The numbers suggest mixed to positive attitudes toward using e-Portfolios from students. Students were able to engage with the e-Portfolio with a sense of control while reflecting upon their achievement (Q7, Q8 and Q9). However, opinions were more diverse in some cases. While close to half of the students believed that the e-Portfolio enhanced effectiveness in learning, over a quarter of the class disagree. Students' opinions on whether useful skills were acquired and whether creating the e-Portfolio helped them to take responsibility for their learning were similarly split, with around 60% of the students agreeing and over 20% disagreeing (Q2 and Q3). It is also an interesting point to note that students of the pilot implementation offered a much more positive self-assessment in these two aspects, with over 70% acknowledging positive impact. A possible explanation to the discrepancy in the assessment of taking responsibility of learning could be the more explicit and restrictive guidelines provided in the second implementation. Other factors contributing to the generally less positive feedback from students in the second implementation remain to be identified.

Table 6.2 Students' feedback on second implementation

#	Question	Strongly agree (%)	Agree (%)	Neither agree nor disagree (%)	Disagree (%)	Strongly disagree (%)	Mean
1	Overall, I found constructing the e-Portfolio valuable to this course	8.51	48.94	34.04	6.38	2.13	2.45
2	I acquired useful skills in creating my e-Portfolio	12.77	51.06	14.89	19.15	2.13	2.47
3	The process of creating my e-Portfolio helped me to take responsibility for my own learning	23.40	36.17	19.15	21.28	0.00	2.38
4	Showcasing electronic media (i.e., text-based, graphic, or multimedia elements) in my e-Portfolio allowed me to demonstrate a more meaningful understanding of my course	14.89	46.81	23.40	10.64	4.26	2.43
5	Overall, I valued the integration of the e-Portfolio into this course	12.77	51.06	25.53	8.51	2.13	2.36
6	Overall, I am satisfied with the way my learning is assessed using the e-Portfolio in this course	17.02	46.81	31.91	2.13	2.13	2.26
7	I was able to engage with the e-Portfolio interface in a worthwhile manner	19.15	53.19	17.02	8.51	2.13	2.21
8	I could exercise choice in how I customized my e-Portfolio entries	17.02	42.55	31.91	6.38	2.13	2.34
9	Constructing the e-Portfolio helped me to reflect upon my achievement	14.89	46.81	27.66	8.51	2.13	2.36

(continued)

Table 6.2 (continued)

#	Question	Strongly agree (%)	Agree (%)	Neither agree nor disagree (%)	Disagree (%)	Strongly disagree (%)	Mean
10	I have a generally favorable attitude toward using the e-Portfolio	29.79	27.66	25.53	14.89	2.13	2.32
11	Using the e-Portfolio enhanced my effectiveness in learning	17.02	31.91	25.53	23.40	2.13	2.62

Other comments from students also came with similar diversity, and such diversity is in line with the instructor's observation throughout the semester. Though described as an "attractive" and "useful" way to show the learning process and generally accepted, if not valued, some students had reservations about the necessity of the implementation. Many saw the e-Portfolio as only a new form of written assignment without appreciating the benefits generally recognized by educators. However, it might be worth to note that, such a response is indeed typical whenever a new form of assessment is introduced in a course. On the other hand, the rationale of linking the presentation with the e-Portfolio was also questioned, though over 60% of the students valued the overall integration of e-Portfolio into the course (Q5).

In their reflections (Entry 4) on the preparation of the presentation, especially the material selection process, most students reported contributions of most group members in the form of sharing of group members' own portfolios. This demonstrates the effectiveness of utilizing e-Portfolios to ensure baseline contributions in a group assessment, though the overall contributions of different members in a group could still vary, as observed by the instructor in the presentations.

Usage and Performance

Over half of the students reported a frequency of reviewing, interacting with or adding to the e-Portfolio at least a few times a month. After working with the e-Portfolios, close to 80% of the students considered themselves to be moderately experienced in using e-Portfolios. In terms of consistency with other assessment components, the students' scores of the e-Portfolio component have a weak to moderate positive correlation (with a correlation coefficient of 0.39) with their total scores of the written test components. This may partially be explained by the different emphasis of the assessment components. Written test components focus mostly on subject knowledge and its applications, with communications and organization as secondary concerns, while the e-Portfolio component emphasizes not only on subject matter but also the presentation of materials in a coherent and logical manner as well as effective communication. Students were also generally satisfied with the overall assessment (Q6).

Background of Students

Students of the course had almost no prior experience with e-Portfolio, with over 90% reporting such absence of experience before taking the class. Such a phenomenon was expected as the course was intended mainly for first year students, and this was indeed the first semester of the 4-year curriculum for over half of the class.

Limitations and Recommendations

Technical issues were one of the major obstacles of the implementation, which is not a surprise given the overall lack of prior experience with e-Portfolio, though it should be noted that some technical issues were platform specific and might have little to do with general prior experience. Sessions in a computer lab are recommended, though some more IT-literate students were actually able to proceed without such arrangements. One fairly common complaint throughout the semester was that the supposedly published content did not show up in the e-Portfolio. Most of such cases were due to a slightly complicated publishing procedure of the Weebly blogs that could give a false impression that the content was successfully published. However, such technical issues notwithstanding, students generally had a certain sense of control over the choices in how the e-Portfolio entries were customized (Q8). Another complaint was that Weebly frequently sent out promotional materials to the students, causing some nuisance. While this might be a platform-specific problem, this could be a point for caution if any free third-party portfolio-building service is to be chosen.

Extra workload associated with the introduction of e-Portfolio was also one of the major concerns for both teaching staff and students. To accommodate such an increase in effort demanded and maintain a similar level of overall workload, some other written assessments were shortened and combined. Such a practice of replacing some existing assessment components with e-Portfolios is recommended and it might also be a good practice to inform the students about such changes to manage students' expectation on workload.

Though the introduction of e-Portfolios provided students with more opportunities to formulate their ideas and communicate quantitative information, further study will have to be carried out to fairly assess whether similar incorporations of e-Portfolios improve students' communication skills.

Conclusion

Incorporating e-Portfolio into a mathematics/statistics course is a challenging task with much potential in transforming traditionally theory-oriented courses to ones driven by authentic examples. Such potential is more apparent in courses intended not to provide training to future mathematicians but to equip a diverse audience with essential numeracy literacy. While technical aspects and students' lack of understanding of the underlying rationale probably will remain major obstacles in the near future, the digital and online nature of e-Portfolios surely makes it more feasible for instructors to facilitate sharing and collaboration among students. With the encouraging feedback and experience from this small-scale implementation, it is hoped that this case study will trigger more similar endeavors by fellow mathematics educators.

References

Albanese, R., & Van Fleet, D. D. (1985). Rational behavior in groups: The freeriding tendency. *The Academy of Management Review, 10*(2), 244–255.

Bairral, M. A., & dos Santos, R. T. (2012). E-Portfolio improving learning in mathematics pre-service teacher. *Digital Education Review, 21*, 1–12.

Bishop, A. J. (1988). Mathematics education in its cultural context. In *Mathematics education and culture* (pp. 179–191).

Boaler, J. (1993). The role of contexts in the mathematics classroom: Do they make mathematics more "Real"? *For the Learning of Mathematics, 13*(2), 12–17.

Fitch, D., Peet, M., Reed, B. G., & Tolman, R. (2008). The use of E-portfolios in evaluating the curriculum and student learning. *Journal of Social Work Education, 44*(3), 37–54.

Gibney, J. (2014). Provoking mathematical thinking: Experiences of doing realistic mathematics tasks with adult numeracy teachers. *Adults Learning Mathematics: An International Journal, 9* (2), 97–115.

Hubert, D. A., & Lewis, K. J. (2014). A framework for general education assessment: Assessing information literacy and quantitative literacy with E-portfolios. *International Journal of E-portfolio, 4*(1), 61–71.

Joyce, W. B. (1999). On the free-rider problem in cooperative learning. *The Journal of Education for Business, 74*(5), 271–274.

Lorenzo, G., & Ittleson, J. (2005). An overview of e-portfolios. *EDUCAUSE Learning Initiative ELI Paper, 1*, 1–24.

Martin, L., Towers, J., & Pirie, S. (2006). Collective mathematical understanding as improvisation. *Mathematical Thinking and Learning, 8*(2), 149–183.

Oughton, H. (2013). *The social context of numeracy. Teaching adult numeracy principles and practice.* Berkshire: OUP, McGraw Hill.

Powell, A. B. (2006). Socially emergent cognition: Particular outcome of student-to-student discursive interaction during mathematical problem solving. *Horizontes, 24*(1), 33–42.

Sfard, A. (2008). *Thinking as communicating: Human development, the growth of discourses and mathematizing.* Cambridge, UK: Cambridge University Press.

Shroff, R. H., Trent, John, & Ng, E. M. W. (2013). Using e-portfolios in a field experience placement: Examining student-teachers' attitudes towards learning in relationship to personal value, control and responsibility. *Australasian Journal of Educational Technology, 29*(2), 143–160.

Stahl, G. (2009). Mathematical discourse as group cognition. In G. Stahl (Ed.), *Studying virtual math teams* (pp. 31–40). New York: Springer.

To, S. K.-M. (2013). *Outcomes assessment in numeracy courses—experience sharing.* E-Learning Forum Asia. 2013.

To, S. K.-M. (2015). *E-portfolio assessment in general education—A practitioner's perspective.* E-Learning Forum Asia. 2015.

Chapter 7
Finding Flow in the Classroom: A Case Study on Instructor Experiences and Likeliness of Continuing to Use Mobile Technology Tools and Gather E-Portfolio Content

Warren S. Linger

Abstract The focus of this paper is to investigate instructor flow experiences when using technology tools to aid interactive classroom learning and create e-portfolios. Tasked with developing university graduates with twenty-first century skills like e-portfolios, university instructors are inundated with new and different technologies to help build these skills. Yet, because these technologies are not easy to learn and use, the instructors are not using them to increase interactive learning in their classrooms. This combination of development pressure, too many choices of technology, and lack of technology understanding, is causing instructors to become increasingly anxious about technology. This case illustrates the process of testing and using two primary tools that were free, easy to learn and use, and yet could be combined in several ways to help curate artifacts for e-portfolios. The effect of using these tools showed it was easier to experience flow-like conditions when using them.

Keywords Flow · Optimal experience · Optimal engagement · E-portfolio · Google Forms · Google HyperDocs

Introduction

Cox and Richlin (2004) introduced faculty learning communities (FLC) as a method of professional development by sharing ideas with other faculty. At Hong Kong Baptist University (HKBU), we used the terminology of academic, structured Community of Practice (CoP). As I had contributed to previous work on e-portfolios (Shroff, Chaudhuri and Linger 2014), I was invited to become a

W.S. Linger (✉)
School of Continuing Education, Hong Kong Baptist University,
Kowloon Tong, Hong Kong
e-mail: warrenlingerhk@gmail.com

© Springer Nature Singapore Pte Ltd. 2017
T. Chaudhuri and B. Cabau (eds.), *E-Portfolios in Higher Education*,
DOI 10.1007/978-981-10-3803-7_7

member of a CoP for student e-portfolios (Chaudhuri and Chan 2016), to share and learn from other faculty who were focusing on generating and validating ideas to improve and implement student e-portfolios. In our CoP we discussed ways to help guide students in searching for and curating artifacts for their portfolios. Although many new technologies and apps have been created to help students learn (Bates 2015; Shroff, Keyes and Linger 2016), few instructors adopt technology to improve classroom interaction and learning experiences. These observations led to this qualitative investigation of tools that were easy for instructors to learn to use to increase engagement and interaction while helping students curate artifacts to be used in their e-portfolios in the classroom.

By December 31, 2015, Facebook reported they had over 1.4 billion mobile monthly active users (Facebook, 2015/12/31). Barrett (2007) outlined e-portfolios and social media similarities including finding and sharing information, and she showed differences as e-portfolios focus on evidence of learning. Peppler and Solomou (2011) found that when learners used social media they developed collaboration and creativity skills that enhance learning. Two important characteristics of e-portfolios are sharing experiences and ownership of learning, and Lewis, Pea and Rosen (2010) showed that social media helped learners develop these skills. Roseth, Akcaoglu and Zellner (2013) found that using computers in the classroom allowed students to curate artifacts and learn from a variety of outside sources. Also, as most universities have university graduate qualities of some kind, Hwang (2014) found developing e-portfolios helped students follow and realize their own skill development as they worked toward attaining graduate qualities.

Westberry and Franken (2012) suggested that by following the ecology of resources perspective, teachers could blend online and face-to-face learning in classroom activities to develop learners' access and retrieval skills for finding outside experts and resources. Also, when investigating tools for helping students collaborate, Chu and Kennedy (2011) discovered Google tools were quite easy to use and were effective at improving interactions. Linger (2016) found that using Google Forms and Docs with mobile devices was useful for in-class tasks to curate content for course e-portfolios, for group e-portfolios, and for individual student e-portfolios. Also, students' in-class learning reflections supported using mobile devices as an effective method for gathering e-portfolio artifacts.

Shroff, Deneen and Lim (2014) asserted that by collecting and showcasing artifacts, essentially becoming curators of their own e-portfolio displays, students built ownership of their learning. Also, the authors found that as students constructed their e-portfolios, the students developed critical thinking and self-evaluation skills, as well as learning and development reflection skills. Linger (2016) found that students appreciate instant feedback as this allows them to understand if they are learning or completing tasks correctly, and in-class exercises can be crafted so students could use their mobile devices in the classroom to curate artifacts for their e-portfolios.

Dewey (1938) mentioned that active and positive learning experiences are influential in assisting learners to continue being lifelong learners. Linger (2002), studying in-service teachers, found that those who had flow-like experiences while learning to use technology tools were more likely to use technology in their teaching. If e-learning tools are easy to use, then learners are more likely to have positive experiences and continue to use them, and if the tools are difficult to use, learners are less likely to continue using them (Hidayanto and Setyady 2014).

Quite often e-learning materials are introduced and evaluated from the point of view of students, but if the instructors do not like technology, find it difficult to learn how to use the tools, or find it difficult to teach students to use the technology, instructors will not use the new technology tools (Bates 2015). Based on my observations and experiences participating in an e-portfolio Community of Practice, instructors use tools they feel comfortable using. While twenty-first century skills are increasingly focusing on technology, instructors and students are working together to overcome the challenge of developing new technology skills. Although there are different lists of skills students and individuals will need to succeed in the twenty-first century, Bates (2015) gives a good summary of what is needed.

The knowledge and skills needed in a digital age, where all 'content' will be increasingly and freely available over the Internet, requires graduates with expertise in:

- knowledge management (the ability to find, evaluate and appropriately apply knowledge);
- IT knowledge and skill;
- inter-personal communication skills, including the appropriate use of social media;
- independent and lifelong learning skills;
- a range of intellectual skills, including:

  - knowledge construction;
  - reasoning;
  - critical analysis;
  - problem-solving;
  - creativity;

- collaborative learning and teamwork;
- multi-tasking and flexibility.

These are all skills that are relevant to any subject domain, and need to be embedded within that domain. With such skills, graduates will be better prepared for a volatile, uncertain, complex and ambiguous world. (p. 434).

Focusing on digital literacies, Dudeney, Hockly and Pegrum (2013) discuss several literacies students will need in the future. These include information literacy where students need to know how to find and work with information to solve problems. Also, the authors outlined collaboration literacy where students need to learn to work together online and in person. Further, the authors described re-mix literacy where students become curators by mixing ideas, images, videos, and other items they have gathered from the Internet.

There are a few models that help us understand factors that influence how individuals select and use technology. Rogers (2003), a professor in Communications, described how opinion leaders are those who adopt innovations first and communicate their experiences to others. Another widely used model for technology adoption is the Technology Acceptance Model (TAM) which primarily looks at two factors individuals consider when adopting technology, and these are perceived usefulness, and ease of use (Davis 1989). Collan and Tetard (2007) developed the lazy user model after finding that people will use technology that is the easiest or takes least effort to use to help them attain their objectives. Because tools are a means to an end, individuals try to focus on the goal and tend to select the tools based on the factor of least expenditure among the three criteria which are cost, time, or physical/mental effort needed.

Csikszentmihalyi (1990) has written studied and written extensively on what is referred as optimal or flow experiences described by individuals who had been engaged in flow activities. These flow experiences occurred when individuals were so completely involved in an activity they reported feeling like they were just flowing with the activity. These flow experiences have been described in the literature as follows:

- intensely focused concentration on an activity,
- merged awareness with the activity,
- lost self-consciousness in the activity,
- feeling of personal control in the activity,
- experience of time awareness is distorted, and
- intrinsically rewarding engagement with the activity.

When individuals are new at an activity, they can experience flow if challenges are low and the skills needed are low. As individuals develop their skills in an activity, they seek higher levels of challenge to experience flow (Fig. 7.1). As flow experiences are positive, individuals who experienced flow reported: developing new skills, reducing anxiety, increasing self-esteem, wanting to return to the activity, and seeking greater levels of engagement with the activity.

Studying students' well-being with ubiquitous technology connections, Salvagno, Taylor, Bobeva and Hutchings (2015) found that user experiences with technology were important. The researchers asserted that students who were less confident with technology seemed to be overly cautious with it. These students tried to avoid the perceived pain of using technology as they felt the experiences were overly demanding. The students who reported being more technology confident described how technology supported their flow experiences in learning activities.

Fig. 7.1 Visual adaptation of skill challenge development in flow experiences (Csikszentmihalyi 1996)

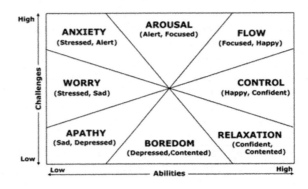

According to Bates (2015) instructors not only do not have time or motivation to research new teaching and learning apps or tools, but also, they do not have time to learn how to use the new tools well enough to teach their students. As most instructors have developed identities as opinion leaders in their own areas of expertise, it seems reasonable that these instructors would not want to change their identities to focus on technology. When instructors attempted to use new technologies, often they report it as not easy to use and not easy to teach the students how to use it. Society, economy, and even governments are pushing instructors to use more technology within the classroom for blended learning.

Methodology

This research aimed to contribute to the complicated field of selecting and using technology to increase interaction with students inside the classroom learning experience. In this case I have focused on creating a map of instructor experiences to observe and understand the Google tool integration process and thus provide a view of this situation. The mapping process focused on Google tool application experiences based on flow characteristics of developing skills, reducing anxiety, increasing self-esteem, returning to the tools, and seeking greater levels of engagement.

Instructor Experiences

This study was conducted in a small Hong Kong university as an instructor who taught students who were enrolled in what is locally referred to as 'self-funded' full-time students in the School of Continuing Education. The Learning Management System (LMS) in use was Moodle, and this version of Moodle was not mobile-device friendly. The LMS was primarily used to distribute learning resources and assignments and to submit finished assignments via Turnitin. The qualitative nature of this study was designed as a beginning point in researching these types of interactive classroom tools and therefore limits the generalizability as a population sample. The following sections present the results of experiences with tools that were designed to help instructors interact with students in the classroom. The articulation step of the situational maps described what had become visible.

Observations of Investigating Interactive Classroom Technology Tools

This section was included because it is important for us, as educators, to focus on decision-making processes that both instructors and students navigate to search, find, understand, apply information, and in this case tools. This process awareness should provide instructors with examples to follow when teaching or guiding students through similar learning and thought processes.

As I am a communication instructor, I am not an expert with technology, so I only looked for technology tools that were easy to set up, easy to use in the classroom, and easy for me to locate the data and artifacts that were curated during the class. During the time of this investigation, over a period of about three years, I had investigated tools that I thought could make my courses more interactive and therefore more engaging for my students. With no budget and a limited understanding of technology, I searched for tools that were easy to use and were quite effective at helping both the instructor and students to interact during their time in the classroom. Although many organizations and universities offer different levels of support for teaching and learning with technology, like most instructors, I do not have time to wait for extra support during my classroom teaching.

My purpose for investigating these tools was to increase engagement in the classroom. Based on previous research (Linger 1997, 2002), I have found it is important to interact with students in the classroom to improve their student learning experiences. As I was instructing students who were not native English speakers (I was told I was hired because I did not speak Cantonese, the local language), and so, I found it challenging to maintain a high level of engagement with all students during my classes. Also, quite frequently, students asked me to speak with them in Cantonese in the classroom like the local instructors, but I told them because the university's medium of instruction was English, speaking Cantonese was against the rules. As Asian students are known for not interacting with instructors during class, I continued to search for ways to breach that cultural barrier. While watching students using their mobile devices to interact with one another with Facebook and texting, I saw this as an opportunity to connect with them using their mobile devices, a tool with which they were familiar.

Google and Specialized Searching with Mobile Devices

I began by asking students to complete Internet searches using their mobile devices during class. At certain points during class, I would ask students to use their phones to conduct Google searches for terms or meanings, find the context of issues, locate background information of topic, and even find historical progressions of problems. At times students would share their findings with me by showing their device to me, and they or I would tell other classmates about the findings. After experiencing some success using the Google search engine, I asked students to use other, more specialized search engines, and this allowed for some critical thinking, in-class discussions about different sources of information. Although this exercise seemed somewhat effective, students continued to question the relevance to helping them prepare for their exams. I explained that this process enabled the class to use these 'real life' examples for learning and discussion. Although students seemed to find this process interesting and it helped them understand the real-world context of the ideas, a few students noted in their semester-end teaching evaluations that they saw little value in doing this. Other challenges with searches were that I had little record of what students found during their searches, and at times, as I walked around the class, I found that they were not using their devices for searching as asked.

Flow Supporters As students were all familiar with Google, they used their phones to search for real-world ideas, solutions, and concepts. This was exciting and therefore generated feelings of self-esteem. Students' searching and sharing helped me develop new skills to enable them to conduct higher level searches using more specialized search engines which helped me develop my skills and I continued to return to these tools, and find more advanced uses for these tools.

Flow Blockers After the initial excitement, students lost interest which caused anxiety. Also, as I could not easily track their findings to give feedback, students seemed to think they were using this technology just to use technology and therefore saw little advantage in searching and finding information. By later in the semester, students had lost interest in searching and indicated that they wanted to focus more on information to help them prepare for their final papers and exams.

Observations Experiences Applying Google Tools with E-Portfolios

As I continued to investigate in-class interactive learning tools, I learned about Google Apps for Education while attending a parallel session at the e-Learning Asia Forum, 2014. The speaker introduced Google tools that were easy to learn (via YouTube) and use, were versatile and therefore useful in many different situations, and were free (no charge) to use. After viewing about 10 YouTube videos, I found the tools were fairly easy to learn to use and to apply in the classroom. Although I began testing using Google Docs first, I realized that Google Forms were easier to use for creating interactive lectures. After a video learning and testing period of 2–3 weeks, I felt comfortable enough to try using Google Forms in the classroom for interactive lectures. Later, I gave Forms to the students so they could give individual learning reflections at the end of class, and I tried using Google Docs with group research tasks within the classroom.

An important aspect of using Google tools was that the students and I could use the tools anywhere we were located when we had a device with an Internet connection. Later, I found that this allowed the students and I to walk around the classroom, or campus, (one student was at home sick when she completed a Form) with a smartphone or tablet and they could curate e-portfolio content wherever they found it. No matter where they were located, I could see what the students were doing, and therefore I could give them advice and guide them to different sources to help them find new information. Also, using the sharing function on Google Docs allowed me to see students work whenever they asked me questions, even when I was not at my desk. Further, although a few students complained about downloading the Google Docs app onto their devices, many of the students told me they were keeping the app on their phones after the course.

Google Forms and Class-Level E-Portfolios

I found that Google Forms were a quite easy to use and simple survey tool. Within a Google Form I could include multiple questions, lecture slides, YouTube videos, links to check outside sources, as well as links to Google and other search engines to have students search for information during class. Soon after I implemented Google Forms, I realized that I no longer needed to teach from PowerPoint slides during the lecture, and I began teaching directly from the Forms. Also, as Google Forms were created in my Google Drive, the students' responses were automatically saved in a spreadsheet in the same folder as the Google Form. This enabled me to quickly look at the students' submissions and find exemplars of good examples that I could immediately share with the class so other students learn from high-quality, creative answers. Further, I was able to identify students who did not understand the material, so immediately I could work with them to help identify their gaps in understanding.

Because the lecture slides were included in the Forms for simultaneous viewing on their devices, students could review previous slides, if needed, before they answered questions. In effect, this interaction helped develop an experience–response in-class learning process that enabled students to immediately reflect on what they had learned and how they responded. This allowed me to observe differences in the way students were learning, thinking, and responding, so I could give them improved feedback on how they were processing or focusing on the ideas throughout the lecture. Although I had experienced success at interacting with students using Google Forms during my lectures, the interaction seemed stronger and more compelling as students knew they were contributing to the course-level e-portfolio.

Shortly after I began using Forms in class, students started asking me to give them access to answers they and other students submitted on Forms in previous classes. I simply gave them a link to share the past responses with them anonymously, so on their own, they could review what was submitted in previous classes. As I began a regular practice of sharing the responses with students, I realized this was the beginning of the class-level e-portfolios. I simply pasted links to the submissions into the class e-portfolio, so students could access the links any time they wanted. After giving them access to responses in the class e-portfolio, I noticed that students became more involved in class by asking more questions about their responses. Also, the quality of student responses improved as they realized that, although answers were anonymous, all classmates would see their responses. After process of sharing students' responses continued for a few weeks, one student created the term 'group note taking' as the classroom was becoming 'one big brain' engaged and sharing in the learning experience.

An advantage of Google Forms was that in a single Form the tool allowed me to ask any combination of many open-ended and closed-ended questions, as well as draw from Internet sources like libraries or even YouTube. By inserting links to have students go search the Internet for information, compare examples, I found this process seemed to encourage higher level thinking and questions from the students as they explored information outside of the normal classroom. This created what seemed to be more learning ownership as I heard students often mention 'our class' responses' as the students curated more diverse and interesting examples for the course-level e-portfolio. Also, the students seemed to embrace Google Forms so strongly that all groups included Google Forms in their final in-class presentations. This enabled each group to interact with classmates by asking questions and giving feedback during their final group presentations.

Flow Supporters As I searched the YouTube videos, I received over 500,000 hits containing different methods to use Google Forms and develop my own skills. Although, there was still a learning curve, I did not have any problems I could not overcome after watching more videos. This held my anxiety in check. Also, the YouTube videos were helpful for guiding me through the process of developing the interactive class experiences, and as a result I spent much more in-class time directly talking with the students as we discussed questions related to their e-portfolios. This was quite satisfying and my self-esteem was boosted through our in-class interactions and also when students referred back to their own answers and the course e-portfolio. Throughout the semester I continued to use and develop the tools by trying more and higher level tasks for the students by returning to the tools and seeking higher levels of engagement. There were several times I lost track of time as I was problem-solving and strategizing new uses for Google Forms.

Flow Blockers As mentioned before, I did experience a few anxious moments where I did not know what to do, but I seemed to find ways to overcome the obstacles by watching the videos.

Google Docs and Group-Level E-Portfolios

After using Google Forms for about two weeks, I felt comfortable enough to share Google Docs (HyperDocs) with groups to use as in-class research guides. The HyperDocs were created to guide the individual members of each group to curate content for their group's e-portfolio. As Google Docs can be shared so several individuals can simultaneously collaborate to research and write, these HyperDocs became group wikis in this situation. To give some background to this assignment, for the past few years, at the beginning of the semester, each group in the class choose a case study problem to solve. Each week the groups would apply the newly learned course content to solve different aspects of their group problem using their Hyperdoc.

In the past, each group created a final PowerPoint presentation, but now the groups were tasked with creating a group e-portfolio that contained possible solutions to solve the case problem. In this new process, every week the members of each group were given a shared group HyperDoc to begin collaborating in writing and researching tasks as in-class exercises. Students began these writing and research processes using their mobile devices in the classroom as they gathered content and helped develop their group e-portfolio. Using group e-portfolios as visuals in their final projects seemed better than PowerPoint because e-portfolios offered more opportunities for reflection, comparison, development, and feedback as e-portfolios were more tangible and permanent.

After students received the weekly in-class research HyperDoc containing various individual research tasks, group members could discuss responsibilities, search for information and examples on the Internet, and then each member would insert her or his findings into the group HyperDoc during class. Group members were asked to evaluate effectiveness of their research and findings, and then later, after class, groups would edit their findings and create for their group portfolios. Also, it is important to note that, even though I could not understand the in-class group discussions which were in the students' mother languages of Cantonese or Mandarin, I could still see what each individual was writing in English on the group research HyperDoc. Also, Google Docs have a revision history feature, so I could identify content that individual students had written and then give those students immediate feedback.

As with Google Forms, students were not limited to remaining in the class to complete their research tasks. They could, as a few classmates did, go to the library, find resource, take pictures with their phones, and then upload the pictures into the group research HyperDocs to share the information they found. There were, however, three incidents when students were absent from class and yet they were still completing their in-class research and writing tasks. Although I was happy the absent students were contributing to their group work, I would have preferred they were in the classroom so I could give them immediate feedback.

As groups were researching information in real time in the classroom, I was able to observe, advise, and guide their critical thinking as they developed the best solutions for their case problem. Interestingly, at the beginning of the semester I was giving a lot more advice on "what kind of" and "where to find" information, and as the semester progressed, students were asking me more questions about application, context, and synthesizing options to solve their case problem and improve their e-portfolios. Building on this, I noticed that as the semester evolved, the group members began giving feedback and support to one another too. Being the instructor, I found that I was interacting with students and answering many more questions than I answered before I had introduced the Google Docs and e-portfolios combination.

While the groups were curating content for their e-portfolios, I could see group collaboration activity on my own device as I watched students in real time. Also, I was able to observe students as they practiced real-time collaborative discussions, work tasks, studies, and reviews within the classroom. In the end, the group e-portfolios were focused wikis containing re-mixed content students curated and put into infographics and memes. Although literacies were not the focus of this paper, it is worth noting that many of the literacies discussed by Dudeney et al. (2013) and twenty-first century skills listed by Bates (2015) were practiced when the students engaged in these shared group research HyperDocs.

In the past, when I asked my students to be creative in class, I could see fear in their faces which was usually followed by questions from them like, "How can we be creative?" The answer to how does one "be creative" is not easy, but with group e-portfolios I asked the students to compare different groups' examples and then have them discuss which artifacts were appropriate, or better for addressing different e-portfolio problems. Also, because all the group e-portfolios were linked to the course-level e-portfolio, at any time the students could see other groups' work as examples. After a few weeks, I saw that students were regularly checking other groups' e-portfolios for inspiration.

Later in the semester, the students were asked to use Google Forms to submit anonymous peer feedback for other groups' e-portfolios. This peer feedback was then posted in the course-level e-portfolio and became the focus of class discussions as we analyzed and discussed students' peer feedback submissions for critical thinking and appropriateness.

Flow Supporters Again, I searched the YouTube videos, I found over 500,000 samples that demonstrated different ways to use Google Docs and therefore viewing a few of these videos helped me develop my own skills and overcome problems. This enabled me to build confidence as well as reduce anxiety. Although using Google Forms enabled me to feel more useful by answering more questions and having more discussions, using Google Docs made this question–discussion interaction flourish in the classroom. Like most instructors, I teach to interact and help my students, so this was a great esteem building exercise and I felt excited to continue using the tools with more and more interesting tasks for students. Similar to Google Forms, there were several times I lost track of time as I was problem-solving and strategizing new uses for Google Docs.

Flow Blockers Although Google Docs were not as easy to use as Google Forms, I was able to learn how to use them with only a few challenges.

Google Forms and Individual Student E-Portfolios

A third level of a portfolio was the individual student e-portfolio. In this exercise, students created their own e-portfolios containing not only, their resume, job search cover letters, but also reflections of valuable knowledge and skills they had learned each day in the course. Near the end of each class student completed and submitted a Google Form to record reflections of what they learned in class and how the learning may be valuable to their personal or professional lives. When students submitted their reflections, they would get an automatic response email containing their submission and then students edited and copied those reflections into their individual portfolios. An added benefit to this was each week I could see what they were reflecting and know how well they were learning. This exercise was similar to the "One Minute Paper" process described in Angelo and Cross (1988). Again, because all of the students' submissions were saved in my same Google Drive folder as the Form, it was easy for me to see students' responses in class immediately after they submitted them. In the past I collected the one minute papers to view and return to students, but now I just read down the column in the spreadsheet. Google Forms eliminated the whole process of students' filling out the 3×5 cards, giving the cards to me, and then my checking the responses on the cards, and returning the cards to the students.

Flow Supporters Similar to the Google Forms and Course-level e-portfolio combination, I developed more new skills and experienced fewer anxious moments than with other interactive tools. By having a quick check and reading the students' responses in the spreadsheet, I felt I was able to understand the students better. I learned a great deal about what they thought was important and how they thought they could apply the information to improve their daily lives, and often, the students found value in areas and applications I had not imagined. This process was quite fulfilling and it helped me continue to look for more relevant uses for the tools as well as develop and improve in-class examples for my lectures.

Flow Blockers As I had learned to use Google Forms before, they were easily adapted to this task with few challenges.

Discussion

Though modest, the results articulate an instructor's experiences using two simple and easy to use applications to curate e-portfolio content and reporting flow experiences in the process. These findings were similar to those reported in previous flow literature. An important key seems to be the combination of using just two simple Google tools Forms and HyperDocs, to help students curate content for their e-portfolios within the classroom. As for this instructor, using the tools was more fulfilling than past exercises using paper worksheets. Also, using the interactive tools in the classroom seemed to help students benefit from increased engagement, instructor interaction, and instant feedback during classroom activities, while the instructor was able to follow student knowledge and skill development more closely.

As two primary characteristics of flow experiences are engaging in an activity and having a goal, it seems using the Google tools to curate content was the activity and the e-portfolio was the goal. Students used the tools to interact with me both in class, and with technology via their e-portfolios, and this process seemed to become a more collaborative experience for all. Future research could focus on quantitative assessment of instructor flow experiences as they learn to use these tools.

References

Angelo, T. A., & Cross, K. P. (1988). *Classroom assessment techniques: A handbook for college teachers.* San Francisco, CA: Jossey-Bass.

Barrett, H. C. (2007). Researching electronic portfolios and learner engagement: The REFLECT Initiative. *Journal of Adolescent & Adult Literacy, 50*(6), 436–449.

Bates, T. (2015). *Teaching in a digital age: Guidelines for designing teaching and learning.* Burnaby, BC: SFU Document Solutions, Simon Fraser University.

Chaudhuri, T., & Chan, W. Y. (2016). "Networked learning communities": A perspective arising from a multidisciplinary community of practice on student e-portfolios. *Learning Communities Journal, 8*(2), 27–49. Online at: http://celt.miamioh.edu/lcj/issue.php?v=8&n=2. Accessed June 27, 2016.

Chu, S., & Kennedy, D. (2011). Using online collaborative tools for groups to co-construct knowledge. *Online Information Review, 35*(4), 581–597.

Collan, M., & Tetard, F. (2007). Lazy user theory of solution selection. In *Proceedings of the CELDA 2007 Conference*, Algarve, Portugal (pp. 273–278) December 7–9, 2007.

Cox, M., & Richlin, L. (Eds.). (2004). *Building faculty learning communities.* San Francisco, CA: Jossey-Bass.

Csikszentmihalyi, M. (1990). *Flow: The psychology of optimal experience.* New York: Harper & Row.

Csikszentmihalyi, M. (1996). *Creativity: Flow and the psychology of discovery and invention.* New York: HarperCollins.

Csikszentmihalyi, M. (1997). *Finding flow: The psychology of engagement with everyday life.* New York: Basic Books.

Davis, F. D. (1989). Perceived usefulness, perceived ease of use, and user acceptance of information technology. *MIS Quarterly, 13*(3), 319–340.

Dewey, J. (1938). *Experience and education.* New York, NY: Macmillan.

Dudeney, G., Hockly, N., & Pegrum, M. (2013). *Digital literacies: Research and resources in language teaching.* Harlow, UK: Pearson.

Hidayanto, A., & Setyady, S. (2014). Impact of collaborative tools utilization on group performance in university students. *TOJET: The Turkish Online Journal of Educational Technology, 13*(2), 88–98.

Hwang, B. (2014). The effects of learning portfolio-based program on learning competencies perceived by pre-service special education teachers. *Special Education Research, 13*(1), 26–59.

Lewis, S., Pea, R., & Rosen, J. (2010). Beyond participation to co-creation of meaning: mobile social media in generative learning communities. *Social Science Information, 49*(3), 351–369.

Linger, W. S. (1997). *Putting immediacy to work: Training teachers use immediacy behaviors in their classrooms.* Unpublished master's thesis, San Francisco State University San Francisco, CA.

Linger, W. S. (2002). *The relationship between immediate communication, flow, and motivation to continue learning and to integrate technology.* Unpublished doctoral dissertation, University of San Francisco, San Francisco, USA.

Linger, W. S. (2016). Driving interaction and ubiquitous learning with mobile devices: A pilot study. *Learning Communities Journal, 8*(1), 99–129.

Peppler, K. A., & Solomou, M. (2011). Building creativity: Collaborative learning and creativity in social media environments. *On the Horizon, 19*(1), 13–23.

Rogers, E. (2003). *Diffusion of innovations* (5th ed.). New York: Simon and Schuster.

Roseth, C., Akcaoglu, M., & Zellner, A. (2013). Blending synchronous face-to-face and computer-supported cooperative learning in a hybrid doctoral seminar. *TechTrends, 57*(3), 54–59.

Salvagno, M., Taylor, J., Bobeva, M., & Hutchings, M. (2015). Ubiquitous connectivity and students' well-being: A situational analysis in a UK University. *Ubiquitous Learning: An International Journal, 8*(3), 1–17.

Shroff, R. H., Chaudhuri, T., & Linger, W. (2014). *Engagement with electronic portfolios: Promising practices and lessons learnt from a pilot.* Paper presented at the eLearning Forum Asia 2014, 28–30 May 2014, National Cheng Kung University, Taiwan.

Shroff, R. H., Deneen, C. C., & Lim, C. P. (2014b). Student ownership of learning using E-portfolios for career development. *Journal of Information Systems Technology & Planning,* 7(18), 75–90.

Shroff, R. H., Keyes, C., & Linger, W. (2016). A proposed taxonomy of theoretical and pedagogical perspectives of mobile applications to support ubiquitous learning. *Ubiquitous Learning: An International Journal,* 8(4), 23–44.

Westberry, N., & Franken, M. (2012). Co-construction of knowledge in tertiary online settings: An ecology of resources perspective. *Instructional Science,* 41(1), 147–164.

Chapter 8
The Use of E-Portfolio for Outside Classroom Learning

Atara Sivan

Abstract This chapter presents a case study on the use of e-portfolio for learning in an outside classroom experience in a university in Hong Kong. It involved two students who were members of an intergenerational learning community where they engaged problems and issues, and work collaboratively to bring about changes and improvements to the community. Together with the coordinator of this community and with the use of Weebly, the students built an e-portfolio which provided a platform for documentation, reflection and collaboration. Interviews with the participants highlighted the contribution of the e-portfolio to students' learning and the development of communication, teamwork and creativity skills. The portfolio's framework and context were regarded as facilitative for meta-cognitive reflection and affective learning while the use of a free and user-friendly platform not only was well appreciated but made the process more efficient.

Keywords E-portfolio · Learning community · Outside classroom learning · Reflection · Affective learning · Weebly · Higher education · Hong Kong

The use of electronic portfolio (e-portfolio) has been recognized as a means for enhancing student learning. E-portfolios could help to understand the goals students set for themselves, the ways they achieve these goals and their relationship with institutional goals (Terheggen et al. 2000). Apart from the product which showcases students' skills and knowledge, the process of creating e-portfolios facilitates students' planning, organization and information management and presentation skills necessary for today's digital world (Abrami and Barrett 2005). With the development of new technologies, e-portfolios serve the purpose of interaction of learning on top of evidence collection and reflection (Bhattacharya and Harnett 2007). With all these advantages, e-portfolios can facilitate the development of lifelong learning (Bhattacharya and Hartnett 2007), which is a significant attribute of university

A. Sivan (✉)
Department of Education Studies, Hong Kong Baptist University,
Kowloon Tong, Hong Kong
e-mail: atarasiv@hkbu.edu.hk

© Springer Nature Singapore Pte Ltd. 2017 117
T. Chaudhuri and B. Cabau (eds.), *E-Portfolios in Higher Education*,
DOI 10.1007/978-981-10-3803-7_8

graduates. As stated by Barret (2007) "with the widespread dissemination of ICT in homes and schools, and the many software tools available to support development, the electronic development is becoming a viable option for dynamically documenting learning and reflection across the life span" (p. 10). Yancey (2009) has found that compared to print portfolios which are mostly course-based, e-portfolios spread to the entire curriculum as well as to outside experiences. In their study on the use of e-portfolio among higher education students, Bhattacharya and Harnett (2007) developed a tool for students to evaluate their development of skills and competencies during formal, non-formal and informal learning. Formal learning refers to the structured education system, whereas non-formal learning denotes organized activity outside the formal education system which aims at achieving certain life skills, informal learning takes place through experiences in various settings and contexts. The present case study focused on outside classroom experiences involving non-formal learning, which took place as part of a specific community engagement project within the Faculty of Social Sciences at the Hong Kong Baptist University.

While portfolios are used for assessment of student learning, arguments were made that the focus on assessment could overshadow the learning process and eliminate students' voices. Barret (2007) has distinguished between portfolios used for assessment of learning and those that support assessment for learning. Whereas the former is prescribed by the institution, structured around a set of outcomes and scored for providing quantitative data for external audience, the latter centres on the learner's engagement and choices. When used as a tool for assessment for learning, the portfolio's purpose and content are determined by the student and they are reviewed by the teacher to provide feedback for enhancing learning. Underpinned by the notion that "a portfolio that is truly a story of learning is owned by the learner, structured by the learner, and told in the learner's own voice" (Barret 2007, p. 441), the present study examined the use of e-portfolio to facilitate students' learning through telling their own stories as members of outside classroom learning community. The following section described the project which served as the context for developing and implementing e-portfolio.

Learning Community Project as Context for E-Portfolio

E-portfolio was developed as a mechanism to enhance student learning from their participation in a project entitled: "Building learning community through a transdisciplinary multi-layered approach". This 3-year project which was funded by the university Strategic Development Fund established a multi-layered intergenerational learning community consisting of academics and professionals, university students, older adults in the community and secondary school students. Using a transdisciplinary approach, participants were empowered to engage problems and issues, and work collaboratively to bring about changes and improvements to the community.

The project was underpinned by the university commitment to whole person development and mission of knowledge transferred to the community (Hong Kong Baptist University 2014). By providing the platform for students to initiate and undertake projects within their community with academic support and guidance, the project aimed at facilitating their development of attributes including: responsibility, citizenship, independence, problem solving skills, and readiness to lead, serve and work in a team. The project also provided opportunities for staff–student collaboration to engage in public and community service.

The establishment of the Community of Practice (CoP) involved a process of exploration, inquiry, learning and identification of community needs, and building a common interest under the theme of "Healthy Lifestyle and Well-being". The university students who were at their first and second year of study, became Healthy Living Ambassadors (HLAs) who together with staff and professionals led a series of activities with older adults in the community. These older adults' age ranged between 65 and 90 years old. They lived by themselves and attended integrated service centres in two places within the district. Activities included stretching exercises, bag making, fun adventures, new dumpling ideas, happy memories and a graduation ceremony. The students were assisted by secondary school students to whom they served as mentors. To ensure that learning took place, students took part in on-site visits and seminars provided by professionals and were empowered to undergo an action learning process throughout their involvement. Each activity included brainstorming, planning, rehearsal and feedback, action and reflection while adopting the transdisciplinary three-layered approach: university staff and professionals, university students and secondary school students.

To facilitate the community process, students were asked to complete reflective journals and also to participate in reflection sessions. Students reflected on the main things that they learned, the questions that they had, the problems they encountered and the ways they solved them. Students also shared their feelings and thoughts about community engagement and learning and their accounts provided a holistic picture of their experiences as members of the learning community.

The E-Portfolio Process and Model

The idea to use e-portfolio was initiated by the coordinator of the learning community project (hereinafter referred to as Coordinator) who is a professor of education and who has been a member of a CoP called: "CoP Reflect", which aimed at the introduction and development of university-wide use of student e-portfolios to support the achievement of the university graduate attributes. During the regular meetings, CoP Reflect members have shared their experiences of using e-portfolio in their classrooms and worked collaboratively on ways to develop measures for assessing learning though this mechanism.

Recognizing the benefits of e-portfolio in formal classroom learning and appreciating the need to provide students with an interactive platform for reflecting on their learning community experiences led to the idea to try it out. Although the existing use of reflective journal served the purpose of learning about students' experiences and facilitated the project flow, the reflective journal did not include an interactive component. It was hoped that utilizing e-portfolio in this context could further facilitate students' learning by empowering them to create their own platform and adding an interactive option.

Since it was the first time for the coordinator to use e-portfolios with students, and there was a need to look into the use of this mechanism in addition to the existing reflective journal, it was decided to try it out with students who took part in the project from its establishment. After discussion with the coordinator about the proposed project and students' involvement, two students from two different departments showed interest in joining this initiative. Students were also invited to provide their feedback on their participation after the end of the project. They were enthusiastic to create e-portfolio on their involvement during the third year of the project and they further agreed to be interviewed to gauge their feedback on the use of this portfolio.

Inspired by Zubizarreta's (2004, 2008) simple model of learning portfolio, the coordinator decided to build on it for the development of e-portfolio. The model consists of three fundamental components: reflection, documentation and collaboration. The reflection focuses on learning by looking at how, when and where it occurs. The documentation part provides a platform for students to show evidence of their learning through different forms ranging from their own writings to pictures and creative displays. The collaboration refers to connection with a mentor who could facilitate students' meaningful reflection. This model aligned very well with the model of the outside classroom learning community where all members have been engaged in a collaborative learning process (Sivan et al. 2016). This similarity led to the idea to regard the students' e-portfolio as a small learning community within the existing large outside classroom learning community.

The e-portfolio process included a preparatory phase, during which the coordinator established a suggested framework for the e-portfolio, and two meetings with the participating students. In the first meeting the framework was presented and discussed. After deliberation, a framework for utilizing the model and its related reflective questions were consolidated. Based on Zubizarreta's (2008) list of questions, a total of seven questions were posted, these are: What have I learned, when did I learn, how did I learn? How did this learning contribute to me? Was my learning coherent, relevant, applicable and practical? What new things have I discovered about myself? What were the best things of my learning? What were the disappointments of my learning? In what ways has my learning been valuable? References were also made to the university graduate attributes for reflection on learning (Centre for Holistic Teaching and Learning 2015).

During the second meeting a discussion was held on the platform to be used for the project. To facilitate the discussion, the coordinator invited the CoP Reflect project officer who had a profound knowledge and experience in e-portfolio, to share and demonstrate e-platforms. After deliberation it was decided to adopt the Weebly platform and one student took the initiative to establish the website.

The idea was to set it as a channel for a collaborative e-portfolio, where everyone could write, reflect and provide feedback and comments.

The website included four sections. The first section described the learning community project. The second section stated the objectives of the e-portfolio and the reflection questions. The third section called: "Our Members" introduced the three members involved in the e-portfolio. The last section of Documentation and Evidence aimed to show some evidences of students' learning. In its description it stated that these evidences could be pictures, writings, feedback, creative displays and all types of products or proof that demonstrated learning and that students could describe in their own words how they learned. Since its establishment, the website was utilized for one semester during the last stage of the outside classroom learning community experience. It started with students documenting and reflecting upon their experience and followed with the coordinator's feedback which led to students' new inputs.

Methodology

The study adopted a descriptive case study which is used to describe a phenomenon and the real context in which it occurs (Yin 2003). The case study involved the two students and the coordinator in their use of e-portfolio within the context of the outside classroom learning community experiences they went through. Participants' feedback on the use of e-portfolio was solicited through semi-structured interviews. Both the coordinator and students were asked to comment on their experience of using the portfolio for outside classroom learning and on the usefulness of the model and the Weebly platform. They were assured the confidentiality of their inputs. The interviews were conducted by a research assistant and were analyzed by three independent readers using conventional content analysis. After reading the transcripts and going through the coding and categorizing processes individually, a discussion was held to arrive at the main themes.

Findings

Five themes were identified in the interview analyses and they are presented below with their corresponding quotations.

Providing a Flexible Channel for Expression and Learning

Students regarded the e-portfolio as a means for expressing their feelings and for ongoing consolidation:

It's like I have something that has its physical existence, so you are not just putting your feeling in your heart but you have like some physical stuff to spell out what you have been thinking about. (Student B)

For me, this e-portfolio is not just only an activity logbook, but the continuous consolidation of my future career preferences and personality building... (Student A)

Comparing the e-portfolio to regular reflection in class, the coordinator added that the flexibility of the e-portfolio facilitated her role as mentor:

This time there was no need for a physical meeting, so in a way I have noticed that students when they have the free time to sit and write on their own, there are basically a lot of things that they can come up with. What I learned from this experience is that using this e-portfolio is much more flexible and perhaps allows students to reflect more. (Coordinator)

While flexibility was highlighted as an important advantage of using e-portfolio, it was especially appreciated within the context of outside classroom learning. Both students and the coordinator seemed to prefer using e-portfolio in that context over a formal classroom learning:

Unlike formal classroom teaching, outside classroom learning is often informal and it lacks an organized mechanism to evaluate the learning process and outcome of both teachers and students. An e-portfolio can record and let participants reflect upon their experiences instantly, and they can easily refer back to their entries (Student A)

In a classroom, the professors and teachers deliver the same stuff. And it's very uni-directional. They teach all the students the same stuff. But, in this e-portfolio, I think different people learned different things in this process, so we have different results. (Student B)

Since the project upon which students reflected was not part of a formal learning, the dialogue with the students was more open than a formal classroom learning and touched on personal issues which may not otherwise be reflected upon. (Coordinator)

References were also made to the small size of the e-portfolio experience which the coordinator found to be a great advantage in facilitating students' learning:

So I think the uniqueness of this experience is that it was a small size and it was a trial which provided a safe environment for all of us who used e-portfolio for the first time. It was a supportive environment to test it out. (Coordinator)

Cultivating Reflection

Reflection was identified as a significant benefit of the e-portfolio. References were made to self-reflection, reflection with the coordinator as well as learning from the coordinator's reflection on students' inputs.

I seldom have chances to have reflections with professionals. Normally I do have reflections but I reflect upon myself on diaries. This e-portfolio can organize my reflection with the Project Leader [Coordinator], in which the on-going reflection is worthwhile to my personal development. (Student A)

I would say I know more about myself—my personal trait—my personality traits because when I was doing those activities with the project, I was not going to think of what have I learnt and who am I. But, after writing these reflections, I am sort of like know more about myself because I will think about it and that links the activities to my life. For instance, like, I have written about my experience with my granny (Student B)

The lecturer [coordinator] has always given us a lot of her ideas on our reflections as well as some insights from her perspective and the portfolio worked well because when I just put on my reflection on the platform and I don't think and then I got the ideas so I referred to them and thought more. (Student B)

The Weebly e-portfolio is an on-going reflection process that teachers and students reflect upon themselves in a regular basis. It is a one-on-one reflection process and students would be able to get professional advices and I believe those suggestions will be very fruitful in future working occasions. (Student A).

The coordinator further praised the students for their reflection which helped her to understand them more and to get to know them better:

I read students' reflection and I praise the students because they wrote a lot, and I am happy to see that. I did not expect that they would write so much… I think what I learned from them is basically that they learned a lot of things about themselves and about their learning. They gained a lot of insights from their participation in this community project, about their own personalities, their own capabilities, how to work with other people, and also how to reflect and take some things out of that too and apply in other situations. (Coordinator)

Contributing to Whole Person Development

The experience of using e-portfolios enhanced students' knowledge and developed certain important skills which aligned with the University graduate attributes. These include teamwork, learning and communication, creativity and citizenship. Student A elaborated how the process enriched his knowledge:

Since teachers and students independently reflect without external influences, the relationships among them will be closed and this is important when it goes to lifelong learning, because both sides know each other for long and reflection outcome would become more precise and useful when time elapses. (Student A)

Student B related to the information technology skills:

Specific IT skills such as website management are acquired when users are fully committed into the portfolio. (Student B)

Students' communication skills were also enhanced through the ongoing use of English while reflecting on their experiences and communicating with the team, as attested by the coordinator's account:

About communication, my students had to write in English, and I think it's definitely provided them with a platform to express themselves in a language which is not their mother tongue. They reflected on their experiences in this out-of-class learning community and also responded to me as part of the mentoring process. Unlike writing academic papers, here there was the communicative element which was highly facilitated through our interaction. (Coordinator)

Both students pointed out that the development of teamwork and citizenship were facilitated through ownership, reflection and sharing:

Because the conceptual framework of the e-portfolio was established by us, so I think it has the element of collaboration. Through this project and this reflection process I know more about the importance of teamwork. Because I start to understand that you cannot do the things on your own and you really need support from others. (Student B)

The whole reflection process encompasses sense of responsibility towards myself and the community in a long term manner. Between reflections, I have shown progress in terms of self-actualization that focuses on well-being and appropriate ways to know the society better, assist people and the needy and so on. The portfolio empowers me to continue serving the society by applying things I learned inside and outside the campus…it is also one of the responsibilities of university students. (Student A)

The coordinator also recognized the contribution of the e-portfolio to the development of team work. At the same time, she raised an interesting point related to the communication flow within the community:

By participating in this e-learning portfolio and sharing their reflections, students illustrated teamwork. At the same time, their reflection was mainly between me and them. Even if there were three of us, they referred to me and not to each other's input. Although they possibly read each other's input, there was not an interaction between them on the plat-form…Since they exhibited teamwork when we met, I do not see this as an issue. (Coordinator)

Participants' accounts also indicated that the e-portfolio facilitated students' ability to think in different ways alongside their ability to genuinely and authentically tell their stories:

The e-portfolio is a platform for students and teachers to think out of the box, since more or less it is a sandbox which allows users to make the portfolio entries more appealing, creative that readers would appreciate. (Student A)

I would say you can write whatever you like to write and just feel free to write what you have in your mind and your heart. Just write down the most authentic, the most genuine feeling on that spot. And I think that is a core-value of doing this e-portfolio—being genuine. (Student B)

While thinking critically and reflecting on their own experiences and how those facilitated their learning, students exhibited creativity. They showed their ability to think in a different way and to look at themselves and what they could take out of their experiences that could enhance their learning. Those are higher level qualities which may not be achieved in a regular classroom interaction. I saw their creative thinking in the stories they shared and the way they focused on their learning process on the top of the knowledge and skills they developed. (Coordinator)

Discovering Oneself and Preparing for Future Path

Students' found that the use of e-portfolio fostered their self-discovery and they also saw its potential contribution to their future learning and career. Student A emphasized lifelong learning, whereas student B also noted the personal growth:

> The e-portfolio acts as a bridge for students to attain self-actualization and observe the outside world. This portfolio enhances, enriches and improves my way of learning since it provides guidance in lifelong learning and future career path. (Student A)

> I think by knowing more about myself—by knowing more about what I like and what I don't like, I will make a better decision in the future. For instance, like, because I know I can interact well with old adults as well as secondary school students. And what I would like to do in future is to become a teacher. (Student B)

Both students referred to the future use of the portfolio for reflection and applications of the things they learned:

> When completing the e-portfolio, I sort of thought about what I have done when doing this activity. And it's sort of like, when I do it next time, I would make good use of the things that I have learnt and have been reflected on and I will apply what I have learnt in this reflection process to the things that I will do in the future. (Student B)

> The e-portfolio provides a knowledge base or time capsule for me and the mentor when both sides find queries and miserablenesses in a new working and/or learning environment. Without this platform, one may not easily organize his or her own merits and de-merits as experiences can be long and complicated and reflections are needed to keep things in mind. (Student A)

Facilitative Framework

All users further attributed the success of the e-portfolio to its underlying framework and its related questions which were collaboratively consolidated. In her account, the coordinator shared how the framework was established together with the students leading to students' active reflection:

> I think that the framework and questions facilitated students' learning….They actually liked very much the opportunity to reflect and get to know themselves better and to understand how learning took place and how they can make use of this learning process in the future. So on the whole this framework and the questions seem to be quite good… the questions seemed to be very useful to them and they actually responded to them in their writing, so it worked very well. (Coordinator)

Students especially valued the questions and the mentoring provided by the coordinator through the reflection process. One student said: "The guiding questions were important for me, they constructed my reflection in a more organized way" (Student B). He further appreciated the coordinator's comments:

I gained insights from what the lecturer [coordinator] has written and kept asking me, what I have been learning and personal insights and knowledge stuffs, and how can I transfer the knowledge and personal insights to the other aspects of my life. I think this kind of interaction allowed me to think more about myself and to think about the thing that are not related to the project. (Student B)

The mentoring part is very important. I would like to see what—what she [the coordinator] thinks about.... I mean, because she is more experienced in doing this kind of activity. I would like to know more about her opinions. So I can learn from her. (Student B)

Student A also acknowledged the usefulness of the questions for his future career:

These questions act as indicators for me to discover my strengths and weaknesses...the questions can examine and scan one's experiences and discover his or her strengths and weaknesses that can become references for individuals. Therefore the questions can be universally applied to other working and/or related occasions for all personnel to reflect, and to help the others in need if they face challenges in personal development. (Student A)

Weebly as a Valuable Platform

The Weebly platform was described as user friendly by both students and the coordinator. In general, all parties saw the advantages of using this platform when compared with paper work and other platforms. Some of the advantages raised related to accessibility:

It's easily accessible, and you can do whatever you like to do on the platform. I think that it is a great platform. I don't think there is any drawback or disadvantage. It is easy to use, the presentation is quite decent and that is good. (Student B)

Users can easily access the e-portfolio content simply by signing up to Weebly. Unlike traditional files, users can easily click the related materials of the website in an organized and quick manner. ...teachers and students can directly access specific reflections and reply entries instantly, rather than the traditional way that people have to search files in a physical directory which wastes time and resources. (Student A)

I like the Weebly very much because it's very friendly. You just go there and click and get the messages and then return, and then response to the students. So I think this was a very much facilitative factor to do this project. (Coordinator)

References were also made to the data storage and to facilitation of creativity in use of multimedia resources:

Data would not easily be lost when it goes to Weebly. Unlike the traditional way that occasionally people may lose a certain amount of documents due to negligence or unknown reasons, specified contents in Weebly will not be easily deleted. Users can focus on the actual reflection matter rather than wasting energy on administrating tedious paper works and storage management. (Student A)

Annotations and multimedia content can be attached into Weebly. It is very redundant and sometimes boring for both teachers and students when it comes to a mere paper reflection, Weebly provides a favourable and user-friendly way to include multimedia resources like Annotations, clips, emojis, etc. in order to make the reflection funnier and easier for all readers. (Student A)

The coordinator also described the advantages of Weebly over other platforms she used for her own teaching portfolio:

For me, Weebly was very friendly. When I had the experience of doing my own teaching portfolio I came across several other platforms that for some reasons were not so friendly. There, the process was more complicated and it took more time to do everything and at times I could not upload the materials. Weebly was very smooth and very friendly from the very beginning. And the fact is that I could just go in and key and then save, that was very good. And I had a good feeling that I could do this by myself as well. (Coordinator)

The coordinator added that the fact that Weebly was an open website did not seem to deter students from using it, which encouraged her to reflect back to the students without hesitations. At the same time she suggested that people should consider this issue when sharing their own accounts:

I know that it's opened to the public, and interesting enough, the students didn't have a problem with that....If somebody is a more private person, then I would advise him or her to be aware that it is opened to the public...when I read the students' accounts, I saw that they were actually very open and they shared very intimate things about family, about interaction, about their feelings and their personality change. So I don't see any disadvantages at this stage for my trial of e-portfolio with students. (Coordinator)

Alongside the favourable views of Weebly, one student raised the need for backup of their work since it is an open platform. He also suggested to carefully set the e-portfolio layout for its best utilization. The student further raised issues related to safety, privacy and convenience when comparing Weebly to another platform utilized by the university:

Unlike Weebly, Moodle is safer in terms of privacy and data preservation as the University has subscribed this platform for a long time. Unless the e-portfolio is fully open to public, actually Moodle can perform most tasks that Weebly could do. Teachers and students can reflect independently on the discussion forum under a course on the Moodle platform. (Student A)

Discussion

The case study presented in this chapter is a small scale trial of using e-portfolios for learning through documentation, reflection and collaboration involving one academic staff and two students who together have been engaged in an out of class intergenerational learning community. Utilizing Weebly as their platform, participants have created the e-portfolio collaboratively as a small learning community within a larger community involving university students and staff, elderly and secondary school students. All parties were new to e-portfolio and were motivated to try it out. Their accounts highlighted the usefulness of e-portfolio for enhancing learning, cultivating reflection and developing knowledge and transferrable skills for lifelong learning and future career. Trying out this e-portfolio has brought to light several issues related to the aim, context and process of using e-portfolio for non-formal learning.

The e-portfolio centered on students' learning. It aimed to develop their ability to better understand the way they go about their learning and how they can best utilize it for their personal growth. Unlike the use of portfolio for assessing students' learning outcomes, the model adopted in this project emphasized the use of a learning portfolio which focused on learning how to learn rather than learning for assessment. Students' views attested to their ability to be engaged in meta-cognitive reflection on their learning which is different from refection on the evidences they provided (Dysthe and Engelsen 2011). It can be argued that the reflection students were involved in during the creation of the e-portfolio promoted their meta-learning (Mummalanei 2014).

The context in which the e-portfolio was used provided a very supportive and safe environment for students' expression and reflection. All participants saw the outside classroom environment as having certain benefits over formal classroom learning for employing e-portfolio. They opined that this context contributed to their documentation and reflection on a range of involvements and various personal aspects which might not have been manifested within a regular classroom context. The intergenerational learning community, which involved interaction with different people through a range of activities related to healthy living and well-being, provided ample opportunities for students to relate to the affective domain of learning which despite its significance for learning, is hardly manifested in formal classroom learning.

Students' involvement in establishing the portfolio framework and designing its website seem to contribute to their learning and satisfaction. The process facilitated their sense of ownership which they might not have in a regular classroom learning. Asking the students to design their website and introducing them to Weebly which they did not use before also enhanced their digital knowledge and skills.

Another essential component in the e-portfolio was the interaction with the coordinator. Students' positive feedback on their coordinator's comments demonstrated the importance of including an interactive function in the e-portfolio. Originally, this function aimed to facilitate both student–student and student–coordinator interaction, however, in practice the interaction was limited to student–coordinator. This phenomenon was also found in the larger outside classroom learning community (Sivan and Tam 2015) and could be attributed to the Chinese culture where power distance plays a significant role (Hofstede 2011). Students followed the coordinator and looked up at her for feedback and comments. At the same time, it is also possible that the lack of student–student interaction had to do with the portfolio being rather an individual activity and students were more attuned to their own reflection. Further studies in other sociocultural contexts could shed more light on this issue.

The use of e-portfolio has contributed to students' self-discovery and to the development of knowledge and skills which are part of the university graduate attributes. These include learning, teamwork, communication and creativity. Students' accounts about their potential use of the e-portfolio in the future shows the significance of this tool for their lifelong learning and future development. These findings further support the need for providing students with channels for reflection on their learning experiences both inside and outside the classroom. While these attributes could be enhanced through formal classroom learning, students' and the coordinator's accounts attested to their continued online facilitation through a flexible channel that did not require classroom attendance. In today's digital world where youngsters use their virtual platform for communication, e-portfolio could be further developed as a regular online sharing and learning mechanism.

As a case study on the development and use of e-portfolio in non-formal out-of-class activity, the project involved two students and one coordinator. Although its findings cannot be generalized, they shed some light on the possible contribution that e-portfolio can make to students' learning as attested by participants' accounts. Whereas students' views may not be regarded as direct evidence of learning, their similarity with the coordinator's view seem to confirm that learning took place. Even though the e-portfolio process involved only three people, it provided a valuable platform for trying out this mechanism in a new setting. Oftentimes academics are recommending to start new initiatives small and keep them simple. The coordinator's feedback showed that starting small was an advantage especially when one does not have any experience in developing and implementing e-portfolio. The adopted model required the coordinator to continuously attend to students' inputs in order to ensure a smooth mentoring process. Students were asked to respond to reflection questions which they had not come across in their regular classroom learning. They were also eager to obtain feedback and learn from the coordinator. Since the content involved personal disclosure, the coordinator needed to be cautious when commenting. The challenge may be bigger if such an e-portfolio is used with a large class especially involving outside classroom learning experience that attends to both the cognitive and affective domains of students' learning. Talking about feelings may not be so easy but that is where awareness is heightened and doors are opened for personal growth. For those reasons, it would be good to use this portfolio after getting to know the students and establishing a good rapport with them. If utilized for reflection on outside classroom learning, it would be useful to start this experience with a small group of students so that ample attention could be given to them in the process of establishing and completing their e-portfolio. Last but not the least, there is a need to set time for preparing the framework, reading and commenting on students' input so as to ensure that learning takes place.

References

Abrami, P. C., Barret, H. (2005). Directions for research and development on electronic portfolios. *Canadian Journal of Learning and Technology, 31*(3). http://www.cjlt.ca/index.php/cjlt/article/viewArticle/92/86. Accessed March 17, 2016.

Barrett, H. (2007). Researching electronic portfolios and learner engagement: The REFLECT Initiative. *Journal of Adolescent and Adult Literacy, 50*(6), 436–449.

Bhattacharya, M., & Harnett, H. (2007). E-portfolio assessment in higher education. In *Proceeding of the 37th ASEE/TEEE Frontiers in Education* (pp. 19–24). Wilwauke. http://www.ied.edu.hk/obl/files/e-portfolio%20assessment%20in%20higher%20ed.pdf. Accessed December 20, 2015.

Centre for Holistic Teaching and Learning. (2015). *HKBU Graduates*. Attributes. Hong Kong Baptist University. http://chtl.hkbu.edu.hk/main/hkbu-ga/. Accessed January 12, 2016.

Dysthe, O., & Engelsen, K. S. (2011). Portfolio practices in higher education in Norway in an international perspective: Macro-, meso- and micro-level influences. *Assessment and Evaluation in Higher Education, 36*(1), 63–79.

Hofstede, G. (2011). *Culture's consequences: Comparing values, behaviors, institutions, and organizations across nations*. Thousands Oaks: Sage Publication.

Hong Kong Baptist University. (2014). *Vision 2020* http://vision2020.hkbu.edu.hk/index.html. Accessed March 17, 2016.

Mummalanei, V. (2014). Reflective essay and e-portfolio to promote and assess student learning in a capstone marketing course. *Marketing Education Review, 24*(1), 43–46.

Sivan, A., & Tam, V. (2015). *Building learning community through a transdisciplinary multi-layered approach*. Paper presented at the Lilly International Spring Conference. Bethesda, MD: College and University Teaching and Learning, 28–31 May 2015.

Sivan, A., Tam, V. C., Tam, E. S., Ho, M., Kwan, Y. W., Louie, L., et al. (2016). Building learning community through a transdisciplinary multi-layered approach. *Learning Communities Journal, 8*(1), 71–97.

Terheggen, S. L., Prabhu, R. P., Lubinescu, E. S. (2000). From product to process: Enhancing through the use of student electronic portfolio. US Department of Education, Educational Resources information center (ERIC) HE 33685. http://files.eric.ed.gov/fulltext/ED448674.pdf. Accessed December 12, 2015.

Yancey, K. B. (2009). Electronic portfolios a decade into the twenty first century: What we know, what we need to know. *Peer Review, 11*(1), 28–32.

Yin, R. K. (2003). *Case study research: Designs and Methods*. Thousand Oaks: Sage.

Zubizarreta, J. (2004). *The learning portfolio: Reflective practice for improving student learning*. Bolton: Ank.

Zubizarreta, J. (2008). *The learning portfolio: A powerful idea for significant learning*. IDEA Paper 44: 1–7. The IDEA Center Manhattan, Kansas. http://ideaedu.org/wp-content/uploads/2014/11/IDEA_Paper_44.pdf. Accessed January 12, 2016.

Chapter 9
Perceptions Regarding the Implementation of E-Portfolio for Students in Sport and Recreation Internship Placements

Siu Yin Cheung, Heather H.M. Kwok and Peggy H.N. Choi

Abstract This chapter aims to investigate perceptions regarding the implementation of Electronic Portfolio (e-portfolio) for students enrolled in the Bachelor of Social Sciences (Honours) in Sport and Recreation Leadership program. Sixty students (Males = 35, 58.3%, Females = 24, 40%) participated in a pilot study by electronically submitting their internship experience portfolio to the Mahara e-portfolio system. A compulsory training workshop was conducted in October 2013. Students submitted their CV, internship information, student reflections and artefacts to the Mahara e-portfolio system during and after the internship in 2014. Students' perceptions and lecturers' comments on e-portfolio implementation were collected and discussed in this chapter.

Keywords E-portfolio · Internship · Sport · Recreation

Introduction

Electronic portfolio (e-portfolio) has been widely used in education and career sectors for the purpose of assessment, reflection on learning process, enhancement of teaching quality and employee recruitment. Temple et al. (2003) defined the portfolio as a systemic and purposeful collection of work and achievement. Weller (2002) stated that applicants could showcase their strengths to the potential employers by the portfolio. Students would be embraced in a constructivist-learning approach which shifts the focus of learning paradigm from teachers to students. The implementation of portfolio empowers students to showcase their learning outcomes and reflect upon their learning experiences (Garrett 2011) which provides a more student-centered and innovative assessment than the traditional examination-centered approach.

S.Y. Cheung (✉) · H.H.M. Kwok · P.H.N. Choi
Department of Physical Education, Hong Kong Baptist University,
Kowloon Tong, Hong Kong
e-mail: cheungsy@hkbu.edu.hk

© Springer Nature Singapore Pte Ltd. 2017
T. Chaudhuri and B. Cabau (eds.), *E-Portfolios in Higher Education*,
DOI 10.1007/978-981-10-3803-7_9

In the mid 1990s, the concept of portfolio evolved into an electronic form (McCowan et al. 2005). The e-portfolio brought along several benefits including storage and greater access to a wider audience for the sharing of ideas and discussion of information (Bruder 1993; Bushweller 1995; Hicks and Nunan 2002). The transformation of e-portfolio from traditional portfolio leads to the increasing popularity of its implementation among higher institutions worldwide, such as Australia and Hong Kong (Cheng 2011; McCowan et al. 2005). Different projects on the use of e-portfolio as assessment or reflective learning have been launched in different higher education institutions with positive feedback obtained from different stakeholders. The e-portfolio allows students to take responsibility for building materials in their own work (McCowan et al. 2005). Students can demonstrate their creativity, their progression in learning, and achievements in the e-portfolio which help them to gain sense of ownership of their own learning. The e-portfolio also allows teachers or outsiders to provide feedback on students' work and with this interactive approach, the quality of the learning experience and outcomes of students can be enhanced.

The use of e-portfolio is still in its early stage of development (Yu 2011) and its benefits are weakened by several factors including the lack of sustainability of students' motivation in completing the e-portfolio, the feasibility for teachers to provide concise comments to all students, and the rigidity of the tool chosen (Rossi et al. 2008). To enhance the effectiveness of e-portfolio, the challenges of implementing the e-portfolio in each institution should be carefully reviewed as each institution is developed with its unique background and structure.

Background of Bachelor of Social Sciences in Sport and Recreation Leadership (SRL)

The SRL program was commenced in 2005 and over five hundred students graduated from the program within the past ten years. As the SRL program aims at preparing students to provide sport and recreation services for the mainstream as well as different populations, including people with special needs, graduates are equipped with special leadership and management skills in sport and recreation which enable them to develop their careers in different sectors and serve diverse populations.

The SRL program emphasizes the needs on serving specific populations, such as elderly people, people with physical or intellectual disabilities and people who require special attention. In order to better prepare the graduates to meet the needs of diverse stakeholders, the SRL program integrates broad-based academic knowledge in sport and recreation with practical training. The extensive professional placements (500 hours of internship over a period of two years) provide students with work integrated learning experiences in different organizations as a special feature of the SRL program. Students would gain valuable working experiences in different sport and recreation organizations that serve both the mainstream population as well as people with special needs within the 500 hours internship experience.

Under the supervision of lecturers, students are encouraged to apply the theories that they have learnt in class to the real work situation. Students are expected to work in partnership with their classmates in planning and delivering activities for a specified group of participants. In order to strengthen the learning experience of students, lecturers evaluate students' performances carefully and provide comments on the planning and implementation of the activities. Students are also expected to conduct effective reflection on their own learning experiences by writing reports for all internship activities conducted and compiling all internship reports into a portfolio. The portfolio enables students to showcase their learning outcomes and reflect upon their learning experiences (Garrett 2011). Shroff et al. (2013) investigated the use of e-portfolios in a filed experience placement for 77 student-teachers in Hong Kong. The results showed that student-teachers' attitude towards learning on using e-portfolios had significant influence on their perceptions on personal value, feeling in control and taking responsibility in learning. Thus, the aim of this chapter was to investigate the perceptions on using e-portfolios in internship field experiences for students of a sport and recreation leadership program.

Method

A colleague of the Center for Holistic Teaching and Learning (CHTL) was invited to introduce the "Mahara" software to 60 SRL students in October, 2013 at a computer room. The content of the workshop included basic concept of e-portfolio, and information based on Mahara e-portfolio version 1.7 user manual: Self-help guide for HKBU Mahara users. Students practiced basic design of template, input data, uploading of video, pictures and artefacts on the portfolio during the workshop. Students received a copy of the self-help guide for HKBU Mahara users and they were encouraged to contact the CHTL for inquiry on the Mahara system.

The students' assignment was to design the e-portfolio to introduce themselves to the potential employer of the internship by curriculum vitae (CV) and to record their internship experience. Students started the internship from November 2013 to August 2014. They submitted the CV, internship information, reflections and artefacts to the Mahara e-portfolio system during and after the internship in 2014.

After the submission of the final e-portfolio of the internship course, students completed a questionnaire on their feedback of the e-portfolio in September 2014. In order to gather more information related to the e-portfolio experience, two lecturers and four students were invited to two focus group interviews.

Results

There were 60 students of the Bachelor of Social Sciences (Honours) in Sport and Recreation Leadership program (Males = 35, 58.3%, Female = 24, 40%) taking part in this pilot study. Their age range was from 21 to 25 years old (M = 22.22, SD = 1.0). The contents of students' e-portfolio consisted of the resume which included personal information, such as education and employment history, certifications and awards, career goals, professional memberships, and work skills. Students also uploaded their internship experiences, reflections and artefacts in a multimedia format (e.g. video clips, sound files, electronic documents, etc.).

Quantitative Result

Survey questionnaires which consisted of 24 items were distributed to students. Students ranked the degree of agreement on each item according to a 7 point Likert scale. The higher the score, the higher the degree of agreement on the statement. The top five and the bottom five feedback statements are listed in Tables 1 and 2.

Students also ranked the overall satisfaction of the e-portfolio experience in a 10 point Likert scale, the mean was 5.64 (SD = 1.97). Table 3 shows the percentage of satisfaction score on the e-portfolio assignment.

Students' written comments on the questionnaire revealed that there were diverse perceptions on using e-portfolio at the internship course. The pros of e-portfolio were as follows: "using the e-portfolio is a current trend in the technological era, it is easier to organize materials, it is environmentally save, it is beautiful, it can digitize all materials, it was practical, and I could add artifacts on the e-portfolio". The cons of using e-portfolio to submit assessment at the internship course are as follows: "It was not useful, no one uses it afterward, hard copy is better than digital copy, it is a waste of time, and it was not convenient".

Table 1 The top five positive perceptions on e-portfolio

Rank order	Item	M	SD
1	My knowledge of technology helped me when creating my e-portfolio	4.73	1.08
2	Control over the e-portfolio content allowed me to showcase my best work in a digitized format	4.64	1.20
3	Overall, I valued the integration of the e-portfolio into the internship course	4.54	1.20
3	I was provided with the appropriate training to assume responsibility for my e-portfolio	4.54	1.13
3	Constructing the e-portfolio helped me to reflect upon my achievement	4.54	1.12

Table 2 The bottom five perceptions on e-portfolio

Rank order	Item	M	SD
24	Overall, I have a favourable attitude towards using e-portfolio for my field experience	4.19	1.21
23	I would welcome the opportunity to use e-portfolio in future courses	4.20	1.32
22	Overall, I found constructing the e-portfolio valuable to my field experience	4.21	1.21
21	The e-portfolio helped me develop a sense of accountability for my learning	4.25	1.11
19	I enjoyed using the e-portfolio for my field experience	4.26	1.18
19	I acquired useful skills in creating my field experience e-portfolio	4.26	1.25

Table 3 Satisfaction rate of e-portfolio

	1 Strongly disagree	2	3	4	5	6	7	8	9	10 Strongly agree
%	1.67	5	8.33	13.33	13.33	18.33	21.67	10	3.33	1.67

As there were mixed opinions on e-portfolio, focus group interviews were conducted for lecturers and students to investigate the effectiveness and perceptions on e-portfolio.

Qualitative Results

Two lectures and four students took part in the focus group interview. All of them stated that it was the first time that they utilized the e-portfolio to design the CV, the report and the reflection of the internship course.

General Perceptions of E-Portfolio

Lecturer A stated that "the e-portfolio and traditional CV are similar, sometimes, students had difficulties on opening the links and it wasted time for students".

Lecturer B also found the problems on the linkage of websites and he stated "the e-CV is better than the traditional CV as it looks better and students can add videos, pictures on the e-portfolio".

Students have different views on the e-portfolio. Student A said "it is a new skill and traditional CV is easier", while student B said" I learnt how to use the system at the workshop, it is easier and convenient to change the content of the CV, the system has different template and I can pick a template and input data".

Difficulties on Using the E-Portfolio

Students reported difficulties on the Mahara system which are as follows:

Student A: "There was only one workshop and we did not know the system well. I did not know how to use the system well...".
Student B: "The system has limited choice, we have so many materials and it is hard to present well at the system".
Student C: "There's a function on the system needs to be unlocked and it caused problem on opening the web site".
Student D: "The system has limitation on the length of the words, when I tried to input the name of the award which I had received on my CV, the name of my award was displayed in two lines instead of one. I think the design does not look good".

As this was the first time for both lecturers and students using the Mahara system to design e-portfolio, they reported difficulties in using the system.

Satisfaction on E-Portfolio

Both lecturers had fair satisfaction on the students' E-CVs and lecturer B stated that "the system has low compatibility and students need to spend lots of time...".

Two students had fair satisfaction on his/her own portfolio, while the other two students commended that they were satisfied with their e-CV. Student B stated that "the e-CV is more beautiful and we can add pictures on the e-CV" and Student D agreed.

Value of E-Portfolio

Lecturer A pointed out that "The assignment has its value; it encouraged students to reflect their experience during the internship". Lecturer B stated "Students could use their creativity to present themselves. I am with reservation on the e-portfolio project if it requires lots of time".

All students commented that the e-portfolio project was very meaningful. Student B stated "It was a good experience for me; I could design and personalize my CV by adding pictures". Student D supported this statement and said "We spent time and efforts on this project, the e-CV is better than the traditional CV, we could add pictures and videos on the portfolio and shared with others".

Student C stated "the e-portfolio provides a media for us to share our experience during the internship, we could add pictures on it, I think it is valuable". Student A agreed with Student C.

Contributions to Graduate Attributes

Lecturer A stated that "[…] students' computer skills have improved, they are more proactive in learning". Lecturer B commended that "this project could enhance the creativity of students…".

Students C said that "From the HKBU whole person education perspective, this project enhanced knowledge, learning and skills […] we learnt new skills, although we do not know whether we are going to use it later on or not, it did provide opportunity for us to learn a new skill". Student A supported Student C and added "It also enhanced creativity". Student B also supported that this project could enhance learning on computer skills and creativity. In addition, Student D agreed with Student B and pointed out that "It also enhanced communication and team work; it provided opportunity for fellow classmates to work together, to share different opinions and communicate better".

Discussion

This project is the first attempt to utilize e-portfolio for the internship placement experiences for students enrolled in the Bachelor of Social Sciences (Honours) in Sport and Recreation Leadership (SRL) program at Hong Kong Baptist University. As students' computer skills are unlike, the Mahara workshop before the project may not be sufficient for some students, who therefore have difficulties in working on the e-portfolio. More tutorial sections should be arranged to better prepare students with technological skills in using the e-portfolio. More sharing workshops or seminars should be conducted to educate both faculty members and students on the use of e-portfolio as it is a new media to showcase students' work, encourage reflection, evaluation and enhance students' future employment opportunities.

Students stated that their technological skills were enhanced, and Wilson et al. (2003) also reported that students' technological skills had increased after completion of the e-portfolio project.

In the present study, both lecturers and students understood it is a new trend on using the e-portfolio, but with limited skills in technology and the amount of time needed for creating the e-portfolio, they do have some reservations on using the e-portfolio for assessment. Whiteworth et al. (2011) found that time was the major barrier to the effective use of e-portfolio for school administrators and educators. Hartwick and Mansion (2014) conducted semistructured interviews for principals on using e-portfolio in the hiring process of teachers. They reported that principals' limited time was the major constraint for not using e-portfolio during the hiring process. But 93% of principals indicated that they would use the introductory video in the e-portfolio during the hiring process. Students should learn how to produce a brief introductory video with 3 min to present himself/herself (Hartwick and Mansion 2014).

The use of e-portfolio is common for some time. As the SRL students are required to develop activities plans for different populations in the different courses, such as the "Planning and leading rhythmic activities", the "Planning and leading water activities", and the "Planning and leading inclusive games", students should upload their activities plans by multimedia format (such as video) to their e-portfolios. This will enhance sharing and discussion of the activities plans, thus improve the final produce. In addition, students learn different sport skills at the program, they should utilize the e-portfolio to show case their sport performances and demonstrate their skills to peers and/or the public. Furthermore, the internship placement report should also be done in the e-portfolio rather than in the written format as to better showcase what students have learnt in the 300 hours of internship in an agency. This assessment may also be linked to their CV to demonstrate their rich job experiences, which would be beneficial to their future job hunting.

Conclusion

Utilizing the e-portfolio is a current trend in the technological era to showcase student's best work in a digitized format. This study supports e-portfolio is a good tool for recording and assessing courses that involves long learning process such as the internship. E-portfolio project can enhance students' computer skill, creativity and even team work. Students are more proactive in learning and the e-portfolio can enhance reflective learning. On the other hand, the major barriers on the implementation of e-portfolio are time and technological skills.

Both lecturers and students have mixed opinions on the implementation of e-portfolio. In order to further promote the use of e-portfolio as an assessment tool for the physical education, sport and recreation programs, more training workshops for faculty members and students is recommended. Finally, further investigations on the effectiveness of e-portfolio and ways to promote e-portfolio in higher education are recommended.

References

Bruder, I. (1993). Alternative assessment: Putting technology to the test. *Electronic Learning, 12*, 22–28.

Bushweller, K. (1995). The high-tech portfolio. *The Executive Educator, 17*, 19–22.

Cheng, C. (2011). Integrative assessment for learning in the classrooms of higher education institutions in Hong Kong. *Hong Kong Teachers' Centre Journal, 10*, 35–43.

Garrett, N. (2011). An e-portfolio design supporting ownership, social learning, and ease of use. *Educational Technology & Society, 14*(1), 187–202.

Hartwick, J. M. M., & Mason, R. W. (2014). Using introductory videos to enhance E-portfolios and to make them useful in the hiring process. *International Journal of E-portfolio, 4*(2), 169–184.

Hicks, M., & Nunan, T. (2002). Generic capabilities and learning portfolios: Practices and developments at the University of South Australia. Retrieved from www.unisanet.unisa.edu.au/directions/abstracts/HicksNunanGQandLearningPortfolio.doc

McCowan, C., Harper, W., & Hauville, K. (2005). Student e-portfolio: The successful implementation of an e-portfolio across a major Australian university. *Australian Journal of Career Development, 14*(2), 40–52.

Rossi, P. G., Magnoler, P., & Giannandrea, L. (2008). From an e-portfolio model to e-portfolio practices: some guidelines. *Campus-Wide Information Systems, 25*(4), 219–232.

Shroff, R. H., Trent, J., & Ng, E. M. W. (2013). Using e-portfolios in a field placement: Examining student-teachers' attitudes towards learning in relationship to personal value, control and responsibility. *Australasian Journal of Educational Technology, 29*(2), 1–17.

Temple, V. A., Allan, G., & Temple, B. W. N. (2003). Employers' and students' perceptions of electronic employment portfolios. Paper presented at the International Education Research Conference, Auckland, New Zealand. Retrieved from www.aare.edu.au/03pap/tem03523.pdf

Weller, M. (2002). *Delivering learning on the net: The why, what & how of online education.* London: Kogan Page.

Whitworth, J., Deering, T., Hardy, S., & Jones, S. (2011). Perceptions regarding the efficacy and use of professional portfolios in the employment of teachers. *International Journal of e-Portfolio, 1*(1), 95–106.

Wilson, E. K., Wright, V. H., & Stallworth, B. J. (2003). Secondary preservice teachers' development of electronic portfolios: An examination of perceptions. *Journal of Technology and Teacher Education, 11*(4), 515–527.

Yu, T. (2011). E-portfolio, a valuable job search tool for college students. *Campus-Wide Information Systems, 29*(1), 70–76.

Chapter 10
E-Portfolio as a Tool to Respond Higher Education Ambitions and Societal Expectations

Béatrice Cabau

Abstract For several years now, we may observe a shift from a traditional knowledge-oriented educational philosophy to the importance for students to acquire skills and competences in the higher education (HE) arena. This echoes the recurrent idea of employability combined with graduates' concern to find their first job and potential recruiters' expectations. Hong Kong is no exception here, and societal expectations and HE ambitions place a strong emphasis on exposure to a range of transferable skills (e.g. team-working, communication, problem-solving) and attitudes that all students will need in their future professional life. This chapter illustrates how e-portfolios can support the reorientation of discourse in HE and societal expectations with a final year seminar with French as medium of instruction as a case study. This seminar focuses on the multi-faceted skills and competences appropriate in a multicultural professional environment. Students are required to compile a reflective e-portfolio with the support of two main activities, such as a simulation project in a French professional setting as well as a professional development plan. E-portfolios and the inherent component of self-reflection/ awareness and other awareness are envisaged as highly valuable tools to better equip fresh graduates for the global world of work.

Keywords Hong Kong · Higher education · Employability · Competences · Skills · E-portfolio

Introduction

Tertiary institutions around the world have to demonstrate to various stakeholders (funding bodies, community members, employers…) that their programmes result in positive outcomes for students (Jones 2010). Hong Kong is no exception here:

B. Cabau (✉)
European Studies Programme, GIS, Hong Kong Baptist University, Hong Kong, China
e-mail: cabau.beatrice@gmail.com

© Springer Nature Singapore Pte Ltd. 2017   141
T. Chaudhuri and B. Cabau (eds.), *E-Portfolios in Higher Education*,
DOI 10.1007/978-981-10-3803-7_10

universities are pressed to enhance the quality of teaching and learning and they need to ensure that the education they offer meets the expectations of students and the requirements of employers. It entails that university education and higher education (HE) modes of learning need to equip students with appropriate skills, knowledge, values and attributes to thrive in the world of employment. It also means that the building and creation of knowledge should be developed together with a reformulation of the concept of knowledge in learning situations and an understanding of working life. The concern for fresh graduates' employability in Hong Kong appears crucial given societal issues, such as the importance given to the concept of knowledge economy, the strong profile of globalisation, the possible shortage of human resources, the intensified access to HE, students' financial burden, i.e. to pay back their study loans, and the increasing demand of European companies for skilled labour force. Hence, HE institutions are at some point responsible to help students accomplish personal and professional growth and develop valuable lifelong learning skills as well as make them aware of employers' needs and expectations. In the light of these new expectations and trends observed within the HE arena, this chapter aims at answering the dual question: why and how can e-portfolios help smooth "the students' pathways from classroom to career" (Flanigan 2006: 110) in the HE context in Hong Kong?

Theoretical Frame

These last years, we can observe a shift towards outcomes-based education accompanied with the redefinition of curricula and assessment in order to include generic skills and graduate attributes in HE. This indicates the importance of the role of universities to prepare students for lifelong learning skills and employment. Lifelong learning skills are defined as "the ability to solve problems, work both independently and in a team, communicate effectively in all formats and on all levels, and self-direct one's learning and professional development needs". (Heinrich et al. 2007: 653) Various terms are used to describe the abilities, qualities and skills expected from graduates who are prepared for lifelong learning in an increasingly international/global environment such as problem-solving, critical thinking, and reasoning skills; information and technology literacy; self-management skills; communication, teamwork, collaboration, and leadership skills; language skills beyond first language; understanding of professional and ethical responsibilities; appreciation of human diversity, cultures and business practices; understanding of importance of lifelong learning and ongoing professional and personal development (Heinrich et al. 2007: 653). This long list illustrates the fact that employers generally expect to see a graduate's achievements not solely related to the subject discipline to be recruited. In fact, "in some employment contexts the actual subject discipline may be relatively unimportant. Achievements outside the boundaries of the discipline (such as the possession of so-called "soft skills") are generally considered to be important in the recruitment of graduates"

(Yorke 2006: 2). Students are then expected to go beyond their study requirements (Heinrich et al. 2007), and skills seem to appear a priority consideration in employer hiring, since "the presence of desirable work skills in new employees means less time and money spent in training and development" (Lumsden et al. 2009: 127).

These considerations are obviously linked to the idea of graduate employability which is defined as "a set of achievements—skills, understandings and personal attributes—that makes graduates more likely to gain employment and be successful in their chosen occupations, which benefits themselves, the workforce, the community and the economy" (Yorke 2006: 8). Universities' reputation is increasingly being based upon, among others, the hiring rate of their fresh graduates. This is the reason why far from being "an intrusion on the proper concerns of academic life" or "being toxic to academic values" as it is often perceived, [...] "a concern for employability aligns with a concern for academic values and the promotion of good learning" (Knight and Yorke 2004: 1, 5). Hence, institutions and employers have to support the students' need in terms of knowledge, skills, attributes, reflective disposition and identity to succeed in the workforce (Kinash and Crane 2015). Hence employability skills include a wide range of generic skills (Yorke 2006). The problem is that academics have various conceptions of generic/transferable/soft skills, which partly explains their limited implementation in university courses (Barrie 2007). This might not come as a surprise, since "universities have seriously underestimated the kind of cultural, institutional and policy change required to implement the graduate skills agenda" (Green et al. 2009: 17). Knight and Yorke (2004) also point to the need to include attitudes to work in graduates' assets praised by recruiters.

For several years now, e-portfolios have been implemented in several universities as a means of enhancing and assessing skills and competencies (Cambridge 2010). A portfolio is "a demonstration of skills and abilities, containing evidence of growth and competence" (Flanigan and Amirian 2006: 103). The predecessors of e-portfolios, i.e. non-digital portfolios, were already considered as supporting constructive alignment, promoting quality learning and bringing about different learning outcomes to those of traditional assessment tasks (Jones 2010). It is important to stress here that the word e-portfolio may cover different realities, depending on the academic contexts and objectives of their use (Hallam and Creagh 2010). Nevertheless, e-portfolios can be classified into three main categories: learning/developmental/reflection/formative/working; assessment; and professional/formal/presentation/representational/career employment portfolios.

Hallam and Creagh (2010) consider e-portfolios as a tool "to assist students become reflective learners, conscious of their personal and professional strengths and weaknesses, as well as to make their existing and developing skills more explicit, with an associated value apparent in the graduate recruitment process" (2010: 186). According to Lorenzo and Ittelson (2005), e-portfolios "allow students to demonstrate competencies and reflect upon the experiences, documenting academic preparation and career readiness. Creating e-portfolios enables students to enhance their learning by giving them a better understanding of their skills, as well as where and how they need to improve to meet academic and career goals" (2005: 1). E-portfolios are even envisaged as a synergy tool between the HE world and societal needs and expectations: "e-portfolio policy and practice can draw together the different elements of integrated education and learning, graduate attributes, employability skills, professional competencies and lifelong learning, with the ultimate goal of developing an engaged and productive workforce that can support innovation and productivity to ensure ongoing national economic development and growth" (Hallam and Creagh 2010: 179). Reflective practice and more precisely, developing skills in reflection appears as a crucial component of e-portfolios for students engaged and responsible in lifelong learning process (Doig et al. 2006).

Contextualisation

Higher Education in Hong Kong: Ongoing Trends

In its report entitled *Aspirations for the Higher Education System in Hong Kong* (2010), the University Grants Committee (UGC) stated that the prime objective of further developing HE is to enhance a nation's competitiveness through nurturing an educated and highly skilled workforce to meet the challenges of a knowledge-based economy (UGC 2010: 24). Students are expected "to contribute in the kind of globalising economy in which Hong Kong must find its place" (UGC 2010: 57). The emphasis put on the necessity for students to adopt an outward vision is justified as follows: "Hong Kong's future relies upon the ability of its best-educated people to understand the wider world and to become persuasive interlocutors with those with whom they do business" (UGC 2010: 58).

One of the consequences is that as in other parts of the world, universities in Hong Kong have been engaged in redefining curricula and assessment and experienced a shift towards outcomes-based education with an increased emphasis on skills to be developed by students (UGC 2010: 78). This was echoed with the alignment of curricula with graduate attributes, learning outcomes and the needs of industry. Under the new four-year curriculum introduced in 2012, universities were expected to devote more attention to whole person education (Cabau 2015b). This echoed the recognition of the importance of skills and knowledge transcending academic disciplines.

Recently, the Quality Assurance Council (QAC) of the UGC stressed the necessity to reconsider students' achievements not only through academic awards, but also other students' abilities which could provide an effective measure of overall personal development:

> In addition to an academic qualification, employers have an interest in how students can apply their learning and in their skills of communication and self-motivation. [...] institutions may be expected to show how they evaluate the needs of employers and other

stakeholders, how they support students in their development during their studies and how their achievements are recorded and publicised (Quality Assurance Council 2013: 7).

This is the reason why the QAC encourages institutions to use external reference points in setting their own academic standards and assessing the achievements of students, among which is the evidence from employers about the expectations for graduate employment (2013: 38).

Last but not least it is worth mentioning here that Hong Kong is not immune to the phenomenon of decline and population ageing. It must therefore deal with a possible shortage of skills in various professions, which are essential to preserve its status as global megalopolis. In various official documents, mention is made of the growing importance of the service sector and increased need for human resources, which emphasise the need to increase competitiveness within HE and develop communication skills and critical thinking of students (Cabau 2014).

HKBU's Vision and Commitment to Graduate Attributes

Hong Kong Baptist University (HKBU) aims at preparing students for the challenges of a globalised knowledge-based economy in order to groom the workforce of tomorrow. Two educational principles are seen here as essential: to nurture students a mindset for whole person development and lifelong learning. As the former president and vice chancellor explained, "HKBU believes 'whole persons' must meet the following requirements: 'solving global problems', 'savvy with technologies', and 'working in successful teams'. At HKBU, it is believed that students who obtain a whole person education also obtain 'employability skills'" (Association of Christian Universities and Colleges in Asia 2012). This is echoed in the University Vision 2020 aiming at improving "employability of students in terms of percentages of employment after graduation and career progression of graduates thereafter" (Hong Kong Baptist University 2014a).

At HKBU, we may observe a growing interest in e-portfolios to facilitate reflection on learning and the university experience. Academic staff is expected to encourage "students to record, access, reflect on and present achievements in ways appropriate to a variety of situations" (Hong Kong Baptist University 2014b). HKBU also supports project-based learning in that "it allows students to construct their own knowledge and skills by working cooperatively on complex and challenging real-life project" (Hong Kong Baptist University 2010a, b).

Employers' Expectations

In the past years, the Education Bureau (EDB) has been conducting surveys on opinions of employers on major aspects of performance of post-secondary programmes graduates with the aim of keeping track of the quality of graduates and employers' views over time. The latest survey covers full-time locally accredited publicly funded and self-financed first degree and sub-degree graduates of 2010 (*n* = 16,615) (Concourse for Self-Financing Post-Secondary Education 2014). Nine major aspects of performance were selected: Language Proficiency in Chinese, English, Putonghua and other languages; Numerical Competency; Information Technology Literacy; Analytical and Problem-Solving Abilities; Work Attitude; interpersonal Skills; Management Skills; Technical Skills Required for the Job; and Knowledge of Current Affairs and Business Issues, Self-learning Ability and Self-esteem. It clearly indicates that Hong Kong employers' expectations go beyond pure academic knowledge to include not only skills but also attitudes.

Amongst the different areas, employers considered Work Attitude to be the most important aspect for the positions held by the graduates, followed by Interpersonal skills. Work Attitude together with Information Technology Literacy was the best rated area. The lowest performance scores could be observed for Management Skills, Knowledge of Current Affairs and Business Issues, Self-learning Ability and Self-esteem, Analytical and Problem-Solving Abilities. The most noticeable gaps between the graduates' performance score and the importance score given by employers were observed for Analytical and Problem-Solving Abilities (3.35 vs. 4.02); Work Attitude (3.73 vs. 4.35), Interpersonal Skills (3.53 vs. 4.10), and Technical Skills Required for the Job (3.49 vs. 4.04) (Concourse for Self-Financing Post-Secondary Education 2014: 11).

The employers suggested further enhancement on Work Attitude, Language Abilities and Interpersonal Skills for improving the performance of first degree graduates in general. Work Attitude was defined as willingness to take responsibilities, making commitment, being more enthusiastic about their work and taking more initiative at work. As for Interpersonal and Management Skills, some respondents recommended that graduates should enhance their team spirit. Employers suggested various ways to improve these aspects, among which more opportunities to develop practical skills, such as speeches, presentations, business writings, promoting contact with the outside world, current affairs and updated professional knowledge.

Overview of the Seminar European Economic and Business Life: Travailler en Contexte International

The specific features of B.Soc.Sc. (Hons) in European Studies Programme (ESP) at HKBU combine a systematic study of European political, social and economic affairs with intensive foreign language acquisition (French or German). The four-year programme comprises two years of full-time study in Hong Kong, a third year spent in Europe with academic study and, whenever feasible, working experience in companies or institutions, followed by a fourth year of full-time study in Hong Kong. In terms of skills, the ESP should enable students "to show familiarity with high, professionally relevant proficiency in one major European language (other than English), so as to apply these skills both orally and in written form to academic and/or professional purposes" (Hong Kong Baptist University 2010a, b). Eighty per cent of the ESP graduates find their first job in the commerce/industry sector (Hong Kong Baptist University 2015a, b).

Final year students of the French stream of the programme want to find a job in a French-speaking environment. It is important to mention here the growing importance of the French community in Hong Kong. The number of French nationals in Hong Kong is estimated at 17,000. They represent the largest French community in Asia and their number doubled during the last decade. There are about 750 French companies in Hong Kong, mainly involved in trade (60%) and banking/finance activities (25%), and hiring more than 30,000 employees (Consulat Général de France à Hong Kong 2014).

"European Economic and Business Life: travailler en contexte international" is a final year seminar with French as medium of instruction taught by the author. It is specifically designed to answer two objectives of the ESP, namely "to train students to become skilled and knowledgeable communicators between Hong Kong/China and Europe; [and] to enable students to contribute to Hong Kong's role as a major international commercial and cultural crossroads" (Hong Kong Baptist University 2010a, b). The seminar focuses on the multi-faceted competences and skills appropriate in a multicultural professional environment to answer students' recurrent concern about their lack of professional experience. Students are hence expected to develop their knowledge about the business world and its environment and to acquire a "know-how" tool set in an occupational context. The course also enhances the students' communication and interpersonal skills in a French-speaking work environment. These multi-faceted competencies build a *savoir d'action* ("how to act") transferable to the world of work (Cabau 2015a, b).

This is mainly a project-based seminar in which students use Web resources to set up a simulated professional situation involving French and local company representatives. The project devised by the students sets the objective to be achieved (e.g. the opening of a French company in Hong Kong) and defines the different steps (micro-tasks) of the mission (macro-task) to be accomplished. The assessment takes place for each micro-task focused on reception, interaction and production of written and oral communication. Each task reflects situations the student may encounter in his/her future work (Cabau 2015a, b). At the same time, throughout the semester, students are required to fill out a document of self-assessment and professional life planning (Etudier.com). It is similar to a personal development planning (PDP), which is defined as "a structured and supported process undertaken by an individual to reflect on their own learning performance, and/or achievement and to plan for their personal, educational and career development" (Jackson 2001).

Introduction of an E-Portfolio

As already mentioned, final year students of the French stream of the ESP want to find a job in a French company in Hong Kong, even if they have generally no clear idea of job nature or sector of professional activity they want to engage in a few months. Moreover, since the introduction of the seminar in 1998, it has looked obvious that they are not fully prepared to enter the world of work, even if they master French at a fluent level. This was reflected in various activities and assignments (project development, interview simulation, CV…) organised in the seminar. As a fact, it appears from discussions with potential French recruiters that it is not the sole proficiency in French per se which is valued: recruiters are expecting fresh graduates to be mature, to take initiatives, to understand and fit in a French company culture, to possess intercultural competences to work with French counterparts, to be knowledgeable about Hong Kong in various domains…

The gap between final year students' competences and skills and potential recruiters' expectations was the pivotal axis for the orientation and format of the seminar as described above. The participation in the Community of Practice working on Learner e-Portfolios at HKBU helped the author grasp the potential of e-portfolios to answer students' needs as a self-assessment/development tool, as a learning tool, and as an employment showcase tool (McCowan et al. 2005: 50). The decision to develop first a reflective e-portfolio was justified as follows: first, reflection was definitely considered as being "at the heart of the process of composing an eportfolio" (Cambridge 2010: 199); hence, a reflective e-portfolio appeared as a promising support in that it would help "students to recognise the variety, depth and ongoing development of their knowledge and abilities, increase their confidence in themselves as an emerging professional, and help them identify skill areas in need of improvement" (Cockburn et al. 2007); second, since the author and students alike experienced e-portfolios for the very first time, it seemed appropriate to focus on one aspect, i.e. self-reflection, as an experimental basis before trying to develop the other two profiles of the e-portfolio.

The reflective e-portfolio was introduced as a compulsory component of the seminar and Blackboard was used as virtual learning environment and course management system. It is supported by three main categories of assignments/tasks given to students, namely the PDP, the project of opening a French company in Hong Kong, and finally the analysis of texts exposing cultural differences between the Hong Kong/Chinese and French/European work environment. It is interesting to note here that class simulations of a typical business environment and the use of e-portfolios were identified among six strategies to enhance graduate employability within the generalist disciplines in Australian universities (DASSH 2015).

Structure and Profile of the E-Portfolio

The e-portfolio was divided into three parts. In the first part entitled "This seminar and me", the reflective prompts focused on students' expectations and needs for this seminar in terms of course format, support tools, knowledge, skills and competences to be developed, the proportion of linguistic versus non-linguistic component to be included, assessment format, and the use of their own and their classmates' experience in France. The second part entitled "My future professional life" focused on students' self-assessment in terms of competences, skills, assets, and weaknesses versus potential recruiters' expectations. Students were asked to answer two questions based upon their reflective work achieved in the PDP as well as in the various tasks they were involved in for the simulation project, i.e. the creation of a French company in Hong Kong. The third part was related to intercultural communication in a professional setting. Given space constraints, only the two first parts will be presented here and their outcomes analysed in the next section of the chapter.

The prompts of the first part of the e-portfolio were as follows:

1. Could you briefly state what you expect from this course?
2. What would be the best learning support tools to help you integrate a professional environment?
3. What should be the share between the linguistic component (the use of French in a professional environment) versus the content part (knowledge, i.e. the work and company culture, economic environment) in this seminar?
4. What assessment formats would be the most adequate to monitor your progress in this course?
5. To what extent can your peers' various experiences (inside and outside the university context, in Hong Kong or abroad) help you for this course?
6. To what extent will your experience in France help you acquire the required competences, skills and knowledge for this course?
7. Do you think this course differs from the other courses you were enrolled in during your studies at Hong Kong Baptist University? If so, please elaborate the reasons by providing some examples.

The prompts of the second part of the e-portfolio are as follows:

1. According to you, what are job applicants' major attributes expected by potential recruiters?
2. State first your assets, then your shortcomings in a professional perspective for the following terms:

Communication
Skills
Competences
Knowledge
Team work

Outcomes and Further Development

A full analysis of the outcomes of the reflective e-portfolio in the above-mentioned seminar is beyond the scope of this chapter. We will discuss the content of students' e-portfolios in the light of two seminar activities and assignments, namely the simulation project and the PDP only.

First of all, it appears that the e-portfolio enabled students to analyse the thinking and reasoning process they were engaged in both activities. For example, students stated in their e-portfolio that the PDP enabled them "to reflect upon our competences/professional future", "to engage in a self-assessment process", "to gain self-awareness of assets", "to better know myself by analysing my interests in a professional perspective", "to understand the necessity to set some professional objectives". Students identified their skill gaps and training needs, for example, their "difficulties to express one's opinions", their "lack of in-depth analysis skills" which became more salient with the regular work on their PDP and the simulation project. They also recognised their assets, such as their proficiency in several languages and their confidence in their abilities "to manage time and stress to provide efficient and good quality services". They were fully aware of the importance of interpersonal skills, where linguistic proficiency is to be accompanied with intercultural competences (Cabau 2015b). In fact, students' e-portfolios sustained their ongoing professional development, to slowly forge a professional identity, which is "a key component of employability" (Cambridge 2010: 153). They complemented the self-assessment work embedded in the PDP.

At the same time, students' self-assessment process was supported by integrating a reflection about an external point of view, namely the recruiters' and/or the company manager's perspective. Students realised the need to ponder about what as job candidates they can offer to the company, what the company needs. In their e-portfolios, they reported their difficulties to present themselves in a favourable way, to show their motivation and dynamism during interviews. As a student explained, "if I know what I can offer the company, I can present myself in a favourable light during interviews". Students also referred to the external perspective highlighted in the simulation project, where they have to anticipate and design tasks that are necessary for French businessmen who want to create a company in Hong Kong.

E-portfolios also appeared to help as a tool for enhancing metacognition (Yorke and Knight 2004) and supporting students' thinking and learning process. Students reported how and what they were learning. Let us take an example: in the simulation project, a student had to present a business plan to a French company manager. In her e-portfolio, she reported the different strategies she used to find and select reliable and relevant information, how she benefited from other students' experiences (business/marketing courses, internship) to incorporate valuable data she would not have thought of. The reflective work she achieved in her e-portfolio was a metacognitive support tool for her between the time gap when the assignment was given and when the assignment was delivered.

In their e-portfolios, students referred to their work mindset: they appreciated the possibility of taking initiative and intervening during the simulation project, which made the seminar "different from traditional courses". They stated that they were eager "to synthesise several skills and competences directly transferable to a professional context", with a predilection for team working versus individual work. Students reported their increased self-confidence and motivation, sense of initiative and anticipation. The regular use of e-portfolio appeared beneficial to help them acquire the skills listed by employers, such as analytical and problem-solving abilities; work attitude; interpersonal skills; management skills; technical skills required for the job; and knowledge of current affairs and business issues. Hence, e-portfolios greatly contribute to help students engage with the course's learning experiences (Barrie 2007: 248), since they offer students the opportunity to ponder about the content and the profile of the graduate attributes such as knowledge, skills, communication or teamwork through learning activities. The e-portfolio with its embedded materialised self-reflection work supports students' personal engagement and consequently consolidates their graduate attributes.

In the light of the positive outcomes of the reflective e-portfolio, the next step is to develop next year a show/public e-portfolio including a combination of multi-media support such as video, audio recording, PowerPoint presentations, reports, digital images, text documents, Web pages, etc. The showcase e-portfolio will help fresh graduates describe to potential recruiters what their strengths are, and "share concrete examples to convince interviewers that they are suitable for the job" (Cheng 2012: 130). The concrete examples here will be among others all the micro-tasks accomplished by students during the simulation project. They will provide "better evidence of their employability skills in ways that are relevant to employers" (Precision Consultancy 2007: 56). At the same time, e-portfolios will be used as assessment tools for the teacher and student peers as for students' ability to interact, adapt, integrate, interpret and negotiate in a French professional setting. These future developments will be operated while paying attention to possible technical problems students may encounter and students' concerns about time management. Furthermore, representatives of a French recruitment company and the French Chamber of Commerce in Hong Kong will be invited as external reviewers to expose their views about e-portfolios' pertinence, format, content as an employment showcase tool.

Concluding Remarks

When analysing the content of students' e-portfolios, findings were consistent with the literature: students reported their increased self-confidence and motivation, sense of initiative and sense of anticipation… But benefits can also be derived for other stakeholders, namely HE institutions and employers. E-portfolios can help prepare students for the transition from university life to work environment, hence enhancing universities' visibility by showing their link to business and industry.

The development of e-portfolios for all final year students would highlight universities' concerns to answer societal demands and expectations. As for potential employers, they would get a clearer picture of the profile, competences and achievements of fresh graduates, especially Social Sciences graduates. Here, a large-scale survey would help determine whether Hong Kong employers would favour the e-portfolio approach as a means to assess fresh graduates' strengths and potential, what kind of evidence e-portfolios should include, and what format and structure would be the most suitable for e-portfolios to incorporate different needs and categories. Students would have a more informed understanding of how to structure their e-portfolios and best present their employability skills according to the type of job they want and the profile of the company they intend to join.

Finally if e-portfolios are to be envisaged as a valuable tool to help fresh graduates smoothly integrate into a professional environment, the contact with potential recruiters can only be fruit-bearing with the first step, i.e. the self-assessment process embedded in the reflective e-portfolio. This is a sine qua non condition for graduates who are expected to have been engaged in their learning process, but also to be ready to engage in their future professional life.

References

Association of Christian Universities and Colleges in Asia. (2012). Report to United Board for Christian Higher Education in Asia. ACUCA Biennial Conference 2012. *Whole Person Education—Trends and Challenges.* http://www.acuca.net/2012/12/Biennial%20Conference%202012%20Report.docx

Barrie, S. C. (2007). A conceptual framework for the teaching and learning of generic graduate attributes. *Studies in Higher Education, 32*(4), 439–458.

Cabau, B. (2014). La mobilité étudiante dans l'enseignement supérieur hongkongais. *Journal of International Mobility. Moving for Education, Training and Research, 2*(2), 45–60.

Cabau, B. (2015a). Rencontres franco-hongkongaises en contexte universitaire. In B. Bouvier-Lafitte & Y. Loiseau (Eds.), *Polyphonies franco-chinoises—Mobilités, dynamiques identitaires et didactique* (pp. 189–199). Paris: L'Harmattan.

Cabau, B. (2015b). The intercultural approach in a Hong Kong academic setting. *The Language Learning Journal, 43*(2), 165–179.

Cambridge, D. (2010). *E-portfolios for lifelong learning and assessment.* San Francisco: Jossey-Bass.

Cheng, C. (2012). Challenges and rewards in the implementation of an e-portfolio project in a higher education institution in Hong Kong. In *International Symposium on Information Technology in Medicine and Education.* http://ieeexplore.ieee.org/stamp/stamp.jsp?tp=&arnumber=6291264

Cockburn, T., Carver, T., Shirley, M., & Davies, I. (2007). Using e-portfolio to enable equity students to reflect on and document their skill development. *Waikato Law Review, 15*, 64–77. http://eprints.qut.edu.au/12480/1/12480.pdf

Consulat Général de France à Hong Kong, Service Économique. (2014). *Présence des entreprises françaises à Hong Kong.* http://www.tresor.economie.gouv.fr/File/402797

Concourse for Self-Financing Post-Secondary Education. (2014). *Survey on opinions of employers on major aspects of performance of first degree graduates in year 2010—Executive summary.* http://www.cspe.edu.hk/GetFile.aspx?databaseimageid=971–0

DASSH. (2015). Graduate employability: How universities can improve students' graduate employability. *Lessons from National OLT Research.* http://graduateemployability.com/wp-content/uploads/2015/10/DASSH-Package.pdf

Doig, B., et al. (2006). Using e-portfolios to enhance reflective learning and development. In A. Jafari & C. Kaufman (Eds.), *Handbook of research on e-portfolios* (pp. 158–167).

Flanigan, E. J., Amirian, S. (2006). E-portfolios: Pathway from classroom to career. In A. Jafari & C. Kaufman (Eds.), *Handbook of research on e-portfolios* (pp. 102–111).

Green, W., Hammer, S., & Star, C. (2009). Facing up to the challenge: Why is it hard to develop graduate attributes? *Higher Education Research and Development, 28*(1), 17–29.

Guide du Bilan Projet. (n.d.). http://www.etudier.com/dissertations/Guide-Du-Cv-Et-Lettre-De/67187056.html

Hallam, G., & Creagh, T. (2010). E-portfolio use by university students in Australia: A review of the Australian e-portfolio project. *Higher Education Research & Development, 29*(2), 179–193.

Heinrich, E., Bhattacharya, M., & Rayudu, R. (2007). Preparation for lifelong learning using e-portfolios. *European Journal of Engineering Education, 32*(6), 653–663.

Hong Kong Baptist University. *EURO 3160 European economic and business life: Travailler en contexte international.* http://www.hkbu.edu.hk/~europe/obtl/EURO3160.doc

Hong Kong Baptist University. (2010a). *Engaging pedagogy.* Retrieved from http://chtl.hkbu.edu.hk/resources/pedagogy

Hong Kong Baptist University. (2010b). B.Soc.Sc. (Hons) in European studies. *Programme handbook.* http://europe.hkbu.edu.hk/european_studies/handbook.html

Hong Kong Baptist University. (2014a). *Vision 2020 statement.* http://vision2020.hkbu.edu.hk/en/Updated%20Vision%202020%20Statement%20(FINAL).pdf

Hong Kong Baptist University. (2014b). *Enhanced learning and teaching using technology: An institutional strategy.* http://chtl.hkbu.edu.hk/elearning/documents/eLearning-Strategy.pdf

Hong Kong Baptist University. (2015a). *Graduate employment.* Office of Student Affairs.

Hong Kong Baptist University. (2015b). *About Hong Kong Baptist University.* http://buwww.hkbu.edu.hk/eng/about_hkbu/about_intro.jsp

Jackson, N. (2001). *Personal development planning: What does it mean?* http://www.northerndeanery.nhs.uk/NorthernDeanery/primary-care/gp-specialist-training/intending-trainer/course-materials/PDP_what_does_it_mean.pdf

Jones, E. (2010). A professional practice portfolio for quality learning. *Higher Education Quarterly, 64*(3), 292–312.

Kinash, S., & Crane, L. (2015). Enhancing graduate employability of the 21st century learner. In *Proceedings of the International Mobile Learning Festival: Mobile Learning, MOOCs and 21st Century Learning,* Hong Kong. May 22–23, 2015.

Knight, P., & Yorke, M. (2004). *Learning, curriculum and employability in higher education.* London/New York: RoutledgeFalmer.

Lorenzo, G., & Ittelson, J. (2005). Demonstrating and assessing student learning with e-portfolios. *EDUCAUSE Learning Initiative.* ELI Paper 3. https://net.educause.edu/ir/library/pdf/ELI3003.pdf

Lumsden, J., Pinataro, C., Baltuch, A., & Reardon, R. (2009). Assessing career skills and competencies with an electronic portfolio. *Career Planning & Adult Development Journal, 25*(4), 126–137.

McCowan, C., Harper, W., & Hauville, K. (2005). Student e-portfolio: The successful implantation of an e-portfolio across a major Australian university. *Australian Journal of Career Development, 14*(2), 40–52.

Precision Consultancy. (2007). *Graduate employability skills*. Melbourne: Business, Industry and Higher Education Collaboration Council.

Quality Assurance Council. (2013). *Audit manual—Second audit cycle*. http://www.ugc.edu.hk/eng/doc/qac/manual/auditmanual2.pdf

University Grants Committee. (2010). *Aspirations for the higher education system in Hong Kong*. http://www.ugc.edu.hk/eng/doc/ugc/publication/report/her2010/her2010-rpt.pdf

Yorke, M. (2006). *Employability in higher education: What it is—what it is not*. In Learning and Employability: Series One, Higher Education Academy. https://www.heacademy.ac.uk/sites/default/files/id116_employability_in_higher_education_336.pdf

Part III
E-Portfolios: The Institutional Perspective

Chapter 11
Using Student ePortfolios to Showcase Students' Learning: Experience from Hong Kong Baptist University

Eva Y.W. Wong, Theresa F.N. Kwong and Peter F.M. Lau

Abstract This paper gives a descriptive account on the pilot in using learning electronic portfolios (ePortfolios) to facilitate students' reflective practice of their learning at Hong Kong Baptist University (HKBU). The opportunities and challenges faced by HKBU are explained to share experience in our continuing endeavour to enhance teaching and learning quality at the University.

Keywords ePortfolio · Learning portfolio · Reflection · Learning-centred experience · Evidence · Outcomes assessment · Whole person education

Introduction

With technologies advancing at a phenomenal pace and globlisation becoming a must, the twenty-first century is exerting great demands on the tertiary education sector, worldwide. Governments and taxpayers expect greater public accountability from higher education institutions. In particular, they are interested in whether their funding has been used effectively to help students learn successfully so that the students, in turn, can make positive contributions back to society. In consequence, simply conferring degree certificates on graduates, showing that institutions have good curricula with good teaching is not adequate. There is an exigence on evidence showing how well students have learned, and how they will continue to learn after they complete their university study. It is hence expected that institutions provide a learning-centred educational experience for students by helping them to become engaged learners, equipped to continue active learning for lifelong employability.

According to Dewey (1933), *"We do not learn from experiences; we learn from reflecting on our experiences"*. So any attempt to show how well students have

E.Y.W. Wong (✉) · T.F.N. Kwong · P.F.M. Lau
Centre for Holistic Teaching and Learning, Hong Kong Baptist University,
Kowloon Tong, Hong Kong
e-mail: evawong@hkbu.edu.hk

© Springer Nature Singapore Pte Ltd. 2017
T. Chaudhuri and B. Cabau (eds.), *E-Portfolios in Higher Education*,
DOI 10.1007/978-981-10-3803-7_11

learned must involve engaging students in documenting and reflecting on their own learning experiences. In this regard, helping students to make use of electronic portfolios (ePortfolios) to collect artefacts related to their academic curriculum and extra/co-curricular activities, then assisting them to journal their own learning experiences and reflections in the same ePortfolios would facilitate evidence collection on student learning.

Within the above-mentioned context, this paper describes a pilot project, the use of ePortfolios to collect evidence and facilitate students' reflection on their learning sojourns at Hong Kong Baptist University (HKBU). The experience of HKBU will be shared to highlight the opportunities and challenges. The paper will start with a brief literature review on ePortfolios used for education purposes. The development at HKBU leading to the ePortfolio pilot will then be outlined. A description of a sub-project under the pilot engaging students in creating and maintaining ePortfolios for a major co-curricular activity will be provided. The paper ends with a discussion on lessons learned from the pilot. It is envisaged that the ePortfolios pilot will continue at HKBU, and that the Student Learning ePortfolios will eventually become part of an overall evidence collection exercise to ascertain how HKBU is fulfilling its education ethos by providing valuable learning experiences to its students.

Student ePortfolio to Help Students Document and Evidence Their Learning

Lorenzo and Ittelson (2005) defined ePortfolio as a digitised, representative collection of one's work or "artefacts", which can be in the form of audio, text, pictures and/or video on a website or on other electronic media. Unlike a Facebook account or personal website or blog, ePortfolios emphasise students' intellectual identity as they relate to their tertiary education.

The utilisation of ePortfolios has the potential to change the nature of learning environments and the ways in which student learning is promoted through different modes of application (Ayala 2006). From a pedagogical perspective, ePortfolios serve to provide a repository of work on which to base subsequent evaluation of students' knowledge, skills, and dispositions relative to their academic programme. Hence, ePortfolios provide a selection of specific artefacts from which evaluation or assessment of specific outcomes may take place and subsequently offers a medium for students to engage in, document evidence of reflective practice and take ownership of their learning (Tubaishat et al. 2009).

Emphasis on the Reflection of Learning Experiences

Reflective thinking is acknowledged as one of the most important aspects of learning and knowledge building in professional practices (Berry et al. 2003).

Reflection not only makes learning more meaningful and relevant, but also helps students own their own learning as more independent, self-directed, lifelong learners.

Barrett (2000) emphasised that "an ePortfolio is not a haphazard collection of artefacts but rather a reflective tool that demonstrates growth over time". It is believed that learning portfolio provides an opportunity for developing students' reflective judgement (King and Kitchener 1994) and higher order or significant learning (Bloom 1956; Fink 2003) that educators desire in students of all abilities. For example, engaging in a process of reflection using ePortfolios may improve learning outcomes such as critical thinking and problem-solving skills because it encourages an individual to generate knowledge connections (i.e. cognitive constructivism) and independently apply new knowledge and strategies that align with his or her value disposition (Chau and Cheng 2010).

For students to develop effective ePortfolios, guidance for reflection is pivotal to reveal how one's own particular increment of learning takes place. As such, it is believed that an intentional design and well-structured learning ePortfolio framework based on the assessment criteria used in graduate attributes rubrics can provide a clear guidance for reflection (Lam et al. 2014).

The Development of ePortfolios at HKBU

Whole Person Education (WPE) at HKBU

Hong Kong Baptist University is one of eight publicly funded universities in Hong Kong. Established in 1956, HKBU celebrated its 60th anniversary in 2016. Since its inception, HKBU has focused on whole person education as its educational ethos.

An education at HKBU aims at developing all aspects of the whole person. In particular, it aims to foster the following seven attributes among its undergraduates who should (Centre for Holistic Teaching and Learning, Hong Kong Baptist University, 2015):

公民 Citizenship	Be the responsible citizens with an international outlook and a sense of ethics and civility
知識 Knowledge	Have up-to-date, in-depth knowledge of an academic specialty, as well as a broad range of cultural and general knowledge
學習 Learning	Be independent, lifelong learners with an open mind and an inquiring spirit

(continued)

(continued)

技能 Skills		Have the necessary information literacy and IT skills, as well as numerical and problem-solving skills, to function effectively in work and everyday life
創意 Creativity		Be able to think critically and creatively
溝通 Communication		Have trilingual and biliterate competence in English and Chinese, and the ability to articulate ideas clearly and coherently
群體 Teamwork		Be ready to serve, lead and work in a team, and to pursue a healthy lifestyle

HKBU is dedicated to delivering WPE that nurtures students to become responsible citizens and caring leaders who possess discipline knowledge and generic skills to succeed in meeting the challenges, and taking the opportunities, of the twenty-first century. In this regard, WPE is not just a concept or goal, but a systematic approach that permeates the University's three major endeavours: quality education, quality research and service to the community. With the outcomes-based approach to student learning fully incorporated into the curriculum, HBKU operationalises our WPE ethos for undergraduates, taught postgraduates and research postgraduates students via three sets of Graduate Attributes (GAs). Hence numerous opportunities, both within and outside the academic curriculum, are provided to deepen students' educational experience to attain the GAs. In this connection, it is deemed necessary to record the development of various learning experiences and generic skills of our students alongside the reporting of students' academic achievements.

The Need for Student Learning EPortfolios

Gathering evidence of student learning is at the forefront of today's higher education initiatives. There is a pressing need to collect direct evidence of student learning for quality assurance and enhancement to address the issue of accountability to public funds. For HKBU, an important element of quality assurance is to show evidence that our students are attaining the GAs as they progress in their study (Chong et al. 2015). This is not only central to the entire implementation of the outcomes-based approach to student learning stipulated by our funding agency, the University Grants Committee (UGC), following the sector-wide curriculum change from a 3-year to a 4-year undergraduate degree, but gathering evidence also ensures the University's continuous commitment to excellence in learning and teaching.

At HKBU, most of the direct evidence of student learning, such as reflective journals and other written work by students are often submitted to, and kept by, individual faculty members or units organising the activities. Under the new 4-year undergraduate curriculum, which offers students more flexibility in their choices of general education courses and courses within and outside their majors, a common platform is required for students to keep a record of their learning experiences holistically and communicate with their teachers and peers. However, knowing that ePortfolios are a good way of providing such a common platform does not mean the implementation can be automatic or even done easily. The concept of using ePortfolios in education is still relatively new. To many faculty members, ePortfolios are entirely within the education discipline and do not apply to other academic areas. Hence convincing the entire University to adopt ePortfolios for student learning cannot be achieved in a one-step implementation, rather, pilot projects on ePortfolios have to be started to let the ideas gradually develop with our community.

Initial Efforts in Using ePortfolios to Enhance Student Learning

The earliest adoptors of ePortfolios at HKBU were certain faculty members in the Department of Government and International Studies (GIS) within the Faculty of Social Sciences. For a number of years, GIS has been offering a successful 4-year 'sandwich' programme in which students spend the entire third year in Germany or France (depending on which major they have chosen) to deepen their language skills and enrich their cultural understanding of the respective countries. As such, students in this programme have to become fluent, both in written form and orally, in German or French within the first two years of study at HKBU, so that they are well prepared to spend the year abroad at the partner institutions. The coordinator of the German stream, in particular, recognised the potential of ePortfolios to assist students in honing their language skills while they are on the HKBU campus, as well as documenting their learning experiences during their time in Germany. Working together with the unit that provides elearning support at HKBU, the Centre for Holistic Teaching and Learning, GIS colleagues in the German stream started experimenting with electronic journal writing in the 2011–12 academic year. At this initial stage, no specific ePortfolio platform was adopted, instead various functions were used in the learning management system, Moodle to mimic an ePortfolio. The aim was to confirm whether students would embrace such a concept and whether they would indeed benefit from developing their own electronic journals to document their learning journeys.

The experiment went well and the response from both staff and students on the German stream was very positive. The experiment and results were shared within the HKBU community and externally at international conferences to the effect that in the ensuing academic year, other colleagues came on board and an ePortfolio pilot project was conducted. The remit of the pilot team was to experiment with selected ePortfolio platforms with the aim of recommending a suitable one for adoption by HKBU eventually. The Mahara ePortfolio platform was on the list as it could integrate with Moodle fairly easily. During that period, the University decided to adopt the Blackboard Learning Management System as a second platform, primarily for outcomes assessment purposes. Blackboard has a built-in ePortfolio system, consequently, the Blackboard ePortfolio was also put on the list for pilot testing. Incidentally, around the beginning of 2013, the UGC provided seed funding for HKBU to set up communities of practice (CoPs) with the aim of further enhancing teaching and learning. The pilot team took the opportunity with a successful application, leading to the establishment of the CoP on Student Learning ePortfolios. The seed funding also supported another CoP on Teaching ePortfolios to document teaching practices and showcase teaching innovations. With work progress and dissemination practices of these CoPs, the University community became more familiar with concept of ePortfolios, both for students and teachers.

Current Utilisation of ePortfolios to Enhance Student Learning at HKBU

The above-mentioned European Studies programme offered by the GIS Department has incorporated ePortfolios as a standard practice for its students to document and reflect on their learning experiences during the year that they are away from the HKBU campus. Apart from this programme, the following outlines further sub-projects under the umbrella of the ePortfolio pilot.

CoP on Student Learning ePortfolio

Colleagues within this CoP are from diverse academic disciplines that have either used ePortfolios as an assessment tool or see it as a viable option for their respective disciplines. Preliminary pilot work has been done by members of this CoP with colleagues leading the GIS programme requiring their students to record their learning activities and reflections using ePortfolios during their off-campus study year. This CoP piloted the use of both Mahara and the Blackboard ePortfolio systems and found both to be suitable hence could not make a definitive recommendation.

Graduate Attributes (GAs) Ambassador Scheme

To help student actualise the seven GAs, the GAs Ambassadors Scheme was established in early 2012 with a generous donation from Professor Albert Chan, the President and Vice Chancellor at the time. The idea is to provide a group of motivated students with training and support so that they can plan and lead activities to assist their fellow students recognise and attain the GAs. Despite the short history of the Scheme, evidence collected from various activities (via ePortfolio and other evaluation methods) suggested that both the ambassadors and their fellow students welcomed the opportunities to work on and reflect upon their achievement of the GAs. It has been demonstrated that the use of ePortfolios can help the GAs Ambassadors re-conceptualise their key learning experiences in this Scheme and student narratives in the ePortfolios could also serve as qualitative assessment tools to ascertain students' attainment of the GAs. This Scheme has also experimented with both the Mahara and Blackboard ePortfolio systems.

General Education (GE) Outstanding Students Award Scheme

To reward students who have excellent academic results in GE courses and their active participation in GE activities and community services, the General Education Office established a "GE Outstanding Students Award Scheme" and encouraged students to showcase their strengths, achievements and reflection on GE and related non-academic experiences through ePortfolios.

School of Chinese Medicine

Due to the good efforts and experience sharing of the CoP on Student ePorfolios and GAs Ambassadors Scheme, plus GIS' pioneering success in incorporating ePortfolios into its European Studies programme, HKBU's School of Chinese Medicine adopted the ePortfolios in the 2014–15 academic year to allow its students to record and document their clinical learning experience while they were away fulfilling their practicum requirement. Interestingly for these students, as their practicum was conducted in a region in Mainland China where Internet access was limited, while they welcomed the introduction of electronic journal writing, the Internet provision had to be enhanced by a good margin before they would embrace the entire ePortfolio concept as multi-media materials could not be accommodated.

Piloting ePortfolios—Experience from a Sub-Project

Implementation of Student ePortfolio in the GAs Ambassadors Scheme

To promote the 7 HKBU GAs within and outside the HKBU community, the Centre for Holistic Teaching and Learning (CHTL) established, in 2012, this student ambassadors scheme to recruit students to support and organise various promotional events. Various training workshops were provided to help students develop certain soft skills, such as teamwork skills, communication skills and project management. Based on their choices of the GAs to promote, the students were grouped into various GA Teams. Having considered the possible positive influences of learning portfolios to independent learning (Mahoney 2007), lifelong learning (Chen 2009) and self-regulation (Yastibas and Yastibas 2015), a team of four students were convinced and they believed that it was a good idea to promote GAs by participating in the ePortfolio pilot project.

The pilot project was carried out in 2013–14. The major purpose was to explore a possible way to implement ePortfolios in a co-curricular programme in order to effectively assess students' attainment of institutional learning outcomes or GAs. An initial idea was to make use of assessment criteria of the institutional GAs rubrics as guidance for student reflection. It is believed that the criteria and descriptions in the GAs rubrics could help guide students to develop structured reflection and ePortfolios. In additional, since ePortfolios could further enhance student learning by supporting the university's academic advising (Chen and Black 2010), the design of this pilot project also considered ePortfolios as a tool to help students set their personal/learning goals, reflect their selected learning experience, and discuss their future action plans.

Unlike the situations in academic programmes, this pilot ePortfolio project was not discipline-based which meant students were not required to write reflection on the specific discipline knowledge or professional skills they learned. Instead, the students set the learning goals which were aligned to their selected GAs from the outset, then they reflected on the attainment of their learning goals and the related GAs after organising and/or participating in selected activities. As such, students had the autonomy to make the decisions to include any learning experience, including learning activities in both academic and co-curricular activities, that they believed were meaningful and constructive to their learning goals.

To achieve the above objectives, the pilot project was designed in three stages: (1) training workshops, (2) building ePortfolios, and (3) showcases and modification.

First Stage: Training Workshops and Consultation Meetings

The first stage of this project included two training workshops (1.5 h each) and some individual consultation meetings (15–30 min each). Since the ePortfolio tool (Mahara) and writing skill for reflection were new to HKBU students, it was necessary to arrange a hands-on workshop to introduce these new tools and concepts. Suggestions on the possible structures of ePortfolios and the submission requirement were also provided. Another workshop about goal setting and study planning was also arranged, which aimed to explain the GAs rubrics and help students connect their learning goals with relevant GAs rubrics. A few individual consultation meetings were arranged for some students who had struggled in setting goals or choosing GAs rubrics. Some students also sought advice on their study plans and appropriate activities in order to achieve their goals.

Second Stage: Building ePortfolio

After identifying the learning goals and starting to participate in the relevant learning activities in September 2013, students were required to write their reflections based on their current learning experiences and build their ePortfolios on a monthly basis. Feedback was given verbally in individual consultation meetings or in written form on the Mahara ePortfolio system.

At the end of the semester, most of the students had developed very comprehensive ePortfolios which were organised in sections (including self-introduction, learning/career/personal goals, reflection, and future actions). They selected suitable work and attached them as artefacts to support their development of certain skills. In addition, some reflective write-ups showed some interesting experience. For example, a Year 2 Translation student mentioned her successful experience of solving a classification problem in translation study, by using an etool that she learnt from a computer course unrelated to her major. She believed that there are always some connections between different disciplines; and having identified these connections, one could develop different creative solutions for problems. Another Year 4 European Studies student wrote in her ePortfolio that she was very happy to realise her new strength of organising concepts and theories in visual form. Furthermore, this new found strength was recognised by her teachers and peers. This showed that students actually benefited through the process of reflection and building ePortfolios.

However, some difficulties were also encountered. Some students did not follow the rubrics criteria when they prepared the reflection because they could not understand the criteria properly. The project tried to address this weakness in the third and final stage.

Third Stage: Showcases and Modification

The final stage was students' showcases which aimed to provide students with the opportunity to present their work and seek comments from different perspectives, teachers and peers. The first showcase event was arranged in the University Library, entitled "How does the eportfolio enhance independent learning and reflective learning?—A show case of student learning portfolios". The setting was informal so as to encourage interaction with the participants. Participants were asked to rate the session using a feedback questionnaire, and the session scored 4.57 for overall quality (1 = strongly disagree; 5 = strongly agree); this was very encouraging to the students.

After the first showcase, the students started to modify their ePortfolios according to the comments from the audience. As mentioned in previous section, one weakness of their work was the structure of reflection. Students were supposed to prepare their reflection based on the GAs rubrics criteria so that they could demonstrate their achievement of that GAs. As such, consultation meetings were arranged to help them address this issue. The students further enriched their ePortfolios by adding some reflection on their previous learning experience in the University. For example, some of them reflected on the learning experience of a year-long exchange programme and HKBU Model United Nations event to ascertain attainment of relevant skills based on the cross-cultural competence and problem solving rubrics.

The second showcase was arranged at an academic conference, Higher Education Research and Development Society of Australasia (HERDSA) 2014 Conference. With the support of the CHTL, two student representatives, Elaine and Panda, prepared an academic poster presentation in this conference. The topic was "Assessing Cross-cultural Competence in Co-curricular Programmes: A Case Study of Using ePortfolio and Institutional Rubric", which demonstrated how a student's narratives in an ePortfolio and institutional rubrics could be used as outcomes assessment tools to evident students' competences in problem-solving and cross-cultural environment adaption. By using their ePortfolio as examples, they demonstrated to the audience how they had used a selected GA rubric's criteria as guideline for reflection. They also explained how their teachers would assess their work with the same assessment rubric. Finally, they concluded the presentation by addressing the benefits to students and HKBU (see summary in Table 11.1).

This poster presentation was very successful, winning them the HERDSA Best Poster Prize in this conference (see Photos 11.1 and 11.2).

Continue Developing Learning ePortfolio

More than one year after this pilot project, Panda still regularly updated her ePortfolio in the Mahara system. She set new learning goals for 2015 and kept

Table 11.1 Benefits of using institutional rubrics in preparing ePortfolio

Benefits to students	Benefits to university
Clear goal setting	Promotes "assessment as learning"
Better understanding of competences to be acquired in co-curricular learning	Helps identify curriculum and co-curriculum gaps
Well-framed reflection under the guidance of rubrics	Enables a systematic collection of evidence and maintain consistency while reviewing portfolios
Accessibility of reflections online and possible reception of feedback from others	Helps the university identify patterns in students' attainment of GAs and reflect on the contributions of various activities to student success

Photo 11.1 Elaine (*right*) and Panda presented their poster at HERDSA 2014 conference. *Photo source* HERDSA 2014 conference website (http://conference.herdsa.org.au/2014/)

writing reflections on her learning experience in both academic courses and co-curricular programmes. Furthermore, she built an ePortfolio to apply for an outstanding student award of the University. Hence Panda has developed a strong ownership to her ePortfolio. This actually echoed Siemens' (2004, p. 6) view on a successful institution-level implementation of ePortfolio, i.e. the effective use of ePortfolio needed to be driven by the learners and their "understanding of applicability and use".

Photo 11.2 Elaine, as the representative, received HERDSA Best Poster Prize in 2014. *Photo source* HERDSA 2014 conference website (http://conference.herdsa.org.au/2014/)

Discussion and Moving Forward

The pilot of using ePortfolios to enhance student learning has been successful as shown by the various sub-projects being established and carried out to fruition. Most notably, two academic units, the Department of Government and International Study and School of Chinese Medicine, have ascertained the value of using ePortfolios to help students record and showcase their learning sojourns while they are away from the HKBU campus. However, as discussed above the integration of student learning across curricular and co-curricular areas is imperative for deepening student awareness of their learning experiences, both within and outside the campus. Hence ePortfolios should be maintained and evaluated over the course of an entire college career and beyond but not on an ad hoc basis. To this end, a position paper to formally establish a Student Learning Electronic Portfolio (SLeP) system starting with freshmen on their entry to the University was submitted to senior management towards the end of 2014–15.

The position paper proposes to introduce the SLeP to support students in the academic advising and mentoring and aims to help students record reflections of their learning experiences at HKBU holistically. Many established ePortfolio programmes in higher education institutions worldwide are introduced during first-year orientation and cultivated throughout the entire educational experience. These programmes often focus on introducing ePortfolio to assist with the advising of students in their first two years prior to declaring a major. While introducing the ePortfolio in academic advising or mentoring programme is a natural starting point for first-year students, the success of a broader and longer term SLeP implementation depends on its integration into the HKBU curriculum and in co-curricular activities related to milestones within the undergraduate learning career. Instead of being a one-time activity never referenced outside academic advising, the position paper envisages that students will continue with their ePortfolios as they transit into their majors. As students continue their learning journeys from freshman to senior years, their learning process and attainment of GAs will be built from one year to another, so students can reflect on their own learning experiences. Intrinsic motivation to maintain the SLeP will become more salient if it is reinforced and reiterated by multiple people and in a variety of contexts over time.

Adoption of new elearning endeavours is a form of organisational change, and often tied to the culture of an organisation. Hence issues such as the timing, dissemination, familiarity and the organisation's readiness for change all come into play. In 2014–15, a quality assurance audit was conducted on HKBU, and then in 2015–16, the ascension of a new President and Vice Chancellor took place. To exacerbate the situation, the University has to decide on a single learning management system as the dual-platform model was deemed resource-intensive for our institution. Thus while the University community may be ready for change, a lot of changes are already happening and the establishment of a SLeP system has not been given top priority. To date, there is still no decision on the SLeP.

Yet despite the uncertainties mentioned in the previous paragraph, the outlook for using ePortfolios to enhance student learning remains sternly positive at HKBU. Enhancing student learning and collecting evidence that learning has indeed taken place, and that the university is adding value to the process, is top priority for institutions around the world. Universities and colleges worldwide have deployed ePortfolios for a variety of purposes, for student-centred learning and reflection, and for the purposes of institutional accreditation and outcomes assessment, etc. Hence the various sub-projects started under the pilot will not come to an abrupt end; the "seeds' planted thus far for ePortfolios, due to the good and hard work of the various colleagues will germinate and continue to grow. Given sufficient time and continuous nurture, the concept of SLeP will take hold and its formal establishment will become inevitable at HKBU in due course.

References

Ayala, J. I. (2006). Electronic portfolios for whom? *Educause Quarterly, 29*(1), 12–13. Retrieved from http://www.educause.edu/EDUCAUSE+Quarterly/EDUCAUSEQuarterlyMagazineVolum/ElectronicPortfoliosforWhom/157386

170   E.Y.W. Wong et al.

Barrett, H. C. (2000). Create your own electronic portfolio: Using off-the-shelf software to showcase your own or student work. *Learning & Leading with Technology*. Retrieved from http://electronicportfolios.org/portfolios/iste2k.html

Berry, F. C., DiPiazza, P. S., & Sauer, S. L. (2003). The future of electrical and computer engineering education. *IEEE Transaction on Education, 46*(4), 467–477.

Bloom, B. S. (Ed.). (1956). *Taxonomy of educational objectives: Handbook 1: Cognitive domain*. New York, NY: Longman.

Centre for Holistic Teaching and Learning, Hong Kong Baptist University (CHTL, HKBU). (2015). *HKBU graduate attributes*. Hong Kong, China: Author. Retrieved from CHTL, HKBU web site: http://chtl.hkbu.edu.hk/main/hkbu-ga/

Chau, J., & Cheng, G. (2010). Towards understanding the potential of ePortfolios for independent learning: A qualitative study. *Australasian Journal of Educational Technology, 26*(7), 932–950.

Chen, H. L. (2009). Using eportfolio to support lifelong and lifewide learning. In D. Cambridge, B. Cambridge, & K. B. Yancey (Eds.), *Electronic portfolios 2.0: Emergent research on implementation and impact* (pp. 29–36). Virginia: Stylus Publishing.

Chen, H. L., & Black, T. (2010, December 15). Using e-portfolios to support an undergraduate learning career: An Experiment with academic advising. *Educause Review*. Retrieved from http://er.educause.edu/articles/2010/12/using-eportfolios-to-support-an-undergraduate-learning-career-an-experiment-with-academic-advising

Chong, K., Thadani, D. R., Wong, W. L., Kwong, T., & Wong, E. Y. W. (2015). A conceptual framework of evidence collection for outcomes assessment: A case study in Hong Kong. *International Journal of Humanities, Social Sciences and Education, 2*(3), 31–44.

Dewey, J. (1933). *How we think: A restatement of the relation of reflective thinking to the educative process*. Boston, MA: Heath.

Fink, L. D. (2003). *Creating significant learning experiences*. San Francisco, CA: Jossey-Bass.

King, P., & Kitchener, K. (1994). *Developing reflective judgment*. San Francisco, CA: Jossey-Bass.

Lam, E., Wong, P., Lau, P., & Kwong, T. (2014). Assessing Cross-cultural competence in co-curricular programmes: A case study of using ePortfolio and institutional rubrics. Poster presented at the Higher Education Research and Development Society of Australasia (HERDSA) 2014 Conference, July 7–10, 2014, Hong Kong Baptist University, Hong Kong.

Lorenzo, G., & Ittelson, J. (2005). An overview of E-Portfolios. *Educause Learning Initiative, 1*. Retrieved from http://www.educause.edu/ir/library/pdf/ELI3001.pdf

Mahoney, P. (2007). Facilitating independent learning using e-portfolios and associated support systems. *FILE-PASS Final Report*. Retrieved from www.jisc.ac.uk/pubication/reports/2007/filepassfinalreport.aspx

Siemens, G. (2004, December). Eportfolios. *eLearnspace, 20*. Retrieved from http://www.elearnspace.org/Articles/eportfolios.htm

Tubaishat, A., Lansari, A., & Al-Rawi, A. (2009). E-portfolio assessment system for an outcome-based information technology curriculum. *Journal of Information Technology Education: Innovations in Practice, 8*, 44–54.

Yastibas, A., & Yastibas, G. (2015). The use of e-portfolio-based assessment to develop students' self-regulated learning in English language teaching. *Procedia-Social and Behavioral Sciences, 176*(2015), 3–13.

Chapter 12
Student E-Portfolios: Unfolding Transformation in University Life in General Education Program

Paula Hodgson

Abstract University students now attend a variety of general education courses to provide a foundation and broader perspective of knowledge across disciplines in Hong Kong. Among the variety of learning activities in such general education programs, students may have undergone different facets of transformation in university life. Students voluntarily prepare E-portfolios targeting the GE Student Outstanding Award and a campus-wide GE Eager to Share award scheme, with award levels through the General Education Office. While students make many instances of gained knowledge and skills in the structured curriculum, evidence of learning transformation through both the curriculum and cocurricular activities are analyzed and discussed from these E-portfolios.

Keywords General education · Transformative learning · E-portfolios · Competence · Generic skills · Metacognition

Introduction

A general education (GE) curriculum was introduced in Hong Kong in 2012, when undergraduate degree programs were converted from three to four years. The University Grants Committee aims to set renewed learning experiences in university study so that there is a need to "strike the right balance between the breadth and the depth of such programs. This would, in addition to helping students master the necessary knowledge and skills for specific professions/disciplines, give them exposure to other learning areas and help them to develop a sense of integrity, a positive attitude, a broad vision and important generic skills" (Hong Kong Education Commission 2000: 9). The goal of the GE program is to promote whole-person education through exposure to a range of transferable skills, guiding principles, and attitudes that students will need in their future professional and

P. Hodgson (✉)
The Chinese University of Hong Kong, Shatin, New Territories, Hong Kong
e-mail: phodgson@cuhk.edu.hk

© Springer Nature Singapore Pte Ltd. 2017   171
T. Chaudhuri and B. Cabau (eds.), *E-Portfolios in Higher Education*,
DOI 10.1007/978-981-10-3803-7_12

personal lives. Students attend courses that are equivalent to 38 out of 128 credits (around 30%) covering more than a dozen three-credit courses for the GE program, which is now a requirement for undergraduate study in the university.

In such GE courses, not only may students build sound foundations for higher order thinking for academic requirements, they are also exposed to a range of learning opportunities. They will experience a variety of learning opportunities in addition to classroom-based lectures. This includes doing fitness tests in a physical laboratory for physical education; taking field trips to outlining islands to explore nature and cultural heritage; exploring city sculptures to examine cultural arts; interacting with stakeholders in communities when doing projects; designing and creating objects in a laboratory; and experiencing new technology applications such as 3D printing or Google Glass.

Apart from this rich mix of learning opportunities, they are assessed through writing essays, project presentations, producing multimedia footage, designing products/objects, quizzes and paper-based examinations on different courses. Among the types of assessment, students build different competences through authentic hands-on projects. They may report on professional practice by interviewing professionals, reflect on the Hong Kong legal system as experienced in the High Court, provide services to communities, and research social issues by conducting surveys and interviews.

In addition to this structured curriculum, they can opt to participate in off-campus GE activities such as taking field trips to interact with indigenous village people on their views on government policy on environmental sustainability, interacting with people playing street football, simulating living with disabilities to experience social inclusiveness, and building social communication and networking skills in small talks circles with business pioneers and students from other institutions. Students can develop transferable skills through such an array of activities.

Learning Transformation

The change to a four-year curriculum has created the opportunity for university students to broaden their horizons through GE. Students can reflect on the process of learning across courses, so that they are made aware of the process of how they make inquiries to meaning-making through metacognition (White and Frederiksen 1998). Students as 'self-authors' create their e-portfolios (Fitch et al. 2008: 51), whereby they can integrate and synthesize what has been learned over time; they can build personal and academic profiles, and evaluate personal interest as they search for their academic pathways for studying majors and gaps in their competence (Miller and Morgaine 2009).

During this transformational learning process, students may critically reexamine and reflect on their beliefs, assumptions, and values while acquiring new knowledge through reframing from a new perspective through the process of personal and social change (Mezirow 2000). Cranton (2002: 64–65) identifies seven facets during this transformation:

1. An activating event that typically exposes a discrepancy between what a person has always assumed to be true and what has just been experienced, heard or read.
2. Articulating assumptions, that is, recognizing underlying assumptions that have been assimilated uncritically and are largely unconscious.
3. Critical self-reflection, that is, questioning and examining assumptions in terms of where they came from, the consequences of holding them, and why they are important.
4. Being open to alternative viewpoints.
5. Engaging in discourse, where evidence is weighed, arguments assessed, alternative perspectives explored, and knowledge constructed by consensus.
6. Revising assumptions and perspectives to make them more open and better justified.
7. Acting on revisions, behaving, talking and thinking in a way that is congruent with transformed assumptions or perspectives.

The first six steps are predominantly a cognitive process in which critical thinking on beliefs, values, and assumptions is reconsidered. However, this would influence what we do and subsequently build new meanings and understanding through reframing from individuals' pre-assumptions in actions and experiences (Clark and Wilson 1991).

Writing E-Portfolios in GE Program

About 84% of members of the Association of American Universities use e-portfolios at the program level to facilitate student reflection on learning and assist program assessment (Mayowski and Golden 2012). Thoughtfully selected artifacts produced by students in GE courses in a program can demonstrate both impact learning and quality accomplishments (Ring and Ramirez 2012). However, it is not common to create e-portfolios for learning or assessment in courses or programs in universities in Hong Kong. While students are encouraged to complete all GE courses in the first two years in Hong Kong Baptist University, they receive a collection of final grades from courses attended. Grades and marks may easily be interpreted as student achievements with reference to the cohort or the holistic criteria, but little is known about individuals' comprehensive cognitive and tacit knowledge.

However, there is much information about individuals' capability and insights gained through a spectrum of learning opportunities. This includes conventional coursework, off-campus GE activities, cocurricular activities, and other forms of life experience such as volunteer activities and internships. Only coursework is assessed, and students are encouraged to do reflections after attending these activities. Information of these events can be viewed at http://ge.hkbu.edu.hk/students/geoffcampus/. To encourage students to build a deeper understanding of personal growth through the GE curriculum, the General Education Office invites students to reflect on different GE learning experiences, and it has created a campus-wide GE Eager to Share award scheme through e-portfolios. Students can build their first e-portfolios from the first year or share reflections on learning outcomes after the completion of all GE courses.

Students are prepared intensively for the format and requirements of writing that is prescribed in the criteria in high-stakes examinations, which is quite different from the academic writing required in university study (Acker and Halasek 2008). First-year students go through a transition from school to university study, which includes learning to evaluate critically the second-hand data available on the Internet, and work through a methodological process of an inquiring research to collect valid and reliable data for analysis. As a first attempt to build student e-portfolios for the GE Eager to Share award scheme, students are provided with guidelines that include eligibility, suggested topics, popular platforms, notes on copyright and privacy, and samples of exemplary past works (http://ge.hkbu.edu. hk/students/ge-share/topics/#eng). Awards are evaluated according to the variety of GE experiences, the depth of reflection, the effective use of multimedia, the language used, and clarity in the organization of content (http://ge.hkbu.edu.hk/ students/ge-share/awards/#eng). A variety of presented e-portfolios from other university students are shown to encourage creativity when building the e-portfolios. Students participating in the scheme can select any public platform to host their work, and they are made aware of the public audience. In addition, in order to promote extended reflections across university study, students have a second chance to submit their work if they are not awarded the highest level in their senior year, and they can choose to include competence gained through learning in their majors as a demonstration of learning transformation in the four-year curriculum. Although the number of first-round submissions was not high, there is evidence to trace some facet of learning transformation.

Transformative Learning Unveiled in Student E-Portfolios

The primary purpose of employing e-portfolios is their use as a 'reflective tool' for learners, who can reflect on the process of standing back from experience and examine how that experience creates personal insights and meaningful knowledge as part of their holistic growth through thoughtful integration into the entire program (Love and Cooper 2004; Challis 2005). A transformational learning process can be observed through the reflective discourse in student e-portfolios. Some students make reflections after they have completed a dozen or more GE courses; some submit their learning journals in which they select topics across college life, and the reflection goes beyond formal and informal learning experiences. Four students using platforms Wix, Mahara, Weebly with self-selected structure, and Wordpress in diary format, have been selected for discussion. In the reflective discourse, students generally describe what they have done to illustrate growth in knowledge or skills instead of changes in perceptions or assumptions.

Students attending core courses such as *English II* or *Public Speaking* have opportunities to practice and debate what they did not have the chance to do in school. Student names have been replaced with pseudonyms 'A,' 'B,' 'C,' and 'D' in this section. Student A: "my first time debate experience in English of which I learned to prepare a good debate speech and how to respond to criticism in an effective way." In the core IT course, students build IT skills after acquiring different educational tools for learning. Student C used "[a] platform called 'bubble us,' and I can manage to organize this complicated and fragile information using a large but clear mindmap." Student A showed her creativity by producing a video with two classmates and posting it on the YouTube platform.

Apart from mastery of different forms of communication, university students are challenged with real-world practice through which they establish heightened awareness of ethical practice in disciplines. In an interdisciplinary GE course, student C learned that the "degree of ethics in a company was interrelated with its profits," and he learned to make judgements on the ethical behavior of employees and the practices of companies.

However, transformational learning is embedded in the cultural context, so learners reflect with reference to psycho-cultural assumptions (Mezirow 1981). Students need to take a course from the core category *History and Civilization*. Student B, a Hong Kong Chinese student, may have had some background knowledge of China as part of his school curriculum but not be able to critically review different primary artifacts to learn about the impact of imperialism and how to interpret these sources through the eyes of modern China until attending university study. However, when exploring between the lines, assumptions can be extracted from those students who were born in the 1990s.

> I learn to analyse various types of historical primary source, including art, literature, material objects and propaganda, so as to explain aspects of China's interactions with the modern world...enhance my understanding of the complexity of China's relations with the world, which ranged from imperialism and violence to artistic and literary exchange...to think in a more internationally-aware way...need to acquire a basic but broad ranging familiarity with the history, literature, regional geography and economics of various peoples around the globe...enhance my sense of a global brotherhood...allows me to gain a more profound sense of my own culture [broadening mindset and attitude]. [Student B]

Student B did not elaborate further on the types of propaganda used, but the scope of his personal view seemed to be more ready to extend to alternatives, i.e., from local to global, while students were expected to assert individual thoughts and demonstrate an awareness of the uses and limitations of different historical evidence in the course.

Apart from the campus-based curriculum, students can participate in off-campus activities that enable them to extend experiences beyond the curriculum. First-hand personal experience as a volunteer can enable these students to interact with people in need in Hong Kong.

I have joined the social service program held by Wofoo. As a student, we could only know the second-hand information reported by the journalist. We went to Kowloon City to visit some subdivided houses. This program enabled me to gain first-hand information on the plight of the lower class, also providing me an opportunity to learn how to help those people in need skillfully. For example, the technique of being a volunteer, communication skills and the correct attitude of being a volunteer. Moreover, it provided me with an opportunity to teach those children English, to help them tackle their academic problems, to make a special connection with the people living in different environments in the same society. [Student C]

The impact on students through community-based learning is notable because they are actively involved in the process of relief actions in which they can learn the psychological aspects and complexity of caregiving (Amer et al. 2013). Through direct contact, student C was in the first stage of transformation, and she personally learned about the gap between reality and news reported by journalists. She had the opportunity to reach out so that she could provide short-term but direct assistance with children living in a substandard environment. She gained tacit skills as a caregiver, although she did not elaborate on the change in her perception of people whom she contacted. However, she gained a heightened awareness of the gap between the environment where she lives and people living in subdivided houses in the same city.

Besides volunteer experiences, there is a wider possibility for university students to participate in exchange programs through which they are exposed to different cultural practices, and the cultural differences provide a good opportunity to question assumptions on ways of doing or ways of working (Wright and Clarke 2010). Students in Hong Kong can choose to experience exchange programs during the summer, and the impact on such students can still be observed.

From Day 1 of the exchange program, I learned not only to be independent, but also to be adaptable and more flexible when a power failure could happen from time to time. Now I appreciate more the stable electricity supply in my home country. [Student A]

It's lovely to teach a group of adorable children in Yingde province. I am teaching them English, while they are teaching badminton skills to me! Such an unforgettable experience! The program not only enhanced my teamwork training and social skills but also raised my sense of social responsibility in seeing these disadvantaged children get educated. [Student B]

Students A and B both realized the prominent divergence of living standards between the place they visited and Hong Kong. Apart from sensing the privileges of living in Hong Kong, experience gained through exchange programs triggers pre-assumptions, that is, a regular energy supply and education for children do not happen around the world. While business students can learn about social responsibility at a corporate level, exchange programs can reach individuals and instill responsibility from curriculum into community.

Nevertheless, the pace of change in the process of transformation varies from person to person. University students as young adult learners have established identities and values, and they were born around the time the United Kingdom government transferred the sovereignty of Hong Kong to China in 1997. These students are at a key stage of becoming independent in terms of thinking and ways of doing things. Student D unveiled a subconscious question about his identify, although he knows that Hong Kong has been part of China for over 18 years now

> I attended another photography class at Communication University of China in Beijing, last 48 hours in Beijing, I still couldn't feel my nationality as a Chinese, but a Hongkongese who started to realize that one day.... [Student D]

Student D certainly did not share the identity of being a Chinese at the time of writing her e-portfolio when she reported off-campus activity in Beijing. The first-hand experience in her homeland did not unfreeze her established belief that Hong Kong is not part of China, although the sovereignty of Hong Kong had been formally handed back after 157 years of British governance. Nevertheless, there is a degree of resistance expressed by student D, and university students are at the stage in their lives where they are building critical analysis and defining individual identity with respect to the historical context (Fairbrother 2003).

Writing e-portfolios is a process of self-reflection, and reflection on actions is one of the most important lifelong learning skills; starting from self-observation and self-reaction, individuals build enhanced self-awareness (Zimmerman 2002). Subsequently, this may contribute to continuous improvement of personal and professional practice (Leitch and Day 2001) and building of metacognition at a personal (Abhakorn 2014) and team level (Nonose et al. 2014).

> I can really experience great team spirit among all our team members. Everyone is doing their best, showing qualities of self-awareness on being confident to oneself, qualities of social awareness on placing empathy on other team members, qualities of relationship management on making good collaboration with teammates and handling conflicts smoothly among members....We are able to voice views that are unpopular and go out on a limb for what is right. [Student B]

> At the end of the day, no matter how good your speeches were, only one passed draft resolution would count as this is why we have a marathon-like conference to discuss possible alternatives for the existing problematic international bodies under United Nations....I realized that how much cowardice I demonstrated as I didn't raise motions frequently. Despite delivering a couple of satisfactory speeches, I was too conservative to raise motions since I feared to say anything wrong. [Student D]

Communication skills, whether spoken or written, are key skills to develop as university students prepare for their future careers. Both students B and D have gone through self-reflection, and they have both addressed the heightened awareness of individual performance when working in different group activities. Student B seemed to have built skills in managing conflicts among team members and can communicate diverse views, while student D felt confidence in making speeches but was still lacking confidence in raising motions. Students reflect on their perceptions of confidence in their communication competence. Nevertheless, growth in language competence can be achieved through continual practice in an immersed environment, which can be shown through reflection in their e-portfolios across years of studying in a university (Buzzetto-More and Alade 2008).

Apart from building language competence, the process of reflection encourages students to revisit established assumptions and original perspectives and make adjustments for alternatives (Mezirow 1990). With a lesser degree of British cultural influence, university students have now been more exposed to Chinese culture compared with their parents. In this university, students have an option to learn more about Chinese medicine practices in GE courses. Courses may cover foundational knowledge of different types of Chinese medicine, Chinese herbal therapy to maintain physical health, acupuncture, and health services in Chinese medicine clinics. Learning experiences in the GE courses serve to build a general understanding of Chinese medicine. However, this provides an alternative perspective to pursue health concepts through Chinese medicine, as claimed by student A: "it is good to learn about health preservation from different perspectives, both the Western and Chinese concepts."

Many students remark on the opportunities to have varied GE learning experiences, including internships and voluntary work. Unsurprisingly, some remark on actions taken after having experiences in GE courses in these e-portfolios. This includes "creat[ing] an online platform for people to exchange or just take the unwanted used items"; "assist[ing] in paddy rice revitalization and other farming-related work in Lai Chi Wo to help to redevelop the rural community there in a sustainable way...changing my lifestyle bit by bit—reducing my daily unnecessary consumption"; "Although it is very common to do assignments for the sake of marks and grades, we decided to keep putting our thoughts and ideas in the blogs after the grading of the 'assignment'...eventually we continue our individual stories in Facebook." Actions are taken because they have established renewal values; students learn to be responsible for actions if they want to maintain a sustainable living habit; and they take continuing action as they redefine assignments as sustainable assessment.

The General Education Office also arranges theme-based off-campus activities, including field visits, guest talks, experiential events, and watching films. Students can participate in these activities without thinking about assessment. Nevertheless, this can have an impact on some students. In one case, a student reflected deeply after watching the drama *Tuesdays with Morrie*, which is a memoir by American writer Mitch Albom, on life's greatest lesson, and he decided not to go for a job interview for a government position because he had learned to redefine life satisfaction, not how much one could earn but how one could work on purposeful academic activities, while many university students build profiles based on a variety of working experiences. While students show growth in skills and knowledge through both curricular and cocurricular activities, they start to build the capability to make informed decisions and take action for themselves.

Limitations in Creating E-Portfolios in GE Program

The variety of GE courses means students can experience multiple exposures and challenges in different contexts in the early years in university life. Reflections through e-portfolios serve as an integral part of different learning experiences (Tosh et al. 2005). The General Education Office aims to encourage them to develop the habit of learning through reflective journal writing using e-portfolios. While some students have had experience in a few GE courses as a requirement to submit the assessment tasks in those courses, many students have little or no experience in building e-portfolios. Therefore, samples selected for discussion in this chapter are very limited, given that all students attend the GE program. Although a briefing session was organized, the participation rate in both the briefing session and the GE Eager to Share award scheme on the first attempt was low. This may be due to a policy that there was no direct email communication from the GE office with individual students while the award scheme was being launched, after all forms of orientation had been completed. Nevertheless, samples of student e-portfolios have been selected, but they are not homegrown examples to provide some concrete ideas on reflection of learning experiences. With hindsight, there can be more concerted efforts between GE educators to encourage student reflection and the use of e-portfolios as tools for continuous learning in addition to the Student e-Portfolio Community of Practice.

Conclusion

Terrel Rhodes, vice president for the Office of Quality, Curriculum and Assessment at the Association of American Colleges & Universities, writes: "e-portfolios are one of the best technologies available to institutions of higher education and their students, as they seek the opportunities to resist the atomization and privatization of education in favor of more integrative and meaningful forms of liberal education— the forms of education that faculty and employers have repeatedly claimed are essential for success in college, the economy, and civic life" (2014: 3). Students can have a variety of learning experiences in the GE courses they attend, including developing competence in service leadership through community service, public-speaking skills through planning structured outlines and paired debates, research skills through making authentic inquiries, digital storytelling skills to produce multimodal reports, and practising critical reflections in blogs. Although these learning experiences may be summarized in the form of grades and marks in different courses, students are encouraged to create their e-portfolios to capture the revealing moments of learning and the representative work they have produced in the first two years of university study.

Generally, these e-portfolios serve to showcase memorable events or activities. Not only do they demonstrate a variety of evidence-based learning (Yancey 2013), but, most importantly, e-portfolios are the testimony for individuals' progress across courses and a period of time (Young 2002; Miller and Morgaine 2009; Yancey 2009). Learning transformation may proceed at different rates and in different directions, it is neither a linear nor a unidirectional path. Students can show the process of personal growth in which they have undergone transformational learning and reflect on experiences that renew their understanding of personal beliefs, assumptions, and values (Ajoku 2015) while they build personal identities through cultural-context activities and set forth on individual academic pathways (Miller and Morgaine 2009). Grades and marks can provide a quick indication of personal attainment, but e-portfolios show the richness of student transformation in their individual learning journeys. These e-portfolios represent snapshots of the early stage of transformation while these students are undertaking the university study. However, there are many more learning opportunities to come, because they need to revisit individual assumptions and perspectives when they attend the senior years. Most importantly, these future graduates are encouraged to start to establish a habit of reflective writing that embraces reflection on actions as a preparation for them to become reflective practitioners in the twenty-first century.

Acknowledgements The author wishes to thank all former colleagues in the General Education Office in Hong Kong Baptist University and with special appreciation of the director, Professor Reza Hoshmand, who provided enormous encouragement in student working on e-portfolios.

References

Abhakorn, M. L. (2014). Investigating the use of student portfolios to develop students' metacognition in English as a foreign language learning. *Journal of Language Teaching and Research, 5*(1), 46–55.

Acker, S. R., & Halasek, K. (2008). Preparing high school students for college-level writing: using e-portfolio to support a successful transition. *The Journal of General Education, 57*(1), 1–14.

Ajoku, P. (2015). Incorporating a transformational learning perspective in action learning sets. *Action Learning: Research and Practice, 12*(1), 3–21.

Amer, M. M., Mohamed, S. N., & Ganzon, V. (2013). Experiencing community psychology through community-based learning class projects: Reflections from an American university in the Middle East. *Journal of Prevention & Intervention in the Community, 41*(2), 75–81.

Buzzetto-More, N., & Alade, A. (2008). The pentagonal e-portfolio model for selecting, adopting, building, and implementing an e-portfolio. *Journal of Information Technology Education, 7*, 184–208.

Challis, D. (2005). Towards the mature e-portfolio: Some implications for higher education. *Canadian Journal of Learning and Technology, 31*(3).

Clark, M. C., & Wilson, A. L. (1991). Context and rationality in Mezirow's theory of transformational learning. *Adult Education Quarterly, 41*(2), 75–91.

Cranton, P. (2002). Teaching for transformation. *New Directions for Adult and Continuing Education, 93*, 63–71.

Fairbrother, G. P. (2003). The effects of political education and critical thinking on Hong Kong and mainland Chinese university students' national attitudes. *British Journal of Sociology of Education, 24*(5), 605–620.

Fitch, D., Peet, M., Reed, B. G., & Tolman, R. (2008). The use of e-portfolios in evaluating the curriculum and student learning. *Journal of Social Work Education, 44*(3), 37–54.

Hong Kong Education Commission. (2000). *Reform proposal for the education system in Hong Kong*. Hong Kong: Hong Kong Education Commission.

Leitch, R., & Day, C. (2001). Reflective processes in action: Mapping personal and professional contexts for learning and change. *Journal of In-Service Education, 27*(2), 237–260.

Love, T., & Cooper, T. (2004). Designing online information systems for portfolio-based assessment: Design criteria and heuristics. *Journal of Information Technology Education, 3*, 66–81.

Mayowski, C., & Golden, C. (2012). Identifying e-portfolio practices at AAU universities (research bulletin). Louisville, CO: Educause Center for Applied Research. Access at http://www.educause.edu/ecar

Mezirow, J. (1981). A critical theory of adult learning and education. *Adult Education Quarterly, 32*(1), 3–24.

Mezirow, J. (1990). How critical reflection triggers transformative learning. In *Fostering critical reflection in adulthood: A guide to transformative and emancipatory learning* (pp. 1–20). San Francisco: Jossey-Bass.

Mezirow, J. (2000). Learning to think like an adult: Core concepts of transformation theory. In J. Mezirow, et al. (Eds.), *Learning as transformation: Critical perspectives on a theory in progress*. The Jossey-Bass higher and adult education series. San Francisco: Jossey-Bass.

Miller, R., & Morgaine, W. (2009). The benefits of e-portfolios for students and faculty in their own words. *Peer Review, 11*(1), 8–12.

Nonose, K., Kanno, T., & Furuta, K. (2014). Effects of metacognition in cooperation on team behaviors. *Cognition, Technology & Work, 16*(3), 349–358.

Ring, G., & Ramirez, B. (2012). Implementing e-portfolios for the assessment of general education competencies. *International Journal of e-Portfolio, 2*(1), 87–97.

Rhodes, T. (2014). E-portfolios in SUNY and the AAU (Association of American Universities), an excerpt from the Progress Report of the General Education Committee, June 2014. Access at https://www.buffalo.edu/ubcurriculum/for-faculty-staff/eportfolio-support/suny-aau.html

Tosh, D., Light, T. P., Fleming, K., & Haywood, J. (2005). Engagement with electronic portfolios: Challenges from the student perspective. *Canadian Journal of Learning and Technology, 31*(3).

White, B. Y., & Frederiksen, J. R. (1998). Inquiry, modeling, and metacognition: Making science accessible to all students. *Cognition and Instruction, 16*(1), 3–118.

Wright, N. D., & Clarke, I. (2010). Preparing marketing students for a global and multicultural work environment: The value of a semester-long study abroad program. *Marketing Education Review, 20*(2), 149–162.

Yancey, K. B. (2009). Electronic portfolios a decade into the twenty-first century: What we know, what we need to know. *Peer Review, 11*(1), 28–32.

Yancey, K. B. (2013). The (designed) influence of culture on e-portfolio practice. In A. Goodwyn, L. Reid, & C. Durrant (Eds.), *International perspectives on teaching English in a globalised world* (pp. 266–278). New York: Routledge.

Young, J. R. (2002). 'E-portfolios' could give students a new sense of their accomplishments. *Chronicle Higher Education, 48*(26), A31–A32.

Zimmerman, B. J. (2002). Becoming a self-regulated learner: An overview. *Theory into Practice, 41*(2), 64–70.

Chapter 13
Library Support for Student E-Portfolios: A Case Study

Christopher Chan

Abstract This chapter explores how librarians can contribute to the use of student e-portfolios. It describes how a faculty member collaborated with a librarian on an e-portfolio exercise for a general education history course. This support consisted of a one-shot information literacy instruction session intended to provide students with the research skills necessary to successfully complete the e-portfolio exercise. In addition, the librarian prepared an online course guide, and was available to students for later consultation. Student work was evaluated by the librarian, and it was found that many students struggled in spite of the intervention. A further interesting finding was that students also sought technical advice from the librarian. Based on this experience, the potential for librarians to provide both academic and technical support for e-portfolios in their role as information professionals is explored and discussed through the theoretical lens of embedded librarianship.

Keywords E-portfolios · Embedded librarianship · Faculty-librarian collaboration · Information literacy

Introduction

E-portfolios are worthwhile additions to the pedagogical toolbox in higher education contexts, however the fostering of an e-portfolio culture at an institution presents a significant challenge (JISC 2008, p. 22). This was recognized by the e-portfolio community of practice (CoP) at HKBU, and the principal coordinator was keen to include nonacademic support colleagues in the group. This included inviting one of the librarians at the University to join the CoP, to which the librarian responded positively. Such involvement is seen by the University Library as an excellent opportunity to better understand the emerging needs of the faculty. By engaging with faculty at the earliest stage possible, librarians can explore what support they

C. Chan (✉)
Library, Hong Kong Baptist University, Kowloon Tong, Hong Kong
e-mail: chancp@hkbu.edu.hk

© Springer Nature Singapore Pte Ltd. 2017
T. Chaudhuri and B. Cabau (eds.), *E-Portfolios in Higher Education*,
DOI 10.1007/978-981-10-3803-7_13

can provide to help faculty achieve their teaching and learning objectives. Another major motivation for the Library was to advance the cause of information literacy (IL) in discussions of how student e-portfolios could be used at the University. Membership of the CoP allowed the librarian to engage in conversations about IL with faculty. From this involvement, an opportunity arose to provide support for one faculty member's e-portfolio assignment. This chapter will analyze the results of this case from the perspective of the librarian, with a focus on the concepts of IL and embedded librarianship.

Literature Review

Many useful outcomes are associated with the use of student e-portfolios, such as supporting learning and assessment, and providing rich evidence of student achievement that can be used to support transitions to employment or further study (JISC 2008). These benefits are discussed at length elsewhere in this volume, so these points will not be rehashed in this review. Instead, it will focus on two areas of particular relevance to this case study. First, the specific use of e-portfolios to enhance IL abilities will be examined. Second, the support of e-portfolio practice will be connected to the concept of embedded librarianship, which has been popularized for some time in the library science literature, but may be less familiar to academics outside the discipline. This will provide an additional perspective from which to analyze the experience and results of the case study under review.

Information Literacy and Academic Librarianship

For decades, IL has been an integral concept to the theory and practice of librarianship. Despite this fact, IL has been notoriously difficult to define precisely, with differing emphases on behavioural and sociocultural interpretations of the concept. The most recent definition adopted by the Association of College and Research Libraries (2015) does well in combining the two approaches

> Information literacy is the set of integrated abilities encompassing the reflective discovery of information, the understanding of how information is produced and valued, and the use of information in creating new knowledge and participating ethically in communities of learning.

No matter how it is defined, it is widely accepted that IL is essential to success in the modern knowledge society. Library and information professionals working in higher educational contexts are constantly searching for effective methods to nurture these abilities in their students, especially in collaboration with faculty members (Mounce 2010).

IL support by librarians has traditionally taken the form of "one-shot" sessions or workshops, however these have fallen out of favour in recent years

(Mery et al. 2012). Such sessions are standalone workshops, typically lasting fifty minutes. Although relatively easy to organize and plan for, by their nature they cannot provide more than a basic overview of library and research skills. More involved approaches, such as the teaching of credit courses, are preferred, and the "gold standard" is a situation in which both librarians and faculty work together as equals in developing the IL components of courses (Sullivan and Porter 2016, p. 34). Working with faculty on the use of e-portfolios to support IL certainly falls into this category.

Supporting Information Literacy Learning with E-Portfolios

The use of portfolios to document and assess IL abilities is not a new phenomenon. As far back as the late 1990s, Fourie and van Niekirk (1999) described a collaboration between the Department of Information Science and the Library Services of the University of South Africa to use portfolios to assess student achievement in a research information skills course. Advantages cited included an emphasis on the learning and growth process and authentic assessment. Authenticity was also cited as a key reason for the use of research portfolios to assess the IL goals of a credit-bearing course offered to students at Penn State University to prepare them for their honours thesis (Snavely and Wright 2003). At the time of reporting, a 'hard copy' portfolio was used, although the authors indicated they were exploring the possible use of e-portfolios. Physical portfolios also appear to have been used by Sonley et al. (2007) in assessing an IL module delivered at the University of Teesside in 2004. They too saw portfolios as a form of authentic assessment, and their application of portfolios illustrates their suitability in the assessment of IL. Students were required to produce a bibliography, but also had to present evidence to demonstrate the process that led to the bibliography. This included search strategy, identification of potential sources, and source evaluation, all of which are fundamental IL abilities.

Somewhat less plentiful are studies that look at the use of e-portfolios in the assessment of IL support. However, it could be argued that from a pedagogical perspective the benefits are essentially the same, with e-portfolios providing essentially administrative and logistical advantages. Buzzetto-More has written extensively on how e-portfolios can be used to build IL skills. She notes that e-portfolio creation requires students to strategically acquire and evaluate information artifacts, reflect on the process, and then synthesize information in the development and presentation of the portfolio (Buzzetto-More 2010). A concrete example of this is given by Florea (2008) in her description of a librarian-designed component of an e-portfolio assignment for nursing students at the University of Rhode Island. Students needed to locate a scholarly article relevant to the research topic they were studying, and include a reflective piece on the content of the article as well as the search strategies they used to obtain it. An important benefit of the project was the enhancement of faculty/librarian collaboration (Florea 2008, p. 426).

The University of Rhode Island case is particularly instructive to the discussion here, as it provides an example of integrating an IL component into a faculty-led e-portfolio initiative, as opposed to a standalone portfolio for research skills. This is closer to the model used by the present case study, and can also be described as an example of embedded librarianship. A brief review of this concept follows.

Embedded Librarianship

The concept of embedded librarianship has been in vogue for several years. The phrase itself is derived from "embedded journalists," a term popularized during the Iraq War to describe journalists that accompanied US combat units during the invasion of Iraq in 2003. Applied to information work, it places the librarian in the midst of where the user is, allowing the on-demand teaching of IL skills as the need arises (Shumaker 2009, p. 239). It has been described as a "distinctive innovation that moves the librarians out of libraries and creates a new model of library and information work" (Shumaker 2012, p. 4). As noted by Carlson and Kneale (2011, p. 167), this model promises to overcome the shortcomings of the traditional "one-shot" library instruction classes that make up the bulk of many IL programmes, by encouraging stronger connections with students and facilitating more frequent and deeper interactions between faculty and librarians.

How librarians actually go about embedding themselves into courses is an area where practitioners need to apply what Carlson and Kneale (2011, p. 168) refer to as an "entrepreneurial mindset." Opportunities need to be proactively sought out, and librarians need to be able to effectively communicate to faculty what they contribute. An early example of this in the context of embedded librarianship is again provided by the University of Rhode Island, where librarians in 2005 had to sell the concept of embedding librarians in their course management system to distance learning faculty (Ramsay and Kinnie 2006). This type of outreach is challenging, and to be successful librarians need to draw on existing faculty contacts and create new contacts by getting involved in campus committee work and social events (Knapp et al. 2013). Stemming from their belief that much can be gained from engaging in the practice of embedded librarianship, Kesselman and Watstein (2009, p. 398) have called on practitioners to explore new embedded roles. One such role could be the support of student e-portfolio initiatives by faculty.

Two points arise from the discussion above. First, while the use of portfolios to enhance IL learning has been fairly well-covered in the literature, additional case studies (especially ones dealing with e-portfolios), would provide valuable additional depth. Second, the use of e-portfolios in IL instruction could be described as an example of embedded librarianship. A description and analysis of a case study using the framework of embedded librarianship could provide unique insights. The remainder of this chapter attempts to address both of these points.

Library Support for a Course-Based Student E-Portfolio Exercise

During a conversation arising from the regular meetings of the CoP, a faculty member expressed interest in incorporating support from the Library into her upcoming general education history course (GCHC 1006—Modern China and World History). In a follow-up meeting, the faculty member met with the librarian to discuss the course content, how the student e-portfolio would be used, and where students could benefit from enhanced IL support. One of the e-portfolio exercises would involve students locating visual primary sources (including an historical photograph and a political cartoon) that they would embed in their e-portfolio along with critical commentary on the source. This was identified as an opportunity for the librarian to provide guidance on locating primary sources using Library-subscribed resources. Undergraduate students are often unfamiliar with the digitized archival sources now available to academic libraries, and such resources would be particularly useful to students on GCHC 1006 looking to enrich their e-portfolios. Useful and reliable free Internet resources would also be covered. Additionally, guidance would be given to students on how to provide proper citations for the primary sources that they discover. This would support their ethical use of sources, which is an important aspect of IL.

The librarian provided this support through two major channels

- **A course-integrated instruction session** where students were guided through hands-on practice with relevant databases. The fundamentals of citing primary sources in APA style were also covered.
- **An online course guide** bringing together all of the material covered in the instruction session for the easy reference of students.

Apart from these primary means of support, the librarian was also included on the Blackboard course site in a teaching assistant role. This allowed him to add a link to the course guide, and provided a means for students to get in touch for help and assistance.

Assessment of Library Support

To gauge the effectiveness of the Library's support, student e-portfolio submissions were assessed against a simple rubric designed to address the following learning outcomes:

- **Make effective use of appropriate search tools** in order to find relevant primary sources for the e-portfolio exercise
- **Construct correct citations for primary sources in APA style** so that they can provide appropriate references in their e-portfolios

The rubric and the results of the assessment are reproduced below (Tables 13.1 and 13.2).

At the conclusion of the course, the faculty member provided the librarian with the relevant parts of the student e-portfolios for assessment. In total, 39 submissions were received, and the results of the assessment were as follows:

Outcome 1—Effective Use of Appropriate Search Tools

The results here were somewhat mixed. Although only a handful of students did not provide any evidence at all of their search, a large proportion only achieved level 1, indicating a reliance on commercial search engines and Wikipedia. Despite being introduced to appropriate free and Library-subscribed sources for their e-portfolio assignment, only about half of the students actually used them to find their historical photograph. An even smaller number (about 40%) used them to find their political cartoon. Nevertheless, to this author even this level of use is anecdotally much higher than would be expected if no instruction at all had been provided. Of course, in the absence of a control group it is impossible to make such a claim definitively.

Outcome 2—Citation Accuracy

For those students who did provide a citation, most achieved quite highly. However, a dishearteningly large number of students (approximately 30% of the class) either did not provide a citation at all or thought it was acceptable to merely provide the URL to an online citation. These results demonstrate the importance of providing guidance on this basic academic practice in lower level undergraduate courses.

As they represent the outcomes of just one course at a single institution, the above results are fit mainly to inform improvements to this specific intervention, should it be repeated in the future. No generalizable conclusions are claimed, however it is hoped that the detailed description of the process and the discussion of the results that follows below will be informative to practitioners.

Discussion

This case study confirmed that portfolios are an effective means to assess student IL skills. The evidence is recorded and accessible. This is in contrast to many other librarian-led IL instruction sessions/programmes, where evidence of student

Table 13.1 Library assessment rubric for GCHC 1006

	No evidence	Level 1	Level 2	Level 3
Make effective use of appropriate search tools to find relevant primary sources	Did not provide a cartoon/photograph **OR** no indication of where it came from	Retrieved their cartoon/photograph from a non-scholarly source (e.g. Wikipedia, commercial website)	Retrieved their cartoon/photograph from an appropriate free scholarly source (e.g., academic/government website, etc.)	Retrieved their cartoon/photograph from an appropriate paid scholarly source (e.g. Library-subscribed database)
Cite primary sources accurately in APA style	Did not include a citation **OR** only provided a URL	Citations are missing key elements (e.g. author, title, date, etc.). Citation formatting includes many errors	Citations include most key elements (missing only one). Citation formatting includes many errors	Citations include all key elements. Citation formatting includes some errors

Table 13.2 Library assessment results for GCHC 1006

	No evidence	Level 1	Level 2	Level 3	Total
Assessment piece 1: Historical photograph					
Effective use of appropriate search tools	7 (18%)	12 (31%)	15 (38%)	5 (13%)	39 (100%)
Citation accuracy	12 (31%)	2 (5%)	9 (23%)	16 (41%)	39 (100%)
Assessment piece 2: Political cartoon					
Effective use of appropriate search tools	5 (13%)	18 (46%)	6 (15%)	10 (26%)	39 (100%)
Citation accuracy	11 (28%)	3 (8%)	15 (38%)	10 (26%)	39 (100%)

learning may go unrecorded. The portfolio assessment experience was also of higher quality relative to other approaches. As suggested by Sonley et al. (2007), the portfolio assessment was much more authentic compared to those with which the librarian had prior experience. Instead of artificially assessing IL learning in isolation, these skills were assessed in terms of how well they were applied by students in the completion of the e-portfolio exercise. Analysis of these results will inform potential improvements to the way that librarians support student e-portfolios.

Apart from the quality of the assessment, one must admit that the support provided by the librarian for the course (i.e. a one-shot instruction session plus an online course guide) was nothing out of the ordinary. However, the case study did provide a glimpse of a potential expanded role for librarians in supporting e-portfolios. As with all library sessions, students were encouraged to contact the librarian with questions. One of them did so, coming to see the librarian in person to seek some clarification on how to cite the primary source she had chosen. Later, however, she also sought advice from the librarian on how to embed an online video into her portfolio. The librarian was able to quickly offer assistance and resolve the student's problem. As faculty often highlight dealing with technical problems as a major hindrance in their adoption of e-portfolios, the expansion of the librarian's role into this type of basic technical assistance could help spur uptake of e-portfolios. It could be further speculated that having librarians rather than technical support staff take up this role would deliver certain advantages. For example, librarians have a better knowledge of pedagogy and are also more likely to be familiar with and invested in the course content. Expertise in information use and research combined with technical skills could allow librarians to deliver effective support for student e-portfolios. It should also be noted that librarians, as information professionals, should be able to handle the types of basic technical questions such as the one encountered in the case study.

Potential Improvements

Based on the results, and after reflecting on the overall experience, the following suggestions are made for improving and further developing the library's IL support for course-based student e-portfolios:

- **Encourage students to make more use of the Library support made available for the course**. Only three students returned to the librarian with questions after the face-to-face session. This is a relatively low number, given that around forty students in total were enrolled in the course. The results show that many students performed poorly on the assessed parts of their portfolios, and would have benefited from further help and advice from the librarian. More interactions could be encouraged by the librarian making greater use of the tools available to an embedded librarian. For example, an area of the course site's discussion forum could be used to inform students of common problems students are having with citations.
- **Truly embed the librarian into the assignment by providing them with direct access to student e-portfolios**. This would have made a practical improvement to the support provided by the librarian, as the faculty would not have needed to spend time extracting student work to send to the librarian for assessment. More importantly, this type of access could improve the quality of the feedback given to the students by providing the librarian with a more holistic overview of the content of the e-portfolios.

  It should be noted that this suggestion is dependent on the e-portfolio platform supporting this type of access. The faculty in charge was prepared to offer such access to the librarian, but the e-portfolio platform used (Blackboard) did not allow for it.
- **Improve the quality of assessment used**. There is room for improvement in the way student IL abilities were assessed in this case study. The assessment of the second outcome (construction of correct APA-style citations for primary sources) was relatively robust as it was possible to unambiguously judge the quality of the citation presented. However, the approach used for the first outcome (make effective use of search tools) is less convincing. Essentially, the quality of the tool from which they found their primary source was used to infer student ability to search effectively. This was the best that could be done given the limited information available in the student's e-portfolio. However, a student who retrieved his/her source using a lower quality tool may have had good reasons for doing so. Perhaps it was the best tool available for their topic, and they evaluated the source for reliability before deciding to use it. In other words, they may have applied their IL skills in selecting the source. Unfortunately, there was no way to tell what the students were thinking when they selected sources for their e-portfolios.

  One enhancement would be to ask students to write up a brief research log where they make explicit their reasons for using particular search tools and for selecting their primary sources. This type of IL assessment can be an effective means for librarians to examine the student research process (Nutefall 2004).

Conclusion

This chapter has presented a detailed description and analysis of a librarian's support for an e-portfolio assignment, which arose from membership of the e-portfolios CoP. Drawing upon the library science literature, this discussion was informed by past work on the use of portfolios to enhance the teaching of IL skills, and also by the concept of embedded librarianship. The experience was certainly instructive for both the librarian and faculty member involved, and as the reflections above make clear, it is hoped that this approach can be further iterated and improved upon in future. The unique support for e-portfolios that librarians bring to the table as information professionals is particularly worth exploring further. By providing both IL skills expertise and technical support, the academic librarian is arguably an ideal partner for faculty members interested in adopting e-portfolios into their teaching. If this proves accurate, and assuming e-portfolios are widely adopted at an institution, another line of investigation will be determining how librarians can provide this level of support to a large number of courses in a sustainable manner.

References

Association of College & Research Libraries. (2015). *Framework for information literacy for higher education.* http://www.ala.org/acrl/standards/ilframework. Accessed July 1, 2015

Buzzetto-More, N. (2010). Assessing the efficacy and effectiveness of an e-portfolio used for summative assessment. *Interdiscip J E-Learning Learn Objects, 6,* 61–85. Retrieved from: http://www.editlib.org/p/44774/

Carlson, J., & Kneale, R. (2011). Embedded librarianship in the research context: Navigating New Waters. *College & Research Libraries News, 72,* 167–170.

Florea, M. (2008). Using WebCT, Wiki spaces, and E-portfolios for teaching and building information literacy skills. *Journal of Library Administration, 48,* 411–430. doi:10.1080/01930820802289466

Fourie, I., & Van Niekerk, D. (1999). Using portfolio assessment in a module in research information skills. *Education for Information, 17,* 333–352.

JISC. (2008). *Effective practice with E-Portfolios.* http://www.jisc.ac.uk/media/documents/publications/effectivepracticeeportfolios.pdf. Accessed March 3, 2016.

Kesselman, M. A., Watstein, S. B. (2009). Creating opportunities: Embedded librarians. *Journal of Library Administration, 49,* 383–400. doi:10.1080/01930820902832538

Knapp, J. A., Rowland, N. J., & Charles, E. P. (2013). Retaining students by embedding librarians in undergraduate research experiences. *Reference Services Review, 42,* 129–147.

Mery, Y., Newby, J., & Peng, K. (2012). Why one-shot information literacy sessions are not the future of instruction: A case for online credit courses. *College & Research Libraries, 73,* 366–378.

Mounce, M. (2010). Working together: Academic librarians and faculty collaborating to improve students' information literacy skills: A literature review 2000–2009. *The Reference Librarian, 51*, 300–320. doi:10.1080/02763877.2010.501420

Nutefall, J. (2004). Paper trail: One method of information literacy assessment. *Research Strategies, 20*, 89–98. doi:10.1016/j.resstr.2005.07.004

Ramsay, K. M., & Kinnie, J. (2006). The embedded librarian. *Library Journal, 131*, 34.

Shumaker, D. (2009). Who let the librarians out? Embedded librarianship and the library manager. *Reference and User Services Quarterly, 48*, 239–257.

Shumaker, D. (2012). Embedded librarians in higher education. *Embedded librarian: Innovative strategies for taking knowledge where it's needed* (pp. 43–64). Medford, NJ: Information Today Inc.

Snavely, L. L., & Wright, C. A. (2003). Research portfolio use in undergraduate honors education: Assessment tool and model for future work. *The Journal of Academic Librarianship, 29*, 298–303. doi:10.1016/S0099-1333(03)00069-7

Sonley, V., Turner, D., Myer, S., & Cotton, Y. (2007). Information literacy assessment by portfolio: a case study. *Reference Services Review, 35*, 41–70. doi:10.1108/00907320710729355

Sullivan, B. T., & Porter, K. L. (2016). From one-shot sessions to embedded librarian. *College & Research Libraries, 77*, 34–37.

Conclusion

Tushar Chaudhuri and Beatrice Cabau

Implementing eportfolios in higher education echoes the need to take into consideration a constantly changing learning environment with new technological tools, the university's tasks to (better) equip students with skills and not only knowledge, community's expectations in terms of academic knowledge and training, and last but not least, students with new demands, needs and expectations. The chapters included in this volume have looked at the affordances and constraints of e-portfolios implementation in higher education from different perspectives and against the backdrop of the research on eportfolios over the last ten years, which pointed out that eportfolios could lead to flexible assessment methods, training of higher level skills such as reflection and evaluation and generally allow learners to take ownership of their learning. At the same time the authors were also aware of the constraints of using eportfolios as assessment methods at the course level. The research already pointed out that eportfolios when taking a top-down institutional approach could easily lead to loss of purpose. Very often students are not aware of why the eportfolio is necessary and how it could help them. In this case the eportfolio is just another assignment and is not able to exploit its full potential.

While the authors in this volume generally confirm both the affordances that eportfolios as assessment bring into their courses and the constraints that go along with implementing them at the classroom level, a more granular picture emerges from these individual and multidisciplinary perspectives. Authors observe that eportfolios in general education courses "reveal students' transformational learning process, their various learning experiences as well as their progress across courses" (Hodgson). They also observe that eportfolios in language and area studies courses "helped students develop their intercultural and reflexive competence in diverse situations, and foster (...) life-long learning" (Chui and Dias). In a business communications course eportfolios were observed to have "enhanced collaboration and interaction between students and between students and the teacher" (Linger). This observation was echoed also in a numeracy course where "eportfolios as a platform for students' constant reflections throughout the course acted as a foundation for further interaction among students" (To). Last but not least eportfolios which were "highly structured and closely integrated with in-class activities were found to be

T. Chaudhuri and B. Cabau (eds.), *E-Portfolios in Higher Education*,
DOI 10.1007/978-981-10-3803-7

most successful" as attested to by observations in a history course (Ladds). Generally the themes "enhanced interaction" and the "need for more structure based on in-class activities" seem to be the most frequently occurring observations throughout the chapters in this volume. From the perspective of higher education and teaching design, authors do seem to agree that eportfolios instil a "sense of empowerment in students and enable them to learn about learning" (e.g. Sivan in this volume). They can also lead to "increased self-confidence and motivation, sense of initiative and anticipation among students" (Cabau).

On the other hand, recurrent themes that emerge are also that students and teachers working with eportfolios for the first time require ready and available support both in terms of technology use as well as the use of pedagogical models in order to see the outcomes set for eportfolios being achieved. Though eportfolios can "facilitate the development of collaborative and participatory pedagogies" (Ellis in this volume) which are essential for the relevance and value of higher education, they must address "key issues such as engaging students and staff and integrating technology at the same time" (Pegrum and Oakley in this volume). Authors point out that though eportfolios ultimately lead to enhanced technology skills in students, more support is required as "lecturers, students and even potential recruiters express reservations that eportfolios can be time consuming" (Cheung et al. in this volume). The resistance to e-portfolios is also identified as being "based in a combination of regional, institutional and entrenched disciplinary cultures but which can be broken through a dramatic cultural shift brought about by the collaborative efforts of the department, the instructor and the institution" (Ladds).

This last point of bringing around a "dramatic cultural shift" through collaboration actually defines the whole purpose of this book. Though based on individual case studies, the picture that emerges through these studies is one of successful collaborative efforts which brought together various stakeholders within the institution based on some common goals relating to eportfolios and assessment which were interpreted individually and then implemented through collaborative effort. First, it was the collaboration between teachers and students which was evident in the discussions and interactions with students on how exactly a portfolio should look like in terms of their profile, content and orientation in order to be effective and support various skills. Supporting various skills also involves collaboration between various units within the same institution. An example of this second level of collaboration to implement eportfolios was the participation of among others experts on information literacy from the library who not only worked with teachers but also with students to make them aware of how using a eportfolio not only enhances technology skills but also information literacy skills which are essential to survive in a technology-driven knowledge-based society. Workshops and mentoring sessions provided by the teaching and learning centre towards the use of the technology itself contributed to a better understanding of technology and in turn to a better rate of acceptance and use in the classroom.

Finally, it was the exchange of ideas and the collaborative search for solutions across the table of the Community of Practice which enabled the implementation of eportfolios across a variety of disciplines but more importantly it enabled the dialogue between academic and non-academic parts of the institution. It is ultimately this dialogue which could lead to the shift in culture which is described in different words by the authors of different disciplines of this volume. The key words that emerge from this volume and should be highlighted in conclusion are therefore *interaction, collaboration, partnership* and *dialogue* to enable students to grasp and assimilate the concept of life-long learning.

Appendix A

Implementing Student E-Portfolios on the course level. A Resource of CoP REFLECT: A Community of Practice on Student Eportfolios Online: http://copreflect.weebly.com/resources.html

Copyright: Dr. Tushar Chaudhuri, Dr. Béatrice Cabau, Ms. Céline Dias, Miss Chui Chi Shan, Prof Atara Sivan, Dr. Catherine Ladds, Dr. Paula Hodgson, Mr. Chris Chan, Dr. Lisa Deng, Dr. Simon To, Dr. Warren Linger, Dr. Dimple Thadani

Would you like to introduce e-portfolios to your course? This might help!
What experts have to say about e-portfolios!
What is a student (e)portfolio?

- A portfolio is a purposeful collection of student work that exhibits the student's efforts, progress, and achievements in one or more areas. The collection must include student participation in selecting contents, the criteria for selection, the criteria for judging merit, and evidence of student self-reflection.[1]
- (An e-portfolio) is a digitized collection of artifacts including demonstrations, resources and accomplishment that present a student. This collection can be comprised of text-based, graphic or multimedia elements archived on a website or other electronic media. Eportfolio encourage personal reflection and often involve the exchange of ideas and feedback.[2]
- In an academic context, these artifacts might include a student's essays, posters, photographs, videos, artwork, and other course-related assignments. Additionally, the artifacts might also pertain to others aspects of a student's life, such as volunteer experiences, employment history, extracurricular activities, and so on. However, while these digital artifacts are important, they are static products. They are simply things that the student has produced or done or experienced, and a good eportfolio ought to be more than just a collection of products. It should also be a process—specifically, the process of generating

---

[1]Paulson, F. Leon, Paulson, P.R., & Meyer, C.A. (1991). What makes a portfolio a portfolio? *Educational Leadership*. 60-63. Retrieved from http://web.stanford.edu/dept/SUSE/projects/ireport/articles/eportfolio/what%20makes%20a%20portfolio%20a%20portfolio.pdf.
[2]Loernzo, G.,& Lttelson, J.(2005). An overview of e-portfolio. *Educause learning initiative*. Retrieved from https://net.educause.edu/ir/library/pdf/eli3001.pdf.

© Springer Nature Singapore Pte Ltd. 2017
T. Chaudhuri and B. Cabau (eds.), *E-Portfolios in Higher Education*,
DOI 10.1007/978-981-10-3803-7

new or deeper learning by reflecting on one's existing learning. It's important, then, to think of an eportfolio as both a product (a digital collection of artifacts) and as a process (of reflecting on those artifacts and what they represent).[3]

Why would you like to start a student eportfolio?

In the context of a knowledge society, where being information literate is critical,

- The eportfolio can provide an opportunity to support one's ability to collect, organize, interpret and reflect on his/her learning and practice.
- It is also a tool for continuing professional development, encouraging individuals to take responsibility for and demonstrate the results of their own learning.
- Furthermore, a portfolio can serve as a tool for knowledge management, and is used as such by some institutions.
- The eportfolio provides a link between individual and organizational learning. (European Institute for E-Learning)[4]

To start developing an e-portfolio for your course, ask yourself the following questions!

Be sure to take a look at the *glossary* at the end.

I. **What are the outcomes for your portfolio?**
   Complete the following two sentences:

   a. The portfolio should be able to help the student to…
   b. The portfolio should be able to help me (the teacher) to assess the following GA(s):_____

   - Citizenship
   - Knowledge
   - Learning
   - Skills
   - Creativity
   - Communication
   - Teamwork

II. **How would you like to assess the outcomes of the portfolio?**
    You can

    a. choose to assess each artifact*/each category/the portfolio using a rubric*.

---

[3]Centre for Teaching Excellence, University of Waterloo. *Eportfolio explained.* Retrieved from https://uwaterloo.ca/centre-for-teaching-excellence/teaching-resources/teaching-tips/educational-technologies/all/eportfolios.
[4]European Institute for E-Learning. *Why do we need an ePortfolio?* Retrieved from http://www.eife-l.org/publications/eportfolio.

b. decide what assessment criteria are important for you:

    i. reflection (on choice of artifact/on alignment of artifact to graduate attribute)
    ii. language
    iii. creativity (in presentation/thinking/problem-solving)
    iv. discipline-specific skill/core competency

c. give different weights to b (i-iv) or even to different outcomes.
d. assess the portfolio once or twice in the course of a semester.

III. What should the portfolio look like?

a. Nature of artifacts
[Note: artifacts, documentations and evidences can be assignments (but not limited to) to be included in a portfolio]

    i. Text (e.g. reflective text (journal/blog, creative text) and/or
    ii. Multimedia/artistic expressions
Append the table:

Outcome	Examples
Critical inquiry (assignment: small scale research task)	Journal entries, (video) blogs, bibliography, evidences of critical use of the internet
Creativity (assignment: solve a problem)	Case studies, assignments, creating an original piece of work such as a literary text or a multimedia artefact
Citizenship (assignment: discipline-oriented community service)	Multimedia and or reflective essay type evidence of extra-curricular engagement (political/social/creative)
Information literacy	Research log, research assignments, bibliography, use of the internet

b. Number of artifacts

    i. Specify the number of artifacts that should be included under a category at the time of each assessment. Is the expectation realistic? For example:
How many reflective journals should the student submit in the course of the semester? Or
How many evidences of extra-curricular engagement, out of class learning, etc. should be included in the portfolio?
    ii. Expect artifacts on a regular basis.
Weekly, Bi-weekly, Monthly

c. Organization and Design

    i. Provide a template* to which students have to stick to. (*reduces workload, helps students to organize their learning*)

    ii. Let students be creative and make portfolio's organization part of the assessment.

    iii. Show examples of well-designed portfolios and explain why they are good.

    iv. Is group work also possible? If so, how would you like to assess it?

d. Highlighting GA(s) where you think is appropriate
Tag* artifacts (to GAs/Core competencies)
In order to facilitate tagging, ask your students to include key words into their artifacts. The key words could be GAs, e.g., Creativity or discipline related words or both.

IV. What scaffolding*(support) would the students need?

a. Technical

    i. introductory session
    ii. technical helpline
    iii. student workshops
    iv. online support
    v. exemplars as practical examples

b. Academic

    vi. guideline of what is expected in order to receive high grade
    vii. show examples of grading by a rubric
    viii. show example of alignment of artifact to expected outcome
    ix. mentoring

V. How would you like to give feedback on the portfolios?
You can provide

a. an interactive communication platform to accommodate the feedback system of the portfolio (e.g. forum)

b. built-in mechanisms for feedback ("Place feedback" in Mahara/class time) (*Note: Personal feedback better than feedback platform*)

c. opportunity to peer-review

d. feedback before or after submission

VI. How would you ensure buy-in for the portfolio?

  a. By embedding portfolios into the curriculum

    i. Embed the use of portfolio system as part of the curriculum and grade it

    ii. Explain the added value to their learning/future career
(See resources for examples)

  b. By adjusting your assessment scheme to facilitate the use of portfolios by replacing an examination/term paper with the portfolio.

  c. By making it part of classroom/curriculum activity.

VII. What platform would you like to use?

  a. **Mahara** (*dedicated portfolio software*)

  b. **My portfolio** on Blackboard (*Assignments on blackboard can be linked to the portfolio, no separate log-in required*)

  c. **Social Networking** sites (*easy to use but not customizable, also too public?*)

  d. **Google docs/sites** (*enable ownership & or collaboration*)

  e. **WordPress/Weebly** (*same as Google but more private*)

VIII. How would you survey students and collect data to revise the design?

  a. Post-portfolio questionnaire

  b. Focus group interviews

Appendix B

Rubric for Student E-Portfolios on the course level. A Resource of: CoP REFLECT: A Community of Practice on Student Eportfolios Online: http://copreflect.weebly.com/resources.html

Copyright: Dr. Tushar Chaudhuri, Dr. Béatrice Cabau, Ms. Céline Dias, Miss Chui Chi Shan, Prof Atara Sivan, Dr. Catherine Ladds, Dr. Paula Hodgson, Mr. Chris Chan, Dr. Lisa Deng, Dr. Simon To, Dr. Warren Linger, Dr. Dimple Thadani

CoP-REFLECT Rubrics for Student E-portfolio*

	Criteria	Indicators	The highest performance level (Max points = 5)
1	Presentation	A. Organization	Collection of evidence is clearly organized according to the portfolio assignment
		B. Page structure	Pages within the portfolio have an attractive and reader-friendly layout which uses elements like headings and subheadings, headers and footers where appropriate. Page is clearly divided into presentation of evidence and reflection
		C. Navigation	Navigation is logical and easy to use. Content is organized under relevant pages. Relevant Graduate Attributes have been added as Tags/Keywords
		D. Use of visual effects and multimedia	E-portfolio contains purposive design and organisational elements (e.g. font, colour, size), media enhances the purpose (e.g. pictures, videos)
		E. Quality of writing and proofreading	E-portfolio is free of spelling and grammatical errors and uses appropriate language for the target audience
2	Reflection	A. Development of knowledge and skills	The student demonstrates that he or she has developed or is in the process of developing his or her knowledge and skills
		B. The connectedness of learning	The student makes connections between classroom learning, learning/research outside of the classroom and the 'real world' experiences

(continued)

© Springer Nature Singapore Pte Ltd. 2017
T. Chaudhuri and B. Cabau (eds.), *E-Portfolios in Higher Education*,
DOI 10.1007/978-981-10-3803-7

(continued)

	Criteria	Indicators	The highest performance level (Max points = 5)
		C. Continuous critical reflection	The student engages in critical reflection on his or her development as a learner. He or she clearly articulates his or her achievements and future learning goals, thus demonstrating growth over time
		D. Articulation of viewpoints and interpretations	The student can provide his or her own viewpoints and interpretations which are insightful and well supported from evidence and argument. Clear, detailed examples are provided, as applicable
		E. Application of theories and concepts	The student can demonstrate an in-depth reflection on, and personalization of the theories, concepts, and/or strategies learned in the course
3	Information literacy	A. Appropriateness of using information tools	Identifies appropriate information tools, investigates the scope and content of different information search engines (e.g. the Library's OneSearch platform, Google Scholar) and selects the appropriate tool based on their information need
		B. Comprehensive evaluation of information sources	Provides evidence of comprehensive evaluation of their information sources and examines and compares information from various sources in order to evaluate currency, accuracy, authority, and point of view/bias. If they largely/exclusively use sources from the free Internet instead of scholarly resources, provides justification for doing so
		C. Appropriateness of documentation style	Consistently applies an appropriate documentation style without significant errors to acknowledge and cite information sources used
		D. Effectiveness of using information	Synthesizes, integrates, and communicates information effectively to accomplish a specific purpose
		E. Ethics of using information	Accesses and uses information ethically and legally, e.g. The copyright of the sources
4	Critical thinking	A. Quality of analysis	The student demonstrates a sophisticated command of analytical skills (e.g. synthesis, problem-solving, evaluation)
		B. Use of evidence	The student draws inferences or conclusions that are supported by abundant, wide-ranging, and appropriate evidence

(continued)

(continued)

	Criteria	Indicators	The highest performance level (Max points = 5)
		C. Use of methodologies	The student uses innovative methodologies to make logical connections across ideas or disciplines
		D. Consideration of multiple perspectives	The student can compare, evaluate and weight the importance of different views or perspectives
		E. Quality of argument	The student engages in creative expression and/or convincingly articulates original arguments

Total Marks: 100

*The rubric includes resources from the Internet, adapted to suit the purpose of assessing student E-portfolios at the HKBU

Note The above rubric is for guidance purposes only. Please adapt it to suit the outcomes of your portfolio and as per the conventions of your discipline

*Glossary

Artifact Artifacts used in ePortfolios are digital evidence of progress, experience, achievements, and goals over time. In other words, artifacts are examples of your work. This might include electronic documents, video, audio, and images. In ePortfolios, digital artifacts are organized by combining various media types into cohesive units that communicate your narrative.
(*Eportfolio Resource Center*. Retrieved from https://sites.google.com/site/resourcecentereportfolio/artifacts)

Rubric A rubric is a scoring tool that lists the criteria for a piece of work, or "what counts" (for example, purpose, organization, details, voice, and mechanics are often what count in a piece of writing); it also articulates gradations of quality for each criterion, from excellent to poor.
(Andrade, G.H. (1997). Understanding Rubrics. *Educational leadership*. Retrieved from https://learnweb.harvard.edu/alps/thinking/docs/rubricar.htm)

Eportfolio template Eportfolio templates enable the immediate customization and creation of ePortfolios. Most of these templates are easily customized in a few clicks. Here are some suggestions on eportfolio templates: Blackboard, Mahara, Google Sites, Weebly, Wix, Wordpress, etc.
(*Eportfolio gallery*. City University of Hong Kong. Retrieved from https://sites.google.com/site/eportfoliogallery/)

GAs (Graduate Attributes) HKBU aims to educate our students into Whole Persons. This is operationalized into Graduate Attributes that you should attain by the time you graduate from HKBU. An education at HKBU aims at developing all aspects of the whole person. In particular, it aims to foster the following attributes among its graduates: Citizenship, Knowledge, Learning, Skills, Creativity, Communication and Teamwork.
(*HKBU Graduate Attributes*. Hong Kong Baptist University. Retrieved from http://chtl.hkbu.edu.hk/main/hkbu-ga/)

Scaffolding In education, scaffolding refers to a variety of instructional techniques used to move students progressively toward stronger understanding and, ultimately, greater independence in the learning process. The term itself offers the

T. Chaudhuri and B. Cabau (eds.), *E-Portfolios in Higher Education*,
DOI 10.1007/978-981-10-3803-7

relevant descriptive metaphor: teachers provide successive levels of temporary support that help students reach higher levels of comprehension and skill acquisition that they would not be able to achieve without assistance.

(*The glossary of education reform.* Retrieved from http://edglossary.org/scaffolding/)

Printed by Printforce, the Netherlands